BITTERSWEET

BITTERSWEET

*Faith Lost and Found, and the DNA Test
that Brought a Baby Back to Life*

BY CHRISTINA MARIE HALES
AND CATHERINE ANNE LEWIS

FOREWORD BY
LATASHA COLANDER CLARK, OLYMPIC
GOLD MEDALIST

XULON ELITE

Xulon Press Elite
2301 Lucien Way #415
Maitland, FL 32751
407.339.4217
www.xulonpress.com

Unless otherwise indicated, Scripture quotations taken from The Holy Bible, New Living Translation (NLT). Copyright ©1996, 2004, 2007 by Tyndale House Foundation. Used by permission of Tyndale House Publishers, Inc.

Paperback ISBN-13: 978-1-6628-4566-6
Ebook ISBN-13: 978-1-6628-4567-3

DEDICATION

I dedicate this work to my mom, Amparo Leonila Salvia Higgins, or as everyone called her, 'Nurse Amy'. The one thing she always wanted was to be a mom, and I'm grateful she was mine.

I would also like to dedicate this book to my good friend, Cat Lewis, my co-author. We have worked on this project together for over 3 years, and we've both been through a lot in that time. Even with the loss of her husband Howard, Cat still picked up the pieces to complete this work for me. So thank you, Cat, Howard, Anna and Howie.

This is a work of creative nonfiction with fiction-alized elements. Some names and identifying details have been altered to protect the privacy of the people involved. These are stories from Ms. Hales' memory and her perspective, and as such, may vary from actual history and other people's recollections.

Acknowledgements

*C*hristi would like to thank her husband John Hales, her son Ian, her writer Cat, her dad and stepmom Mike and Debbie Mercado, her mom Amy, and her sisters Sandy and Judy. She would also like to thank Arlene Kimmel, Janice Barr, Latasha Colander Clark, Bishop John and Mrs. Hortense Colander, Cousin Samantha, Aunt Karen, Cindy, Diane, and the rest of her Arkansas Family. She thanks the following for their encouragement and support: Gina and Flo Kidd, Gloria Reed, Phyllis Jewel, Je, Donna, Kathy and her sisters at Papillon the salon: Victoria, Sandra, Ann, Ya, and Yolanda. And, her Lord.

Cat would like to thank her beloved late husband Howard, and her daughter Anna and son Howie who supported her throughout this endeavor. She would also like to thank Christi for sharing her testimony so boldly. Cat thanks the following: developmental editor Mary Weber (*To Best the Boys*) with kn literary arts; line editor Sue Mulligan; Xulon Press for their support over the years of my dad's writing and now mine; Val Stone Photography; Latasha Colander Clark with

Christ Studios; Hope Edelman (*Motherless Daughters*) with the Iowa Summer Writing Festival; The Friday Morning Writers led by Polly Hamilton Hilsabeck (*American Blues*); and, Whit Trumbull for workshop intensives. Special thanks to those without whose support Cat would not be standing upright in her storm: Cyd and David Ferris, Leanne and Clint Knight, Karin Lawin, Jenn McLaughlin, Tricia and Matt Day (and the Ashley Downs neighbors), Michelle Foy, Kathy Hess, Tami Clark, Pat and Ron Nobles, Jen Dobridge, Mary Smith, Maria Dezenberg, Women Reborn Sisters, Kelli Doby, SBS Owl Sisters, Camille and Ray Bell, Kath and Barry Winston, Dana and Max Irvin, Deanna and George Lewis, many other friends near and far, and most of all, God.

TABLE OF CONTENTS

FOREWORD

*A*n inspirational and compelling read, Christi's story pulls on your heartstrings and takes you on an amazing journey. It challenges you to love yourself unconditionally, and also to love others with the passion of Christ. It is an intriguing story of a beautiful woman name Christi Hales, who, through the miraculous power of God, was transformed from the woman she was before, to the woman God purposed her to become today.

This thought-provoking and heartfelt read will make you cry, challenge you, encourage, and motivate you. It reveals the secrets that only the brave would dare to revealed, and the challenges overcome, only by the grace of God. This book will cause you to reflect on your life, the choices you make, and question what sacrifices you will make to fight for your life and ultimately your destiny.

Christi's life empowers people to come out of the dark and into the marvelous light with boldness, power and purpose.

We are all destined by the choices we make in life, the work we put in and the endurance to continue on our journey to our purpose. Christi's story is a testament to that, and I encourage every woman, man and family to read this book and consider your choice to overcome the odds and choose to WIN.

Latasha Colander Clark
Olympic Gold Medalist and CEO & Founder of
Christ Studios
christstudios.com

INTRODUCTION

The Gift

When Christi messaged me on Facebook a few years ago and told me, "We have to meet for lunch, because it's time to write our book," I got the butterflies. I'd been waiting for that offer for fifteen years.

I was thrilled because I was in a place timewise to do it, and she was at the part in her story where it made sense to document the journey. Our alignment was perfect, but I was scared too, because the project was daunting.

It's hard enough to write in your own voice let alone in someone else's. To the extent that Christi's voice comes through in this story is a credit to God's ability, not mine. I had ghostwritten some other projects and books, mostly in the business or ministry arenas, so I knew how to mimic a person's style and pop in key words and phrases they would use, but I'd never undertaken something so deeply personal. I had to get inside her head, and at times I felt like I had walked in on someone's private conversation. Of course she would wave me off as being too timid; that's how bold and open she is with sharing her experiences. Christi wants everyone to know that it doesn't matter how bad it gets, there is always a road back because God makes a way.

While we were working together I leaned on the honesty she had with her reality. While some people try to mask their weakness, she turned the spotlight directly on it. Since I came from a tribe of people who care deeply about "appearances," it took me by surprise how comfortable she was with her truth. She spoke plainly and bluntly, so I listened and kept my focus on the outcome: telling Christi's story showing God's amazing ability to use any situation to draw us closer to Him, even as we stray far from His path for us.

As Christians we are called on by God to share our testimonies. Author Sara Mae offers this insight: "Stories thread us all together, and God uses the voices of victors to reach the hearts of hearers." To "*testify!*" (you have to hear that in a Southern preacher's four-syllable pulpit cry) is a statement of faith. It's sharing your relationship with God and how that relationship has changed your life. For that matter this book is more than just Christi's story; it's her testimony.

I believe that everyone has a story to tell, and that they should tell it. That means you, dear Reader. *You* have a story to share and you should tell it. How that happens and who you tell depends on your story, so don't limit yourself to a specific format. It doesn't have to be an Amazon bestseller or the movie that rocked Hollywood. It could be as unassuming as publishing a collection of poems online, recording a vlogging serial, or explaining your journey over a cup of coffee with a friend at a local coffeeshop.

Memoirs are one of my favorite ways to hear a story and I've been on the receiving end of some great ones over the years. I don't read physical books anymore, because I simply don't have time, so I binge-listen to as many audio versions of books as I can download, while I'm traveling, working out, or running between meetings. There's nothing better than a tale of adventure or a poignant, childhood reflection. I'm all ears—quite literally with my buds inserted—whether I'm listening to Tara Westover's journey from rural poverty to the halls of higher learning in *Educated*, or laughing at the eccentric townsfolk in Haven Kimmel's *A Girl Named Zippy: Growing Up Small in Mooreland, Indiana*. Or, even biking along the spine of the Andes Mountains with Anna McNuff in *Llama Drama: A two-woman, 5,500-mile cycling adventure through South America*. I've been taken on the most awesome journeys to find out what happened to someone and what changed in them because of it, and how their story affects me and my life. Does it spur me to make changes or try new things? Does it remind me that time flies and I need to make the most of every moment? Does it awaken something inside me that had been dormant? The questions that arise while we read about another's adventure or heartbreak and how we answer those questions determine its impact. Is a memoir just a story about someone else's experience, or do we make it part of our own experience by how we react and adjust our own lives based on it?

On a personal level I know the priceless value of telling one's story. My sister and I were gifted my father's unpublished memoirs upon his death. Since my sister is the public speaker and I'm the writer, reading and editing his files fell to me, and over the past few years it has been an emotional challenge. I've cherished revisiting stories that he shared with us for decades and I've also found a few surprises in those pages that made me gasp out loud—*really!*—things that were so uncharacteristically my dad that I wondered if he'd gotten a little daffy in his old age. But I knew he didn't, because it was his body that failed him; his mind was sharp enough to give university lectures and write a book the year before he died at the age of 83.

My dad's stories comforted me during that time of incredible loss and he continues to live on through them for me and my children. They are more than something my sister and I received legally in his estate, they are a treasured gift of himself to his family. And that's what a memoir is, it's a priceless gift of yourself to others.

Likewise, Christi's memoir is her gift to you.

Catherine Anne Lewis
Apex, North Carolina
catherineannelewis.com

PROLOGUE

Stillborn

Stop wailing," Jesus said. "She is not dead but asleep."
They laughed at Him, knowing that she was dead. But
He took her by the hand and said, "My child, get up!"
Her spirit returned, and at once she stood up. Then
Jesus told them to give her something to eat.
~*Luke 8:52-55 (NLT)*

*J*t was January 1969 when the daughter called her
mother. Snow fell lightly against the window
pane as the temperature dropped to the low teens. The
daughter was in a sterile hospital room in Kingston,
New York. She hadn't seen her mother in a very long
time. She had left home at a young age and fell in love
with a boy. The usual things happened when a girl and
a boy fall in love. They made rushed decisions and their
life took twists and turns and landed them all the way
up in New York state. In a hospital.

The mother was understanding of her daughter's
absence. She had a houseful of other and younger children to feed and clothe. One less mouth at the table and

one less Sunday school dress to buy was a blessing, even as she missed her daughter. But the daughter was headstrong and didn't color inside the lines of life. Sometimes it was easier with her gone.

In Arkansas, the mother had been doing dishes at the sink when the ringing phone summoned her from the kitchen. Her daughter's voice was low and somber and the mother was concerned. This wasn't the type of phone call she'd been expecting. It was supposed to be a joyous time, even if God's rules were bent.

The daughter was direct. "Ma, I lost the baby."

The mother spoke soothing words to her hurting daughter. Their conversation did not linger because of the expense of a long distance telephone call where every minute incurred new charges. The mother asked her to visit when she could. The daughter promised she'd try.

The mother returned the receiver to its cradle and sobbed into her dishtowel.

CHAPTER 1

THE DNA TEST

We may throw the dice,
but the Lord determines how they fall.
~Proverbs 16:33 (NLT)

Present Day

Cary, North Carolina

Winter

"*Y*ou need to get a DNA test." Arlene pestered me as I applied color to her gray roots. She was sitting at my chair in my shop, Papillion the salon.

"Don't you wonder about your history?" she asked.

No, I don't. It wasn't something I wanted to know and I had other things on my plate. Going on a DNA hunt to discover the source of my olive-toned skin or dark brown eyes wasn't something that interested me, but it sure had Arlene excited. To tell the truth, it almost felt like a slam against my own parents. I never wanted to hurt them by looking for my birth parents because my parents, my real parents, adopted me. It didn't matter to me that I didn't share genetics because they loved me either way.

"I'm probably Cuban or Greek, I dunno. It doesn't matter." I never understood her insistence to find my roots as I worked on hers.

"You need to know for sure, honey. It's your *people*." She spoke in her New York borough accent with the missing "r's," and talked much too fast for someone who had been living in North Carolina for well over a decade.

"Well, my people are Cuban." My abuelo and abuela (grandfather and grandmother) had emigrated from Cuba to the US before Castro ruined the country and they settled in Ybor City, Florida, where they had my mom. That was my heritage as far as I knew it from what my mom had told me.

"That's your *adopted* family." She always brought up the adoption, as if my family were somehow not related to me because we didn't share genes and I didn't quite see her point.

"Irregardless, my dad is Irish Catholic."

"The word is 'regardless,' she corrected. Once a school teacher, always a school teacher. "And, he's your *adopted* father. Don't you want to know who your birth parents are?"

"Meh." It didn't matter to me, and it shouldn't matter to anyone else that I was adopted. I never understood why people who wanted kids but couldn't have them biologically didn't jump at the chance to adopt. I was adopted and had a great life. I felt loved and looked after by my parents, and while they weren't perfect— my dad had some issues—they took me in and raised me as their own.

The funny part is that they didn't want me, a girl, they wanted a boy, but they got me instead and they were happy. There are so many children stuck in the system for a long time. The Department of Social Services deals with kids all the time that are stuck because they didn't have great situations in their homes, or maybe they were orphaned. They don't have an opportunity for a home and family like I ended up having. Thankfully, I didn't spend my childhood in the foster system. I was only a foster child until I was 9 months old. Because my parents adopted me, I grew up in a home with a mom and dad and sisters. I experienced a full family life, so it's sometimes very difficult for me to see a parent who tries so desperately to have their own 'DNA child.' I'm on the other aspect of it, because, as an adopted child, I was treated as if I were my mom's and dad's very own. I didn't need a DNA test to find my parents because I already had parents.

The back and forth with Arlene about getting a DNA test was a dance we did over quite a few months. She would come in for an appointment and tell me to get a test, and she'd use that motherly stare she had that was supposed to make me buckle. It didn't. It was just our dialogue when I did her hair and we caught up on our lives.

It was nearly New Year's when Arlene came in again with what I'll assume she thought was her trump card. She entered the salon with two large bags holding fresh food from her kitchen. That was my gift from her *casa* to mine. Like many snowbirds, Arlene and her husband Lou left for Florida after the holidays, missing our prime month in North Carolina for winter cold. A few times a year, or maybe one, we get snow here. But if we get it, it lasts for only a day or so until it melts. Even though it's only a bit of snow, it will still shut everything down. People stay home and businesses shut down. That's the 'two inches of snow' we get that the rest of the country makes fun of us for. But, we don't have a fleet of snowplows or people knowing how to drive in snow, so that's why only two inches of snow will shut us down. Now, if those two inches are ice, it's another story. Ice storms coat houses, roads, trees, and powerlines in thick layers. It's gorgeous when the sun shines on the crystal, sparkling like Christmas decorations, but it can be deadly. Neighborhoods and entire towns can lose power, trapping people in their frigid, dark homes for days. Traveling the roads is like navigating a hockey rink in your minivan so we just forget it.

Light a fire in the fireplace if we can, bundle up inside our homes, and cook meals and pots of coffee and hot chocolate on the grill.

Arlene set the grocery bags she'd brought me on the counter filled with the food that wouldn't last the months they would be gone. Then, she took out a white box. She worked her way into my salon chair, her body frail from chemo because she'd been surviving stage 4 cancer for 15 years, and in her bejeweled hands she held that box. I stared at her wondering what she was up to because there was this sneaky look on her face. The box made me upset because the food was gift enough and she didn't need to get me a Christmas present. I was kind of teed off at that. Then I had to think, was it a Christmas present or was it a Hanukah present? I wasn't sure, because she celebrates both. "It's all to the glory of God," she would say about holidays. She grew up going to parochial school, even though she was Jewish, and her family always had a Christmas tree. Today, Arlene and Lou are Messianic Jews, which means they believe Jesus is the Messiah.

I draped her in an iridescent blue barber cape and pointed to the box. "What's that?"

"Lou surprised me with a DNA kit." She told me that *ancestry.com* ran a buy-two-get-one-free sale, and she and her husband had each taken one test, which left an extra kit. She wanted to give me the kit.

In the early 1980s, *ancestry.com* was started as an organization to help people trace their family roots. They say that they're the largest company in the world that gives people historical records and photos, family trees, DNA test results, and genealogical links. Through their DNA test services, members can find their genetic makeup and that's what Arlene and her husband had done.

Here you go, honey, time to roll the dice and see what you get." Arlene handed me the white box. It sported green writing and the *ancestry.com* logo with its cartoonish leaves and was surprisingly light.

"Now you can find out if you're Cuban, or Mexican, or maybe Greek, ehh?" She shrugged and gave me that knowing grin. She'd pulled a fast one on me.

I sighed.

She became serious. "Christi, God is in control of this. He'll guide it, you don't have to worry."

"Okay, okay, you win, I'll do it!" I threw up my arms in the air.

That was Arlene, she always got her way. She was like a second mom to me, always guiding me, giving me advice, and pushing me. I loved that lady.

Leaving work for the day, the box sat in the seat next to me in my purple Scion like a little passenger. I almost felt like I should strap it in.

Just me and my DNA kit driving down the highway.

My husband and I lived in a small house in Smithfield, a small town outside of Raleigh, North Carolina, and had moved there to be closer to my mom and help care for her. Smithfield isn't much more than a speck on the map, but its claim to fame is that it's the hometown of a famous Hollywood star, Ava Gardner. She made films from the 1940s through the 1980s and her museum in Smithfield is packed with her memorabilia, pictures and clothes. She was married to Frank Sinatra and had a longtime on-and-off affair with Howard Hughes. She died in London, where she chose to live after her career. I thought it was pretty amazing that she lived such a large life coming from such a small town.

At home, I placed the DNA kit on the breakfast counter between the kitchen and living room, where it continued to stare at me for the next few days. It was like an adopted pet, looking mournfully at me every time I entered the room. It probably wanted me to feed it, or pet it, or give it a nice bed. I would immediately ignore it and go about my household routines. I had to clean bathrooms, work on the books for my business, cook dinner sometimes for two and sometimes for more, and do all the laundry. I didn't have time to worry about completing Arlene's DNA task.

One night, I had a dream about it. The box had become a white terrier dog and it was whimpering and tugging at my hand. Only I didn't know what it wanted or what I could do for it. I felt so helpless because it was

7

a sad little dog and it wanted me to do something, but I was paralyzed. I couldn't figure out how to help the little thing. It whined and I wanted to cry.

Okay, subconscious, you don't have to spell it out.

The next morning, as the coffee was brewing, I grabbed the DNA kit from the counter and opened it. It was filled with pamphlets and paper, a vial, and seemingly easy instructions: *To perform the test accurately, you must fill the enclosed vial with your saliva.*

I thought that was pretty doable.

But, no, it wasn't. It took me close to 45 minutes to get enough spit into that little devil of a vial. I nearly gave up, but I kept hearing Arlene's voice in my head prodding me on, so I kept spitting. Finally, I placed the saliva-filled vial into the envelope, thankful I didn't have to spit anymore. I dropped it off at the post office on my way to the salon and watched it disappear through the slot.

I thought that this could end up being very interesting, or it could open up a whole can of worms. I felt like I almost didn't have the right to look into my DNA and what it would say about me and my family tree. What if my biological father was a murderer? Or, I was my aunt's love child? I made a decision that I shouldn't think about these things because wherever the DNA test led me, it wasn't going to be to people. I didn't want to know anything about anyone connected to my DNA, because they weren't my family. I already had a family.

I had a mom and dad, and sisters, and they were my family. I wanted to know my ethnic background but not my family tree. There probably wasn't anything to know anyway, so I decided to forget about it. The test would tell me what race my bio parents were and what countries their ancestors came from and that's it.

I'd wondered about my ethnic background for my whole life. My adoptive parents were Irish and Cuban, so that's what I clung to because I didn't know anything else. When I was a little girl I went to Florida to visit my mom's Cuban relatives, so I knew a little bit about Cuba. I was a little bit excited to find out what my own blood would say. Would I be Cuban, too?

Over the next weeks, *ancestry.com* kept sending me generic messages apologizing for taking longer than usual. I guessed that they'd had a backlog due to the holiday season where more people than expected had placed thousands of brightly wrapped DNA test kits under Christmas trees. The delay didn't bother me too much at the time because my own life was so hectic. Holidays are a huge time in the salon business. I figured, it'll come when it comes.

When the apology messages stopped showing up in my inbox, I really forgot about the test. Life was busy at home and work. I lived a little less than an hour away from the shop, so long commutes were part of my routine. I wasn't thinking too much about my heritage. Work was busy with paying bills, collecting rent from my salon gals, and serving my own clients, plus the hours on the road. I didn't have a lot of free time to sit around and ponder stuff.

Arlene came back from Florida at the end of March, before Easter. She hobbled in, but yelled out excitedly, "Did you get the DNA results? Where did the dice fall? Are you Greek or Spanish?"

"Um…no," I stammered.

She shuffled herself into the chair. "Well, tell me! What are you?"

"No, I mean, I don't have them. I don't have the results."

"What? Didn't you look? Why didn't you look?"

I gave her an exaggerated smile. "And, by the way, hello there. How are you?"

"Yes, yes, hello, fine, whatever. Good to see you, too, honey. Now, the app. Open the app."

"The app?"

She tsk'ed at me and sighed. "The results are on the app. That's where you need to check them. Get your phone and look at the app."

"Ohhh." Things were starting to click in my head. All this time, I had been waiting for the results to be sent to me, so I thought they'd show up in my mailbox. It seemed logical to me that since I mailed my vial to them that they'd mail me back my results. But, the whole time they were waiting for me on the app. I didn't even think of an app.

"Give me your phone," she ordered. Because if Arlene wants you to check for your results, you check for your results. She helped me upload and log in to the app. I found the list labeled *DNA Story for Christina*. After nearly 50 years of not knowing, I held in my hand the nationalities that make up *me*. I felt a tug in my stomach looking over them. In that moment, I was suddenly the same Christi, but a different Christi.

The DNA results said I was of Hispanic descent, and my family was most likely from Puerto Rico. I thought, well, that's kind of cool because my mom's side emigrated from Cuba and they're sort of in the same area down there in the Caribbean. My mom and my older sister Sandy both speak fluent Spanish. I never had the chance to learn more than a handful of phrases, because I didn't grow up with my mom's family in Florida like Sandy did. She was a young teenager when my parents moved to New York and I was adopted.

Looking at the smaller percentages of my DNA makeup, I also had English, Wales and Northwestern Europe in my mix. The list was really long and included Native American, Basque, Ivory Coast, and many others. These were *my people*. My stomach wavered. I was either excited about this, or I was hungry, or both.

Whether excitement or needing lunch, the fact remained that this changed everything. What I had lived with for nearly fifty years, all the ideas I had drummed up in my head, were now irrelevant. It was time to give up the fantasy that so many kids of adoption invent, the one that I was the love child of a famous celebrity. I'd had a specific singer in mind since I was a kid, but my DNA profile didn't match her ethnicity. She is Armenian. Just as well, because it would be impossible to contact her. Like, how would that work? I'm a hair stylist in North Carolina and she's famous and lives in Los Angeles. We don't just live in different worlds, we live in different universes.

I looked at Arlene through wide eyes that matched hers. I kept looking back to the list. "This is who I am. This is what I'm made of. These are my roots!"

"Yes, that's you, Christi, that's you!"

We spent the appointment talking about the different nationalities and the percentages I was of each. It was so much fun. I couldn't believe that for the first time I finally knew what caused my eyes to be brown and my skin to be olive. I hugged and thanked her when she left. Arlene gave me a great gift. And, mystery solved, I could go back to life with our DNA dance finally finished. I knew that eventually Arlene would find another subject to dance with me about, but for today we were done.

The following morning, I received a message from *ancestry.com*. Someone was looking to make a connection with me.

Well, that's interesting.

I had just arrived at the salon having driven my commute in blinding sun. On the way in I had been listening to Christian radio and I was humming a song that had stuck in my head about what it would be like to meet Jesus. The temperature had risen, and the morning was muggy as is typical for Spring in the South. As I was setting up for the day and prepping my station, I received the message from the *ancestry.com* app that a girl named Samantha wanted to connect with me.

I don't understand much about the internet and you hear about people getting scammed, so I was wary. As far as I knew there weren't any connections to my profile, so I was pretty sure that it was a scam. I finished a quick men's cut on my long-term client, Gary, and wondered what I should do. I didn't know whether to ignore it or find out what she wanted. After thinking about it a while, I decided to reply. Since I knew I wasn't going to give her my credit card number it would probably be safe.

Samantha, where are you? I was direct. No sense in beating around the bush.

She replied back. *I live in Arkansas.*

Well, I'm from upstate New York, so unless you know somebody from upstate New York, I don't see how we could possibly have anything in common with each other.

Her next text provided the confirmation I already knew. *I'm not from upstate New York.*

Well, I guess we're not related. Bye.

She was in Arkansas and I was adopted in New York, which are worlds apart. I'll bet she was trying to rip me off after all. I brushed off our exchange as a good dodge on my part, and turned to matters in front of me. As salon owner, I often had to play mediator and resolve the never-ending "whose turn was it to wash the towels?" battle. That's the fight where one party never, ever washes the towels and the other party washes the towels every, single, solitary week. Plus, my 10:30 highlights client was sitting in the reception area. Needless to say, between finding someone to wash this week's towels and serving my clients, the entire probable scam was long forgotten.

Two hours later, "Samantha the scammer" messaged me again.

I talked to my mom. She said that her sister had moved to Buffalo, New York with her husband and she was pregnant, but the baby had died. Mom said it was the late sixties.

A little jolt ran up my spine. This was a strange coincidence. I was born in 1969, adopted from upstate New York, and *ancestry.com* seemed to think Samantha and I are related. I wasn't sure how I felt about that, so I didn't answer her. Frankly I wasn't sure what to say because I had chalked her up to a swindler.

She wrote me again. *Would you mind looking at your DNA track to see if you have anyone with the last name Tidwell or Mercados?*

To be honest, I never looked at the DNA track because I didn't even know it was part of the results. I didn't look for it, because I wasn't looking to connect with people. I was looking for what percentage Cuban I was, which, as it turns out, I'm zero percent Cuban. So, I looked at the DNA track on my phone. Samantha's name was there as a DNA match and, about five people down, was someone with the last name Mercados. That struck me. The last name Mercados is not a name like Hill, or Smith, or something generic or widely used. It was an unusual name, and the fact that she told me to look for it meant something. In a split second, this went from being a con job to being freaky.

So I messaged her. *Apparently, we are connected. Mercados is a name on my list, along with yours. What does that tell you?*

Samantha typed back. *I'm not sure, let me talk to my mom.*

Samantha told me that she had gotten married recently and had been working on her family tree. She was trying to fill in some of the blanks of her family history on her dad's side through *ancestry.com*. I figured since she was probably thinking of starting a family, she wanted to know more about her relatives.

I waited for Samantha to talk to her mom.

Samantha pinged me again. *What year were you born?*

1969. Why?

Then, Samantha revealed something interesting. *I'll tell you what, Christi, I think you might be my first cousin.*

First cousin?

Yes, and if that pans out, and you and I are related like I believe we are, then you also have a full-blooded brother.

A brother? My hands were shaking as I held my phone.

Maybe. Would you mind sending me a picture of you?

I quickly typed back. *Only if you send me one!* Which was absolutely the most ludicrous thing I could have said. Like, how would having a picture of Samantha help me at all?

Despite my misgivings, Samantha sent me a picture, but it wasn't of her, it was of my supposed biological mother, a woman named Wilma Faye. So, I sent Samantha one of me.

Samantha texted me. *You look like Aunt Wilma.*

I could barely see it, but Samantha seemed sure. And, maybe I was sure, too, as I looked carefully at the details of her face. Her skin was not the same tawny brown as mine, but her nose was the same shape, and her brown eyes, were set in, just like mine. Her head was topped with a mass of wild hair, like my own. I swiped out of the picture and clicked off my phone. My heart raced and I needed to catch my breath. Everything was happening so fast.

I thought about what my conversation with Samantha meant. The picture she'd sent me of Wilma Faye sort of looked like me. Wilma Faye had lived in Buffalo, New York, near Kingston where I was born. She had been pregnant the same year I was born in 1969. But, the baby had died. What did that mean in relation to me? Samantha's DNA test linked us as close relatives. I was related to both the Mercados and Tidwell families, the very names that Samantha had asked me to search. I blew out a long breath. The coincidences formed into an idea that I wasn't sure I could ignore.

Am I the 'dead' baby?

Chapter 2

Messes Into Miracles

And we know that God causes everything to work
together for the good of those who love God and are
called according to his purpose for them.
~Romans 8:28 (NLT)

Past

Kingston, New York

Christi/Tina age 6-11

"*Y*ou know what? You're *adopted!*" my older sister
Judy yelled at me, in that snotty way siblings
do when they want to poke at you and make you mad.

"Am not!" I pushed her into the wall. She wasn't
expecting it and slid down barely catching herself
before she fell, and she snaked up the wall to stand.

"Are, too, Tina!" I was Christened 'Christina Marie'
but as a small child my family called me 'Tina'.

"Nuh, uh," I sing-songed back to her and pushed her again. What she was talking about must be pretty bad if she accused me of it.

"Mom! Mom!" Judy yelled for help, but popped me on the arm with her fist out of Mom's line of sight.

I shot her one back before Mom walked in. She let out an exasperated sigh. "Girls, stop it! You're *both* adopted. Now, separate and find something to do."

I didn't have tears in my eyes, because I was tough and didn't give into self-pity, but my arm stung where Judy punched me and I was confused. I tugged on Mom's sleeve. "What does ''dopted' mean?"

She told me what adopted meant and promised me that it was a good thing. She and Daddy had adopted both Judy and me as babies about four years apart. She said that she and Daddy loved us very much and we were her miracle babies because she always wanted a houseful of kids.

I was still mad at Judy, but I felt better. Mom had a way of doing that, of making bad things better so that no matter what trouble I found myself in, she was there to take care of it. She mended my doll's ripped dress, sewed my teddy bear's tail back on, and glued my china teapot back together. She took all my broken stuff and made it whole again. Mom gave me a kiss on my head, and left the room to get back to her sewing. I went to my room to color with my crayons, and Judy went back to resenting being adopted.

We lived in Kingston, New York and were Catholic, but we were not one of those big families of eight or ten members that we'd greet in the St. Joseph church parking lot before Mass; the ones who climbed out of conversion vans or wood paneled station wagons in descending birth order. Our family was just five of us: Mom, Daddy, our older sister Sandy (who Daddy had adopted when he married Mom), Judy, and then there was me.

Our mom had given birth to Sandy back when she was married to her first husband. I found out later that her first husband was in the military and, after giving birth, Mom had hemorrhaged so they'd performed a hysterectomy. She said that it's just the way they handled it back then. I'm not sure if she was talking about medical protocols or military hospital ones, but either way, what chance she thought she had for the large family she desperately wanted was gone. At least that's what she thought at the time.

Mom and her first husband were together for only a short time because she said he was a 'player'. The type of guy I picture spending too much time in the mirror combing his hair and hounding pretty girls on the street. She'd caught him being unfaithful a number of times, and after his 'last chance,' she left. Mom said no woman should put up with that and when I was older she warned me to avoid unfaithful men. She also said that her best three years of marriage were when he was in Korea.

My mom was first generation American. Well, *sort of*.

She explained it this way: her dad had emigrated from Cuba, but he was already a U.S. citizen because he was born when Cuba was part of the United States. Don't take my word for it, because I was never any good at history, but mom taught me this: She said it was because of the *Cuban War of Independence*; that is, Cuba from Spain. The U.S. sent a battleship called the *USS Maine* to Cuba to protect the sugar plantations because Cuba produced more sugar than anywhere else in the world and the U.S. needed its sugar. In early 1898, the *Maine* exploded and sank, killing hundreds on board. No one knew who or what caused it to explode, but since the U.S. wanted Cuban independence—*because of that sugar*—they blamed the explosion on the Spanish. That's how they came up with the slogan: *Remember the Maine, to hell with Spain!*

The whole disaster created *The Spanish-American War of 1898*, which oddly only lasted a few months. At the end of the war, Spain gave Guam, Puerto Rico and Cuba to the U.S. through a Treaty of Paris. I did learn that there are like over sixty Treaties of Paris, which confuses me because you'd think they could come up with some original names for each one if they're going to have over sixty of them. Anyway, the *Treaty of Paris 1898* specifically gave the United States control over Cuba. That lasted four years, until Cuba purchased its independence from the U.S. It was during those four years, in 1900, that my *abuelo* (grandfather) was born making him a U.S. citizen. Which allowed him to move to Florida easily.

My abuelo was awesome. I loved him. Everyone loved my abuelo. He had white hair, a flashing smile and soft blue eyes that hugged you when you looked at him. He was the whitest Cuban man I'd ever seen.

"Aldofo! Que pasa?" they'd shout from tables and doorways as he walked by. I'd clutch his thick, rough hand as he led my sister Judy and me past the shops and diners in Ybor City. This was the Cuban neighborhood of Tampa, FL, where people would sit fanning themselves on the turquoise iron balconies overlooking the streets. The air smelled sweetly of fried plantains and cigar smoke. We'd stop in our usual diner and Abuleo would order us a Cubano. They made a Tampa version of the traditional Cuban sandwich with pork, salami, Swiss cheese, pickles and mustard. He'd cut one half into two portions, one for me and one for Judy, and the other half he'd place in front of himself. We'd share our hot treat at a table by the window, watching the people walk by. He didn't speak much English and we didn't speak much Spanish, but it didn't matter.

Mom's real name was Amparo, but everyone called her 'Amy.' Mom told us when she was little that she was sick with rheumatic fever. During her sick spells, her family lived in Ybor City where Abuelo worked in the cigar factories. The mild temperatures eased her symptoms and nearby family made life easier. When my mom was well and able to live up north, Abuelo and Abeula (grandmother) moved the family to Spanish Harlem in New York City. Abuelo made more money up there, working in the restaurants, while Abeula and my mom and Aunt Nora could work as seamstresses. That extra money was needed so that they could survive down in Florida when my mom needed the different climate for her sickness. Mom said that extra money was the miracle from God that they needed to travel between the cities to help her health because they couldn't afford doctors and hospitals.

It was the Depression and they were poor, even with the extra money, and they led what was considered a Bohemian lifestyle. Abuela had two kids from her first marriage, and two kids from her second marriage, then, some time after she had my mom, she decided she better get married to her third husband who was my Abuelo. After they were married, they had my aunt Nora. Abuela was a medium and saw visions. I had never seen visions, so I never judged that. It's what my mom told me. Mom named me after her, as her Christian name was Christina. But, Abuela never liked the name Christina and she called herself Christina-Paulina. I never met my Abuela because she died before I was born, so I only know about her from what my mom told me. Mom referred to me as 'Christina' because she liked the name so much, but everyone else called me 'Tina.'

Aunt Nora married Merv, a jazz musician who talked like a 'cool cat', wore a beret and played the saxophone. He wore sunglasses all the time, even in the dark, and grew "oregano" in their backyard. He played in the clubs at night until the early morning hours and he slept all day. Their kids were Sandy's age, much older than me, but their grandkids, who were my second cousins, were my age and we hung out and played tag and round robin in the backyard and swam in their swimming pool. When we traveled to see them in Florida, we became one large, happy family. I loved those times because I felt I belonged to something bigger than our little household from up north. Of course, no one could get a word in edgewise because everyone was always talking at once, mostly in 'Spanglish'. When we came back to Kingston, we all had Spanish accents and they took a while to fade.

As a young child in the Seventies, I only saw the pastel colors of Ybor City around me. It seemed so bright and alive compared to our gray street in Upstate New York, where it was always winter. I failed to notice the decaying and empty buildings, the chipped paint and the economic depression that followed the collapse of the cigar industry that had originally brought my family to Florida.

Ybor City was revitalized decades later as young Bohemian-types rented the cheap studios inside vacant buildings. Bars and shops popped up in the empty storefronts, catering to the resident artsy crowd demanding alcohol and cheap wares. As the neighborhood rebounded, developers came in and created a bustling neon nighttime attraction with restaurants and nightclubs. Today, it's a tourist destination but in my mind, it's home.

We stopped going to Ybor City after my abuelo died. My Uncle Armon and my mother had an enormous fight after the funeral. I didn't know about it at the time, in fact, I didn't even know I had an Uncle Armon until I was much older, because my mom and he didn't speak for years.

One morning in our house in Kingston I awoke to Judy screaming at me.

"What's wrong with you?!" She was shaking me.

"Wha-aa." I didn't know where I was. Daylight was pouring through the windows, but I couldn't wake up.

"Get up! Look! Look!" Judy kept shaking me.

"Stahhp!" I wanted her to go away so I could go back to sleep.

"You've got crumbs all over your bed and you ate all the cookies *again*!" She was mad as spit.

I cracked my eyes, but couldn't get them open. Sunlight filled our shared bedroom and overwhelming the lightweight yellow curtains trying to keep it at bay.

"Get up!" She flung my bedspread to the floor.

I sat up on one side. The prickly crumb bits poking into my elbow.

"I'm telling mom," she hissed at me, then yelled down the hall, "MOM! MOM!"

Mom rushed into our room ready to put out a fire. "What is it? What happened?"

"Tina ate all the cookies last night!" Judy declared indignantly.

"Oh, is that all?"

Mom surveyed the scene and I could tell she wasn't the least bit mad, which probably made Judy even madder. Judy flung herself on her bed.

Mom patted my head. "Were up again last night, Christina?"

I nodded. I didn't even remember getting up and grabbing the cookies. Mom gave me a hug. I had terrible bouts of sleepwalking and would do all sorts of things during the night and not remember a thing.

"Let me clean those sheets," she said, pushing me up and grabbing at a tucked corner. The sheets had chocolate smudges. She carefully bunched the sheets so she didn't spill out the crumbs, and took them downstairs. Judy stormed after her protesting about how unfair it was that I could do something like that and not get into trouble. I was still in a fog, trying to wake up, but wondering if it was still a dream, too.

Sandy got her own room, but Judy and I shared a room. When I was a baby, she begged mom to let me sleep in her room. But, as I got older, she resented it because of the added work. Sharing a room with me meant Judy had to watch me at night due to my sleep-walking. Most of the times she would catch me, like if she found me trying to pee in a potted plant, she'd have to guide me to the bathroom. But, other times, like with the cookies in bed, she slept through it and awoke to my mess.

As much as Judy resented being my roommate, even more she hated dressing like me. My mom was a seamstress and she often made us matching dresses. One year, she bought a Simplicity dress pattern, and made us Holly Hobbie dresses. They were all the rage. She sewed the primitive prairie dresses, frilled pinafores, and big, floppy bonnets that tied under our chins. My dress was a blue print, similar to the original Holly Hobbie, and Judy's was a green print, like Holly's friend Amy.

Judy was tolerant of the style, but I was in heaven. I loved and wanted everything Holly Hobbie, the cat-loving girl with the patchwork pinafore and big, blue bonnet. Her likeness was on everything from greeting cards to toy tea sets. I had a china box with her image on it, but I desperately wanted a rag doll, and I kept begging Mom to get me one.

Besides Holly Hobbie, I idolized my older sister Sandy. She was a teenager, with her own room and her own pink princess phone, and she was cool. She would let me sit on her bed while she painted her toenails bright colors and listened to 45s on her stereo turntable, pretending to sing along with a "microphone" of a long tooth comb. I wanted to be one of those singers with a silky voice like Donna Summers.

Sandy collected stuffed animals, the large ones that people win at the fair, and I would play with them. "Here, kiddo." She piled some of her stuffed animals around me. "It's like you're a little stuffed animal, too." I felt like I was drowning in their fur. I had breathing problems, and with the stuffed animals all around me, I couldn't catch my breath. Mom really let her have it for that.

In New York, we lived in a three-story house set into a wooded hill near Kingston. It had a walkout basement with sliding glass doors that led out into the backyard. Above that, on the second story deck, we had an above-ground pool. Sandy would sunbathe there in a bikini and rub oil on her body and spray lemon juice in her hair. I watched everything Sandy did, memorizing her moves like I'd have to pass a test someday on how to be a teenage girl.

Two weeks after the cookie incident, Sandy asked mom if she could go to a drive-in movie with her boyfriend, Jim. Mom was making rice and beans in the kitchen. Daddy was traveling, as usual, and when he did, we ate Cuban food.

Sandy, begged, *"Please?"*

"Only if you take Judy and Christina with you," Mom told her, probably thinking it would prevent any hanky panky.

"Sure." Sandy didn't mind because she knew what mom didn't: we would fall asleep during the movie. She took us to see *Pete's Dragon*, the original. Jim paid for the carload and parked off to the side.

"Come on, girls, let's go to the Snack Shack." Sandy led us off by our hands.

The Snack Shack was a beacon of fluorescent light and greasy aroma in the dusty, dark parking lot. There we could buy pizza, popcorn, candy, or those hot dogs than twirled on a metal roller. Sandy bought us each a candy bar and a container of popcorn to share. We were in our pajamas, and took our treats to the playground while she and Jim "set up the speaker." Judy and I were clueless at the time. We watched pre-movie cartoons from the playground, and we could almost hear the sound from the loudspeaker from atop of the concessions building.

We watched the movie from Jim's backseat and I remember about half of it. Judy fell asleep, sprawled on the backseat, and I was next to her on the floor, scrunched to one side of the hump. Jim started up the car to head home and they let us sleep. These were the days before seatbelts were the law. That's how Judy fell on top of me during the accident.

On the way home from the movie, a deer darted out in front of our car. Jim swerved across the road and landed at a 45-degree angle in the opposing ditch. The front of the car was completely crushed against the opposite embankment. Later, when Sandy and Judy recounted the story, Judy would always imitate herself crying and yelling, "Tina, oh no, Tina is dead!" Initially, Sandy, Jim and Judy had all thought I had died in the accident.

Obviously, I hadn't. I'd slept through the whole thing, and even the jarring hit against the embankment, the loud crunching metal, the sirens of the emergency vehicles and the paramedics and firemen checking me over didn't wake me up. I slept right up until the time the officer handed me to my mother on our front porch. My mother said it was a miracle from God that we survived such a bad wreck without serious injury. The big tank of a car was totaled.

Well after the 'miracle' of us surviving the accident, my mother set out on a mission to help me find a talent. I had none. Sandy was the smart one, the good girl who spoke two languages and could master any subject thrown at her, especially the hard ones like science and math. Judy was the popular, athletic one in the family who was a cheerleader and had tons of friends. She was short and fit, and she could make her body do anything. She was on the dive team, the gymnastics team, well, basically all teams. Judy could pick up any sport and master it, from softball to lacrosse to volleyball to cheerleading, and I was super jealous.

My mother decided that she needed to help me find something I could do. Unfortunately, I failed most

31

everything she signed me up to try. I was so bad in tennis that they had to cut my racquet handle shorter to give me more control on the court. It didn't work, so they cut the racquet shorter. And, they had to keep on cutting it shorter and shorter until there was nothing left but what looked like a ping-pong ball paddle. At that point, Mom stopped taking me to tennis.

I tried swimming, ballet, jazz, volleyball…I tried everything and failed, sports and music and even Girl Scouts. How do you fail at Girl Scouts? Well, I found a way.

It wasn't until Mom put me on a horse that I finally found something I could do. I finally felt like I wasn't a failure. I could do something well and enjoy it.

"I want to take horseback riding lessons tomorrow, too," Judy told Mom.

"No, this is Christina's activity," Mom said, shutting down any hope of Judy outshining me at the stables.

I was secretly happy because I finally had something all to myself. And, so Mom let me have horseback riding lessons a few times a week. I learned to trot and canter and take care of the animals by brushing them and cleaning their hooves. I had to perform 'barn duty' where I cleaned out the stalls and fed the horses. The barn became my second home.

Three days before Christmas, Mom accidentally set our house on fire. Daddy was on a business trip with IBM, and Mom wanted to surprise him by decorating for Christmas all by herself. Daddy usually put the lights on the tree, so Mom didn't know which ones to use and she ended up putting the wrong lights on the tree. They were the big ones, the outdoor lights, and somehow they caught the tree on fire.

Judy and I had already gone to bed when Mom started yelling for us to get out of the house. Judy shook me but I didn't wake up. She begged me and pleaded with me. "The house is on fire, Tina! We're going to die!"

I mumbled something. Mom called the fire department from downstairs and screamed for us to get out. Sandy came in to our room to help Judy get me out of bed. Sandy tried lifting me and Judy slapped my face, but I couldn't wake up.

"You can wear my ballerina pin!" Judy blurted out. That was really clever of her because she knew I coveted that pin. She had earned it in dance class, and it was shiny and pretty and I wanted it so badly. The promise was enough to get me to half awake so that they could both drag me out of the room, down the stairs, and outside into the freezing night air.

Mom said that if she hadn't still been awake, she's not sure we would have made it to the ground floor to get out of the house. "God looked after us and provided us a Christmas miracle."

As an adult I appreciate that God was watching over us and saved our lives. As a small girl at Christmas, it was a horrible sight to see your gifts burned and mangled. On the day before Christmas Eve when we returned home to find the living room a wet, black mess. We dug through the rubble under the tree, the charred remains of our Christmas. Mom wanted to see if there was anything to salvage before Daddy got home. Mom handed me a present. The paper was damp and the box was scorched. I opened it. Inside was a Holly Hobbie rag doll that mom had sewn for me. It was burned and scary looking. I felt sick.

"I'll make you another one, sweetie," and she hugged me.

Her hugs made things better.

Later that winter, after we'd gotten a lot of snow I came up with a plan. We had an old log trail in the backyard and every winter the neighborhood kids invaded our woods because it made for the best sledding. The older kids sprayed water on it, creating icy moguls and speed zones for some serious tricks. Most X Gamers today would be shocked at their parents' skills.

I wasn't allowed to go up higher than a certain tree when sledding because I was so little, but I had other ideas. Early one morning, I pulled on my boots and parka, and slipped outside into the frigid air. I dragged my sled behind me like a dutiful puppy and made my way to that tree. It had a large, curved branch near the bottom which made it stand out from the others. My parents had been specific that this was as high as I should go. Patting the tree trunk, I looked down the trail at my short ride. I would barely get going, then it would be over. I'd seen the older kids zoom by this very spot where some of them would catch air and they'd shriek with joy. I wanted to go fast and fly, too.

I looked around to be sure that I was alone. It was too early for the older kids to be awake, and the younger ones, who were my age, were watching cartoons and eating Trix cereal or PopTarts in their pajamas. So, I walked right on by my marker tree as I stepped into the larger boot prints leading me farther up the hill. Soon, I was at the top where the fallen tree lay, the one that older kids used to kick off their runs. I sat down on my wood and metal sled and it was one of those that could be steered with the front bar, though I obviously never mastered that feat.

I felt that little thrill you get when you're disobeying your parents and looking forward to an adventure. One push off the decaying bark, and *whoosh!* The steel runners slid over the icy snow and I went so fast that I was sent airborne at my marker tree, landing back on the trail with wobbly thuds. I careened down the slope in an uncontrolled dive and stopped only when my sled spun around like a top, slamming it and me into the pile of firewood stacked next to our shed.

Mom ran out of the house wearing only a nightgown and socks. She'd been watching me from the second story kitchen window, and must've flown down the stairs to run out the basement.

She cradled my face in her hands. Was I okay? Was anything broken? Did I hit my head? Tears wet her cheeks. That's probably when she decided to become a nurse. She took me to the emergency room where they put about a dozen stitches in my head. It hurt like the devil, and I wanted them to stop. I thought maybe God could help me, so I tried to recite a Hail Mary, but I couldn't remember all the words. The only prayer I knew by heart was the dinner blessing, but that didn't seem like the right prayer for being in pain. I knew a little bit of the Our Father prayer, but not the whole thing, so I tried to think if I knew any other prayer. Before I settled on what to pray, it was over, and somehow by not even praying God took the painful experience from me. Looking like an angel, the nurse held out a pail of lollipops for me to choose. They were the good kind, the brightly colored round discs with looped rope handles. I picked a red one, because cherry was the best.

I never did sled past that tree with the curved branch again because that summer we left New York and moved to North Carolina, leaving behind our house on the hill with its log trail perfect for sledding.

In some ways, moving from New York to North Carolina felt almost as jarring as that sled crash. It was hot as Hades, I missed our backyard pool, and I still wasn't any good at besting Judy.

"Race ya, Tina!" My sister Judy was already in the lead. Although smaller than me, she was older and more athletic with well-tuned legs that propelled her bike with the banana seat down the sidewalk at a good clip. Her lime green towel flew out behind her like a cape, and I thought if I could get a little closer I would grab it, and she would pull me along. But I never got closer, and she always beat me to the pool.

It was our first summer in North Carolina and it was so hot I thought we must be living closer to hell. You could see the heat rise up in shimmery waves from the streets and it was hard to breathe. There was no wind, only searing sun and thick air. Ours was the fourth house built in the Farmington Woods neighborhood, which in another life had been old-growth pine forest. I missed our very own pool in New York, speckled with dead leaves that bobbed in the water like little boats.

Mom sewed Judy and me halter tops which kept us cooler in the southern climate. She had one pattern, and made over twenty of them in different colors and patterned fabrics. We wore them every day, even to school when we started in the fall.

I pretty much did what I wanted to as a kid, because back then parents had a different mindset. They weren't really pushing their kids to advance, like today. Parents took care of their own lives and interested themselves in their own activities. They didn't focus on us kids. Sure, mom would get Judy to her dance classes or gymnastics, but it wasn't a main focus. So, Judy and I ran around a lot in the neighborhood on our bikes.

We would put on our swimsuits with cutoff jeans and the halter tops and bike down the sidewalk and across the main road to the racquet club and pool. Today, Kildaire Farm Road is a main thoroughfare and it would take an experienced biker to navigate the dangerous lanes of really busy traffic. But back then, it was a quiet road named for the dairy farm that had relinquished its cow pastures to trimmed suburban lawns and brown and beige painted split level homes.

We threw down our bikes in the grass where they joined the rainbow collection of other two-wheeled steeds left by kids already in the pool, and we made our way through the breezeway to a sign-in desk. The teenage girl who was there to greet us, didn't. Instead, she chewed her gum and flirted with a tan lifeguard in red trunks leaning coolly against her table. He didn't wear a shirt, and his bare chest was mocha and smooth like Mom's coffee, except for his nose which was pure white from the zinc oxide which was the mark of a lifeguard. The girl giggled at him and popped a bubble.

"Our last name's Higgins," Judy said after writing it carefully in the log.

The girl flipped through the pages of her directory, found our name, or pretended to, then waved us in with a dismissive hand tinkling with rings and bangles.

Judy and I bunched our towels and clothes into a pile next to the chain-link fence and we did that quick run-walk you do at the pool, where you're not supposed to run, but you have to move fast because the concrete burns your feet.

We jumped in. The water was temperate at best, but being wet was preferable to sweating at home. We spent the afternoon in the water, our fingers white and wrinkled, taking breaks by baking in the sun on our wet towels. Judy bought us popsicles and we drank warm water from the drinking fountain. By the time we'd head home, our eyes would be stinging and red from the chlorine and our ears would slosh with water. After a few weeks, our hair, like everyone else's, would have green-silver highlights from the chemicals.

At home we threw our wet stuff on the bathroom floor and combed our hair. I wrapped myself in a large towel and walked down the hallway to my upstairs bedroom which was mine alone. Judy had her own room, too. I passed by Daddy's office on the way. It was dark, with only some light seeping in through the nearly closed burgundy curtains. The magazines were there, and Daddy wasn't. I crept in, pulling the towel tighter around me and sat down next to the bookcase by the open door, which I closed slightly with my toes. I stared at the cover of the top issue. A dark-haired woman in a sheer dress smiled out at me. She had a rope tied around her dress like a Roman goddess from my history book, and she held an American flag that waved behind her. The banner across the bottom said, "Happy Birthday,

America!" and the top read, PLAYBOY, in all caps. I knew what was inside and I wanted another look.

Pretty women with lipstick smiles filled the pages. Some of them wore frilly leggings with no panties, or long scarves around part of their bodies, so you could barely see what was underneath. I wondered if my flat chest would pop out big breasts or little nubs? Being adopted, I had no way to know what was in store for me, so there was no use looking at Mom for an example.

I flipped the magazine on its side and freed the centerfold from her paper prison. She sprawled out on the carpet like a summer goddess, dangling on a rope with high, large breasts that reached up as if for a pat. Everything seemed both dangerous and okay at the same time. I allowed a little pat that she seemed to want, my pool-soaked digits touching her nipples, then tracing her bikini tan line down to a pair of wildly patriotic socks. I wondered about those socks, the only clothes she wore. *Did she wear them because her feet were cold?*

"Dinner's ready!" mom yelled from the kitchen. I shoved Miss Centerfold back into her issue and on top of the collection. I tiptoed down the hall and pulled on clothes, leaving my wet towel behind, and raced to the table. My whole body was flushed—from the sun, from the run down the hall, and from seeing the picture of Miss Centerfold.

I didn't fully understand the sexually explicit books and magazines that Daddy had left out in a very public area of his office, easy for anyone to see, but I found them fascinating.

On most Saturday nights, Daddy was home and the house was full of loud people, platters of finger foods and various colored spirits in short-stemmed glasses or tumblers. We threw lots of parties, and all the devout couples at IBM showed up. They were known as the "IBM Catholic Crowd." The company had been responsible for our move down south to Cary. Relocation was normal for IBMers during those years, and they all joked that IBM stood for: *I've Been Moved*.

On party nights, I would sit at the top of the stairs with the other younger kids as our parents partied below. The older kids would hang out with Judy or wouldn't come at all. We would remain hidden in the shadows of the upstairs hallway because that's where we got the best gossip. We could overhear the private conversations which took place away from others in the party room. They thought they were speaking in secret and had no idea that their sneaky children heard every word.

I didn't understand everything, but I got the gist of what was going on. So-and-So's son had marijuana in his locker at school and the police brought him home to his parents. I'll bet he got a spanking. So-and-So's taking the pill. I didn't know what kind of pill that was, but the way they were talking about it made it sound bad. So-and-so's daughter got an abortion. An abortion? I wasn't sure what that was, but I knew it was something Catholics weren't supposed to do. Mom had said something about that, about how the Pope said abortions aren't allowed. So, how could her daughter get one? How could a Catholic do something the Pope said they weren't supposed to do? I had to ponder on that one.

Later, after we got bored with the gossip, the other younger kids and I would fall asleep in my room listening to Top 40 music on a digital radio alarm clock, punctuated with drunken laughter and glasses clinking from downstairs. Daddy was the life of the party and they came 'because of him. He was 'that guy.' He's been dead for years now and in some ways, to a lot of people, he's still 'that guy.'

As a young man, Daddy attended university in Vatican City because he had a calling to become a priest. That's the Jewish mom's equivalent of your son becoming a doctor or lawyer, *maybe even better*, so you can imagine my grandmother's delight. The Vatican has about 65 universities in Vatican City and around Rome, but don't ask me which one he attended. Friends and relatives always revered Daddy because of this close connection to the Pope. I'm not sure he ever met him, but everyone assumed since Daddy was at 'Catholic Ground Zero' (otherwise known as the Vatican), he was somehow more blessed than the rest of them.

To the disappointment of my Irish Catholic grandmother and granddad Higgins, Daddy decided that maybe the celibate life wasn't for him. After graduation, he came back to the States for good and met my mom. She was a petite brunette attracted to his lean, tall frame that was topped by rich auburn hair which dusted silver over the years. He spoke 4 languages and had a Mensa IQ, which probably impressed my mom. To the shock and horror of his parents, my daddy proposed to this divorced, Methodist, single mother, who accepted his offer. To ensure a Catholic wedding, her first marriage would have to be annulled and she would have to convert. She provided a declaration of her first husband's infidelity, and together, with a probably large check to the diocese from my grandparents, the tribunal approved the annulment. White dress, wedding Mass and all, my parents' holy union was sealed.

Right after the vows, Daddy adopted mom's daughter Sandy, and because mom wanted a big family, they eventually adopted Judy, and then me. They probably would have kept going, but Daddy was done. So, Mom busied herself with rescued pets, rescued kids from the Freshair Child program, sewing, and nursing school. She supervised the household while Daddy firmed his position in the IBM corporate hive, buzzing around the country on silver jets to close deals with handshakes and martinis. Then, home on the weekends for parties, grilling and suburban lawn maintenance.

My grandmother Higgins, who we were told to call 'Grandmother,' taught us all about the Vatican and how to make beds properly. To this day, I can't go to sleep unless my sheets are folded and tucked in with military corners.

Grandmother would tell us about the Swiss Guard, the military unit that protects the Pope. She showed us pictures of them standing watch like court jesters, in bright blue and gold striped uniforms with red accents. They wore berets, cocked to the side, or helmets like Conquistadors, topped with huge, brightly colored feathers.

"Dyed ostrich feathers," she would tell us. I would picture those ugly, long legged birds with the large, pretty eyes that I saw in the encyclopedia. I felt awful they had to kill them, because how else would you get "died ostrich feathers."

She told us that the Swiss Guard were trained military men, armed and ready to protect the Pope with their lives if necessary.

I think it's a pretty good scheme to conceal such a deadly force in those frilly costumes. Who expects the court jester would be packing heat?

I had a knack for punching my daddy's buttons, even when I wasn't trying, like when I had to finish my lima beans. Lima beans are the most disgusting food on the planet as far as I'm concerned.

"You're going to sit there, Christina Marie, until you finish every last lima bean on that plate," Daddy ordered from the head of the table. He always called me "Christina Marie" when I was in trouble.

I stared down at the disgusting green things that looked like bug pods and felt my stomach churning. "I can't. I'll throw up!" I protested. I was a projectile vomiter who could make herself sick by willing it.

Daddy pointed his finger at me. "Young lady, you *will* eat them."

I pointed my finger back at him. "No, they'll make me sick."

He clenched his teeth and that vein on the side of his head started to bulge, the one I could get to work out like a little worm from his skin. Pointing my finger at him was like adding fuel to his fire, but I knew I'd be sick if I ate them.

He pushed out his chair, stomped into the kitchen and came back with the entire pot of beans. He ladled most of the remainder of the beans onto my plate.

"There. Now eat them. Every. Last. One." Daddy plopped the nearly empty pot on the table and sat down to watch me eat, that little vein still bulging on his temple.

I knew I had to sit there until I finished the lima beans. The mass of them on my plate seemed impossible, like climbing Everest. But, I wanted to leave the table, so I ate them. Their slimy hard shells slipped off like beetles' wings in my mouth and caught in my cheeks. Pulpy innards stuck to my teeth as I tried to mix the two consistencies into a form that I could swallow. I used milk to help get it down, until my glass was empty. Then, I started popping them whole, like big pills the doctor gives you when you're really sick, until they were all gone.

"Okay. You're done." Daddy sounded satisfied, like he'd won a mastermind battle of the wills. He left me at the table and climbed the stairs to his office.

I picked up my plate and walked into the kitchen. After placing it on the counter, I promptly threw up the lima beans into the trash can. *Every. Last. One.*

So, really, who won *that* battle?

Chapter 3

Cowgirl at the Burlesque

Jesus replied, "You hypocrites! Isaiah was right
when he prophesied about you, for he wrote,
'These people honor me with their lips, but their
hearts are far from me.'"
~*Mark 7:6 (NLT)*

Past

Le Celle Saint-Cloud, France, 1980s

Christi/Tina age 11-15

*D*addy was told by IBM to move to the Paris office,
and so he did. And, so did we. We did not sell our
house in Cary, North Carolina, because mom wanted to
keep it. So, we moved most of our things including the
furniture to France and left the house behind.

"We've stayed in one place longer than most," Daddy had told me, as if that were a consolation for us moving across the entire ocean, far away from all of my friends and my school.

If we'd moved earlier, it wouldn't have hurt as much.

I thought back to when I was little and we'd moved from New York to North Carolina and it didn't seem that bad. But, I was seven then, not eleven, and I hadn't met close friends. North Carolina had become the place "where I am from."

Daddy was explaining that IBM needed him in France, and it would be a great adventure for us all to live in a foreign country. You could tell he was excited about the move, and even Mom pepped up. I was sad because this was one adventure I did not want to have.

When we first moved to France we lived at the Hilton hotel for almost three months. It was Mom, Daddy, Judy and me as Sandy had already graduated college and she was married and living in Florida. Every afternoon, I headed down to the Hotel lobby to savor vanilla ice cream in a tall glass with mint and chocolate syrup. I gained a lot of weight on this snack plan, but it was my daily treat.

We ate in restaurants most of the time then, too, which wasn't helping my waistline. On our very first outing to a French restaurant, fresh off the plane from the States, I ordered a hamburger. It wasn't on the menu, but they made it special for me.

"Un ham-buh-guh." The waiter spoke in a thick, French accent.

The burger he set in front of me was nearly raw. I told Daddy I couldn't eat it. He spoke in fast—and I would assume perfect—French to the waiter, who, with a quick clip, scooped up my plate. A few minutes later he deposited it again. The burger was still too raw for me to eat.

The second time we tried to send it back, the waiter left the plate in front of me, and disappeared into the kitchen. There was a loud clang from within and the chef came shooting out the swinging doors and approached our table. He stood over me and his massive belly, tightly wrapped in a soiled apron, was practically thrust into my face. A white chef's hat teetered atop his nearly balding head and when he bent down to look me squarely in the eyes, I thought it was going to fall off onto the table. He poked his finger at me and then he yelled at me. In French. His round face was red and sweaty and he spit out little bits of saliva as he sputtered something I could not possibly understand. Daddy didn't say anything or try to intervene, so I nodded at the angry chef, picked up my burger and took a small bite. Seeming satisfied, he did an about face and stormed off, the hat swaying on his head all the way back to the kitchen.

That was the first time I tried new food and eventually, after some trial and error, I found that I enjoyed eating different things. I found out that the food in France was actually delicious, as everyone else knows, but that took me some time to figure out.

When we first arrived in France, Judy and I were miserable. We hated leaving our friends in North Carolina, and we sat around pouting like children much younger than ourselves. Mom and Daddy offered to give me horseback riding lessons, but I flat out refused.

"They'll just speak French and I won't know what they're saying." I decided I was going to punish them for making me move by not learning French. No matter what, I wasn't going to learn it.

And, Judy was no better with her attitude. She wouldn't even answer our parents when they asked questions. She sat there with her mouth closed and her eyes elsewhere. Our attitudes made Daddy cry. He actually cried. I think he thought that we'd love France like he did. But, we were too bitter about all that we'd left behind.

Our stuff was in shipping containers locked up in customs after crossing the ocean on a freighter. So, we were still at the hotel when mom sent us off to school at the American School of Paris, or what we called the ASP. The school was filled with mostly IBM employees' kids. Some of them were American and some from other countries. The kids with no ties to IBM were American military brats. Most everyone at the school was transplanted from somewhere else. Despite this, I was still a little chicken because I was the 'new kid'. And, I didn't even have Judy to lean on. I was in elementary school and Judy was in upper school, which is their version of high school.

The ASP was an English-speaking school, but with required French classes. I was to learn to speak French while learning world history, math, art, science, and whatever other important things they wanted us to know. All I know is that I was never meant for school. Like, in no way possible. So, instead of just struggling like I did at my elementary school at home, I was going to be struggling *and* learning a foreign language.

Mom, Judy and I took a bus to the school campus, which was in Saint-Cloud. The school was a typical brick school building sitting on a freshly cut green lawn crisscrossed with sidewalks and bordered by rugby fields. We dropped off Judy first at her building and I sat in the hallway on a bench while Mom checked her in. Then, we headed over to the elementary school where I was set to start sixth grade.

I was feeling pretty good about myself. I wore the Bananarama-style, off-white, courderoy jacket with big shoulder pads, a ruffled jean skirt, and cowboy boots. It was the look we'd all adopted. It was the "Who Shot JR?" days of *Dallas*, the most popular show on TV. Everyone who was fashion conscious owned a jean skirt and cowboy boots, just like Sue Ellen from the series. My friends and I were allowed to watch *Dallas*, a night-time soap opera, because our moms wanted to watch it. So, we pretty much rocked the Texas oil baron wife's look, right down to the huge hair with the requisite 'mall bangs' of the eighties. Big hair was essential to balance out those puffy clothes.

The principal left my mom to fill out paperwork, while he escorted me to class. My high-heeled boots echoed in the empty hallway. The room, which had been filled with students' chatter, became uncomfortably quiet when we walked in. I shook the teacher's hand like Mom told me to do, and the teacher introduced me to the class. I told them my name was "Christi," because I was sick of being "Tina." I could hear the sing-song chants echoing in my head: "Tina, Tina, bal-ler-ina."

No, I was going to be Christi.

The teacher pointed me to a desk and chair unit near the window. Everyone stared at me as I clicked and clacked my boots across the linoleum and wrestled my ruffles into the seat. The other kids were dressed in little kids' clothes: pants with button down shirts and cardigans. I felt very large, very adult, and very out of place. They continued to stare at me, even after the teacher called for class to begin. I held my breath, wanting to melt into my chair.

Back home I wasn't one of the popular set, but I was the lead of a pretty good crowd. We were a tight band. We dressed cool and had our own slang. I was known and I was comfortable and school was social and fun. But bulging out of this tight seat, dressed like an over-fluffed American TV character, I felt like the kid who showed up for the party in costume, only it wasn't a costume party.

The boys in the class checked me out. I definitely wasn't dressed like a child like the other girls in class, and I was developing. The girls threw me dagger eyes.

"Hey, cowgirl, where'd you get those boots?" Janine sat behind me and she wasn't interested in becoming friends.

Angelique, a thin, petite girl with shiny black hair and icy blue eyes gave a little snort. She had graceful hands and a model's face. Even her snort was elegant. "Je crois qu'elle est bête. You know what that means? Are you stupid?"

The students sitting around me laughed. The teacher shushed the class.

I was not stupid and I wanted to smash in her pretty, pert face with a brick. I stared at my desk and prayed for the bell to ring or for God to send lightning striking down to destroy the school. Either one would have been fine with me. The clock on the wall moved with the speed of the Box Turtles back home in North Carolina. Box turtles would cross the road and people would stop in their cars, right in the middle of the street, and get out and transport them to the other side. If you were driving along and you saw a stopped car with their door open, you knew someone was saving one of those turtles.

I tried to ignore the whispers and busied myself with classwork. *There was so much work!*

For lunch I didn't have to wonder if anyone would sit with me because our school didn't have a cafeteria. The younger classes brought their lunches, but since we were still at the hotel and Mom didn't have a kitchen, I had to buy my lunch with the older kids. Mom had given me some Francs and told me to buy my meal from Le Comnionette, which was basically a food truck. While the elementary students ate their lunches from paper bags or metal boxes, I walked all the way over to the upper class drive and bought mine at the food truck. By the time I got back, lunch was over. I learned to eat it on the way back.

The day was painfully slow, and I prayed to God to make it over. When the last bell rang—*finally!*—I waited for everyone to leave the class before I got up so they wouldn't stare. When the room was empty, save for the teacher making notes at her desk and ignoring me, I pulled my ruffled skirt from the desk and clicked and clacked my cowboy boots across the room.

"What's wrong, Sweetie?" Mom had found me lying face down crying into my pillow in my room. I was having a show of teenage drama.

She rubbed my back. "Tell me what's going on."

"They hate me."

"They don't hate you."

She had an annoying way of disagreeing with my version of events. "Yes, they do! They're different and childish. I'm dressed in all the wrong clothes, and I want to go home!"

"Honey, this is our home, now. We can't 'go home' because we're already there. This is home."

"MAHHHM!" She wasn't helping. Plus, it wasn't fair that Judy was doing so well when I was the odd man out. Judy's classmates had learned she was a terrific cheerleader and athlete, so she became part of the 'popular set' in no time. Life was easy for her in the high school because she was skilled and had a big personality. But for me down in the elementary school? Not so much.

"Listen," Mom continued in her soothing voice, "you probably need some new clothes for school, so let's the three of us go to the stores, and I'll buy you and Judy some new things."

From the Hilton Paris Opera to La Défense was only a short metro ride. La Défense was a business and shopping district just outside of Paris and it was also where Daddy worked. IBM France and IBM International both had offices there. We would walk past the ongoing construction for the Grande Arche, a gigantic, open cube that was part monument part building. Then, across a busy intersection to the shopping mall. There was Benneton and other cool stores with the latest fashions.

There were also restaurants that offered quiches and salads and long baguettes with ham and butter.

I sat up on the bed and looked at her. She had that expression she got when she understood that I was in pain and she wanted to make it better. It was the perfect look for her profession as a nurse.

"Okay?" she asked.

"Yeah. I could use some different shirts, maybe some pants. Oh, and I can I get a haircut?"

"You sure you want to cut it? It took you so long to grow it out and—"

"Yes, I do! It's, um, it's too much work right now." I pictured the girls in my class with their simpler, shorter styles that didn't pouf out like mine.

"Okay, I'm sure we can find someone to cut your hair."

I fell into her arms. "Thanks, Mom."

"Of course."

Monday I walked into school dressed in chic, European clothes and my curly hair was bobbed. Now, every eye in the classroom stared at me, but I stared back. They quickly turned to face the front of the room. I had read somewhere that "clothes don't make the man," but I'm not so sure of that. My change of clothes didn't make me instantly popular, but at least my classmates stopped making fun of me.

When we finally left the hotel, we moved into a large house in Le Celle Saint-Cloud, on the other side of the Seine from Paris. The streets were lined with trees and the old buildings and houses were built of grey bricks with rust colored roofs. Everyone had cheery doors that were painted bright red or blue. It was like a picture-perfect French town.

But our neighborhood wasn't like that. It was a new development occupied by many IBM'ers and other non-natives. The modern houses stood out, and not in a good way, from the charming French architecture around it. There were a total of about forty or fifty houses in our gated community, though the gate was only for looks as it didn't work or keep anyone out. The only good thing about the houses was that every window had working shutters that opened and closed, which I thought was pretty cool. Our shutters back in North Carolina were only for looks. They didn't do anything but sit there and need painting. My bedroom window in our French home opened onto a roof ledge, which, once I reached middle school, gave me a perfect place to crawl out on to sneak a cigarette.

We would hit the bakery at the bottom of the street every day for skinny baguettes and heartier du pain. Every Wednesday and Saturday we'd go to the fresh market at the top of the street for ripe cherries and crisp apples and all kinds of fruits and vegetables. Grocery shopping didn't mean like going to the Piggly Wiggly once a week like in North Carolina. In France we picked up 'this or that' from small shops nearly every day.

The first big thing that happened in France was that my daddy bought Mom a puppy. We named her Sadie. He bought the long haired teckel dachshund pup at a local bar in town and even wrote the check on top of a pinball machine. It was like a big city 'deal' going down. Then, we came home with the puppy. Sadie was Mom's, because she was the caretaker of all things, but it was my responsibility to walk her every day. Whenever we were out walking, if Sadie was finished with the walk, she would lay down in the middle of the road. So, when I'd turn back for home, I'd have to carry her all the way. Making me walk Sadie was my parent's way of putting me on an exercise program to help me lose the hotel ice cream fat.

Things were getting better, but I still refused to learn French and I didn't have any friends. Judy-the-cheerleader had her own set of friends. My birthday was coming up and without any friends, I wasn't looking forward to it.

"Let's plan your party!" Mom said with a little too much excitement.

"Why have a party if no one's going to come?" I retorted.

Mom thought for a moment. Then she stated, "We'll see about that."

Mom got on the phone and called the mom of every girl in my class and invited them to my birthday party. All 20 of them. And, they all showed up. Back then, moms could make their elementary schooler girls attend a party even if the girl didn't want to go. It was all about how these things reflected on the mom, not what the kid wanted.

"I'm Celia."

"Christi," I replied, as if we were meeting for the first time and we hadn't spent the last few months in class together.

"Show me your room."

I thought it was a pretty bold thing to say. But, here was a real, live girl asking—no, demanding—to see my room, and that made me pretty excited.

"Down this way." I lead her down the hallway.

"We'll come, too." A girl named Delphine tugging on the arm of her friend and constant companion, practically her Siamese twin, Nina. Another girl named Lisa joined them.

We listened to cassette tapes of pop hit singles by artists like Blondie, Dr. Hook, Christopher Cross and Pink Floyd. We ate junk food and watched videotaped movies, movies which would be considered inappropriate for our age on the VCR. My big sister Sandy, who was married and had remained in North Carolina, sent us Mel Brooks movies, like *Blazing Saddles*. We talked about the boys in class. Cecilia had a crush on Pierre. Delphine thought our classmate Luke was dreamy, but not as dreamy as Shaun Cassidy.

School was better, and I had kids to sit with at lunch now that mom packed me one. I had friends to copy homework off of, and pass notes to, and share secrets with. I felt like I was finally fitting in. Except for the mouthful of orthodontic bands and wires the French dentist maliciously stuck in my mouth, I was feeling pretty good about being in France.

But, I still refused to learn French.

And, that was a sticking point with my parents. I refused to learn French at school, and I refused to learn French when they signed me up for private lessons. So, when I got to 7th Grade, Mom and Daddy sent me to summer camp. I spent two months living at a camp where they only spoke French. I guess my parents fig-ured a full-immersion experience was probably the only way I was ever going to learn to speak French.

The camp was in the Alsace region of France, near the border of Germany. Our camp occupied a smat-tering of older stone buildings tucked into the woods on a hill above the Rhine River. The counselors took us on hikes in the woods and tours of local historical sites, and they gave us packet tubes of condensed milk and crackers for our snack breaks on the trail. We spent a lot of time outdoors climbing the hillsides, sleeping in open-air tree hammocks, horseback riding bareback and exploring the ruins of old buildings and churches. Other times, we hung out like typical teenagers eating, playing cards and dreaming about what the future held.

There was only one other girl at camp that spoke English as her first language. Her name was Maureen and we went to school together. But it was our similar circumstances at camp that made us close friends: she also did not speak French.

I found out that her father worked for IBM, too, and it didn't take us long to put two and two together. It seems that our fathers got into cahoots and sent us to this particular camp to learn French by necessity. It worked, because even though Maureen and I could speak English with each other, we still had to speak French to communicate with the counselors and other students. So that was the summer I learned to speak French. None of it was proper French. A lot of it was slang and bad words, because, let's face it, it was the other teenagers who taught Maureen and me to speak French.

At the camp, they had a Turkish toilet. Now, a Turkish toilet is sort of like an outhouse. It has your typical outhouse hole in the ground, but the kicker is, a Turkish toilet does not have a seat. Well, I wasn't going to be doing that. So, Maureen and I had to figure out a solution because standing was not an option for us American girls.

"Follow me," I ordered Maureen, as if I knew what I was doing. All I knew was that I wasn't happy with the toilet hole situation and I was determined to find a solution. Behind the main building was a barn, and behind the barn was a dump area littered with discarded furniture and broken equipment. We trekked around back and marched through the tall weeds and rusted metal trash to see if we could find something to better the situation.

"Ouch!" I cried. A wheel spoke from an old bicycle poked my leg and blood dripped from the wound.

"I hope you have your shots," said Maureen, half joking.

"Probably." They'd given me a bunch before we left for Europe, so I was hoping that at least one of them would protect me from the rusted spoke. "Which one is it again that prevents you from getting sick when you get cut by metal?"

"Tetanus. I think if you don't get the shot it makes your jaw freeze or something like that."

"Well, if my jaw freezes, I guess I won't have to learn French!"

We both laughed.

"Look, there's a chair!" she called out.

And, there it was. Our summer savior of rusted metal with white chipped paint and a seat warped from rain.

"Excellent!" I shouted and ran to it, blood trickling down my leg from the scrape. But, I didn't care. I picked up the chair and jammed the foot of my other leg into the back side of the seat. It popped out and landed in the weeds.

We took turns carrying our find back to the out-house, where we sat it down over the hole. We had our toilet seat.

And, we became quite popular for it.

Daddy wanted us to see as much of the country as we could. So, when I returned from camp, he took us on a trip to the south of France. On our first day at the beach, I got a shock. Nearly all the women at the beach were topless.

"Looks like we'll have to adjust to the way they do it here." Daddy turned around to look at Mom. "I think you and the girls should take off your tops."

"Alan, you're not serious?"

"It's their custom. We don't want to seem out of place, do we?"

Mom set her bag of towels down on the sand and sighed. "I don't know."

"It would be rude, don't you think, not to go along with what they consider normal?" Daddy laid out a blanket and grabbed the suntan oil.

"Well, I guess, if that's what they do..."

"C'mon girls, we're going to be French today!" Daddy grabbed the tie on Mom's bikini top and pulled it loose. Two strings fell down where once had been a bow.

Judy and I took off our tops and put them in Mom's bag. It felt awkward to be wearing only bikini bottoms at the beach. Daddy helped Mom slather our bare torsos with oil and I wondered if my chest would burn.

On Sundays we attended Mass at an English speaking church in Paris. One day I walked through the doorway and I was overcome with an intense hatred for everyone inside. It seemed like everyone lived a different life inside the church than outside of it. Their prayers left their lips easily in Mass, but in their daily lives they were far from God's decrees. I felt like the church people were a bunch of hypocrites.

They all made me sick. As we walked down the aisle as a family, the four of us with Daddy in front, I looked at the rows of supposedly devout Catholics. People worked rosaries in their hands, they greeted each other, and some sat in reverent awe of the altar. To me, they were a bunch of fakes and phonies.

You say you don't believe in abortion, but when your daughter gets pregnant, you take her for an abortion. You say you don't believe in birth control, but after you've had your sixth kid, you take the pill. You're not living the life you're telling everyone else they should be living.

We slid into our pew, near the front, of course, so Daddy could do the reading. He was a Lector, a lay member who read the gospel to the congregation during Mass. A prominent position was required for someone as revered as Daddy who had attended college at the Vatican. And that seemed weird. He was put on a pedestal for nearly being a priest, yet here he sat in the cathedral with his family: his daughters and a wife who was a divorcee. The service started and I went through the motions. Standing, kneeling, sitting, repeat until communion. We didn't walk out after communion like so many did. No, we stayed until the very end.

And the minute I get old enough that I don't have to come back to church, I'm outta this place. I'm not going to go to church with hypocrites.

On Sundays we attended Mass, which I really didn't like, but on Tuesdays we went to the burlesque, which I did. We would hop on the train into Paris and Daddy would take us to a burlesque show. It was a thing that people did. You took your family to Paris and out to dinner, then to the Moulin Rouge or Le Lido. Topless dancers with feathered headdresses would kick about the stage, and the parents would order cocktails brought to the seats. Daddy loved taking us there.

As I got older, I could take the train into Paris all by myself, my parents trusted me that much, and Paris was a safe city then. I had friends to go with me and we'd take the train to eat in the ethnic restaurants in the various sections of the city. After, we would walk around Montmarte and go into the shops. In Little Africa we'd eat Thieboudiene, which was a pungent rice and fish dish, or Chicken Yassa with onions and lemon. Or, we'd wolf down some crepes from a busy café before drinking in the bars along Rue Oberkampf, since the drinking age then for beer and wine, which included champagne, was 16 years of age in France. Other nights, we'd head to the Latin Quarter to eat real Spanish food and hit the Flamenco clubs after. My taste in foreign cuisine had really expanded since that raw hamburger incident.

One day, I'd gone into the city alone to do some shopping, but I missed my train heading back to La Celle-Saint-Cloud so I had to take a later train. I was standing at the station waiting for the train, a lit cigarette stuck out my mouth when I looked up to see Daddy was standing next to me.

"What do you think you're doing?" The little vein on the side of his temple started to bulge.

He looked down at me and I felt small. Trying to be casual, I took the cigarette out of my mouth and threw it on the pavement, extinguishing it with a deliberate step of my army boot.

He grunted, but didn't say anything. I figured that I was going to be in a world of hurt when we got home. The train arrived with a rush of wind and I wished I could get caught up into the blast of air and blow away down the rail line far away from Daddy and my crushed cigarette on the ground.

"Let's go home," he said sternly.

We boarded the train and took backwards seats next to each other. But the odd thing was that he never said another word to me about the cigarette. Not on the train, and not at home. We never spoke about it ever again. I felt like I dodged a bullet with that one.

About a month later, we were having dinner in our large dining room in our house in La Celle-St.-Cloud. Mom had made a certain baked chicken, called a *Poulet Roti*, roasted squash and Brussel sprouts, with baguette. It was a normal weekday night, and I had some homework to do, but mostly wanted to watch a movie. Sandy had sent a us a new video cassette.

The dinner conversation was ordinary. Judy had been talking about a school trip coming up, and I was telling Mom that I needed new ski pants for the season.

Daddy interrupted our chatter by clearing his throat. "I have an announcement to make." He spoke as if he were giving a presentation for a crowd. "In a few weeks, we'll be moving back to our home in North Carolina."

The room went silent. We stopped chewing. I wasn't even sure the grandfather clock in the living room that we'd brought over from the States continued to tick. I looked at Mom, but she looked at Daddy. She had known, of course.

"No! No! No! I'm not going with you." Judy started to cry.

I started shaking. "Leave France? Now? Why?" I couldn't believe it was happening. I wanted to scream or throw something. So, I threw down my fork, where it clanked and rattled on my plate in the quiet of the room.

How could he do this to me? To us? I've got friends and parties…and bars…and cigarettes. I wanted a cigarette. They'd spent so much time, money and effort making me fit into French culture, and now they were taking it from me. It was unfair and they were hypocrites. I even learned to speak French. For what? What was the purpose now?

I pushed back from the table, my chair falling behind me, and stormed off toward my bedroom. A pack of cigarettes was hidden underneath my mattress and I planned to sit on the window ledge, drawing in that soothing grey smoke, and plot a way to get out of this move. There had to be a solution. I would stay with Maureen or Celia, if their families would have me. I could finish school and join my family later, after graduation. Judy would be going off to college anyway, so it really didn't matter. Let Mom and Daddy live in North Carolina. Judy and I could live anywhere in the world we wanted.

But, I knew it was a false hope. My parents would never leave me in France.

"I don't wanna go and you can't make me!" I yelled down the hallway as I slammed my bedroom door shut.

Chapter 4

Dead Ringer

This I declare about my Lord: He alone is my refuge,
my place of safety; he is my God, and I trust him.
~*Psalm 91:2 (NLT)*

Present Day

Cary, North Carolina

March

*I*t was a busy Saturday in the salon because the
following day was Easter. Women needed their
fresh hair to complement their Easter attire. This is the
South, and on Easter, you dress up. If you attend certain churches, you might even wear a new hat. *Not me*.
Everyone usually gets a new pair of pumps or maybe
sandals, which we wear even if it's freezing because
regardless of the temperature, it's Spring. The sanctu-
aries are packed with bright colors and shiny fabrics,

the people sitting should-to-shoulder in pews like rows of flowers in the garden.

After Easter services, we feast. Most families serve sweet ham or turkey or both, and every side usually has bacon in it. Bowls overflow with dishes like collards with bacon, green beans with bacon, beans with bacon, brussels sprouts with bacon, well, basically anything with bacon. I once ate a slice of chocolate pecan pie with bacon. It was overkill, but really good overkill.

Between clients, I stared at the photo on my phone. Arlene would be thrilled to see the picture of my possible birth mother. Should I call and tell her? I felt some obligation since this was all her fault anyway, and she'd want to know.

"What you looking at?" Victoria, another hairdresser and my partner in crime even before Arlene, leaned over to peek at my phone. "She's pretty. Who is she, Christina?" Like my mom, Victoria always called me 'Christina'. When we met many years ago, when I first saw her rich auburn hair and sparkling blue eyes in the salon. I introduced myself as 'Christi,' but she asked me for my 'given name' and she'd used it ever since. We became friends in salon school and she was the peanut butter to my jelly, the friend who followed me from salon to salon. She rented a booth from me now at 'Papillion the salon', which I owned. Victoria sidled up beside me and gave me a half hug with one arm, while her other hand held shears that pointed to the ceiling.

"You won't believe this, Victoria. I have a picture of the woman who might be my bio mom."

Ann leaned her tiny frame over an empty chair and asked, "What did that girl Samantha send you?" She was another stylist friend of mine who now rented from me, even though I'd rented from her in the past. We've known each other for about three decades.

I started to show my phone to Ann when Victoria snatched it from my hand. "Me first!"

Sandra whirled around and said, "Lemme see that pitchur!" She spoke in a thick, Southern drawl, her dimples dancing as she smiled. Her station was behind mine.

The entire shop had been following along the DNA journey with me. They knew my journey, from Arlene's pestering me about getting a DNA test, to getting the results yesterday, and now this connection in Arkansas. My DNA journey had become like a soap opera, and everyone, stylists and long-time clients alike, wanted constant updates. I was spending as much time working as I was sharing Samantha's messages over-and-over to a new audience throughout the day.

Who needs a TV show when the real deal is playing out in the workplace?

"She said that might be my bio mom." I pointed to the phone in Victoria's hands. We all stood in a semi-circle and stared at the picture of Wilma Faye.

Victoria tapped her long, red fingernail on the screen. "That *is* your mama."

71

Sandra grabbed the phone from Victoria and stared at the pic. "Y'all do look alike."

"Yes, she looks like she could be your mom." Ann brushed a lock of thin blonde hair from her eyes with the back of her gloved hand.

"Christi you look like your mother—um, yeah, your *mother*." Sandra winked at me and handed back the phone.

"Maybe…" I held up the image of Wilma Faye to the mirror to get a side-by-side view. "I don't know. What do ya think?"

"I think you look a lot like her," said Victoria in her matter-of-fact way. She nodded in agreement, but not one lock of platinum hair moved from its sprayed perfection.

They were convinced, but I wasn't sure I could see the match. I squinted into the mirror again looking at my face and then the screen. When I scrunched up my nose to see my reflection better, I thought I saw a hint of the woman on my phone.

"Did she say anything else?" Ann asked, eyes wide, looking the part of the scatterbrained blonde.

Before I could answer, Victoria chimed in. "Is she going to put you in touch with her?"

"I don't know. She just sent me this picture. And, if what she suspects is true, she said that I might have a full-blooded brother."

They gasped.

"I know, right?" I didn't start this journey looking for people, but now there were people.

"I've only had sisters. What do you do with a brother?" I asked them. I really didn't know. It seemed an oddity at this point in my life to have a male sibling.

"They're pains in the ass." We all looked at Sandra, who then realized that maybe it wasn't the right time for raw honesty. She held up her hands in surrender. "Alright, y'all, I'm sure he'll be fine."

Victoria pointed her finger at me as if giving me orders. "You've got to contact Wilma Faye. Talk to her first before the brother. Have Samantha give you her cell."

Ann bobbed her blonde head in agreement. "Oh, that's a good plan, do that."

"Okay, I will." So I texted Samantha. *What's the next step? How do I contact Wilma Faye?*

While waiting for her reply, we all went back to business.

My stylists had always been my family, going through whatever storm raged in my life, and there were some really big ones. We were there for each other. My husband says the value of my salon is due to the decency of the people in it. When my life was out of control, they helped get me back to a safe place and they gave me great advice. My entire local stylist community had been there for me, whether they rented a booth from me, I'd rented a booth from them, or we'd just crossed paths, they had been my rock and my fortress in the storms.

Ping. Samantha messaged me back.

My heart fluttered. The experience was so overwhelming and I had all sorts of emotions, it was hard to keep them in check. I've always prided myself on my independence, on being on my own and taking care of myself. And now there were these connections and it was hard to keep a clamp down on everything. I was going to talk to my biological mother. It was really happening.

I opened the conversation and read Samantha's text.

Christi, the picture I sent you of Wilma Faye was used at her memorial service.

No. No. Oh, God, no.

What?

Samantha explained. *Wilma Faye died of brain cancer two years ago.*

My heart ached. I knew brain cancer. And I knew I would never meet Wilma Faye. I lost out on the chance by two years. Two years? The what-ifs started creeping in my head. What if I had taken the DNA test sooner? What if I pursued finding my bio family like my sister Judy had? What if I could go back in time?

No, I had to stop thinking like that. I remembered that a week ago I wasn't interested in any of this. Plus, it wasn't helping me or the situation to ponder over things I couldn't change, so I turned to God. *Lord, why is this happening? Why did you put this in front of me just to have it snatched away? What is the purpose here?*

While I waited for an answer, I felt the weight of it all settle on me. I was angry and disappointed. I had a reunion with my birth mom right in front of me, so near I could almost feel what it would be like, and now it was gone. It was like the time my cone of cotton candy got caught in a summer rain shower. One minute I held a fluffy, pink treat and the next moment grainy, sticky liquid dripped over my hands.

The one awesome thing about not knowing your bio family is that there's less work. When I was at the doctor's office and I had to fill out my family history forms, I drew a line across the page and wrote, "Adopted!" I'd never, ever had to fill out any of that stuff. That totally had saved me time and effort, and that was one of the perks of being adopted.

But now I've found out that my biological mother died of brain cancer. I can't just draw that line anymore because now I have to write cancer. And while I'm writing that word and explaining why she died, I have to deal with the feelings of knowing that I missed meeting my biological mom by a couple of years. All because of cancer. Cancer had altered my life before. *Cancer sucks.*

I turned to Victoria. "She's gone."

"What? Who's gone? What's going on?" Victoria looked over at me with a puzzled expression.

"Wilma Faye. She died two years ago."

"Are you serious?" Victoria left her station and flung her arms around me. "Oh, I'm so sorry, Christina!"

"Wilma Faye passed?" Ann came running around the corner followed by another client, Sybil.

I updated them, choking back emotions trying to escape out of me. "Brain cancer. Two years ago."

The happiness I felt connecting with my new family had turned to grief. My chest felt heavy and it was hard to catch a good breath. All the while, my brain scolded me for how my body was reacting because the emotions weren't logical. Was it possible to grieve someone you've never met? Someone you were never going to meet? I wasn't sure what the right response was to something like that. I felt grief for a woman who I never met, but she had given birth to me. Was I sad for her, or sad that I had missed out? She was just a stranger, after all, someone who lived in a different state and who, except for a DNA test, I would have never known about or met.

"Christi, what is it?" Sandra came in from the back storeroom holding a stack of folded towels (*those towels!*). She had just come back from lunch and missed the latest update.

I'm sure my face said a lot. This wasn't some made up story, this was my life and it was happening to me.

"Wilma Faye's dead," I blurted out.

"Aw, honey, that's awful! I'm so sorry!"

My salon family rallied around me as I processed the news. Most of all, I felt discouraged and I wasn't sure what I was supposed to do or feel next. My story wasn't going to offer a happy ending. It was a downer headline: daughter finds bio mom two years too late. Well, *if* she would have wanted to meet me. I guess I assumed she'd have wanted to connect with me. What if she didn't? I could be placing more on this than I should. She might have had reasons for keeping me secret, and she might have told me to "get lost." I think that would hurt more, so I chose to assume that she would have picked up the phone.

Every good soap opera has a surprise twist, and this was mine. Wilma Faye was gone and unlike fictional characters in movies or TV shows, she was not coming back. No 'Bobby Ewing in the shower' moment for me. Up until this point, it had been an interesting and exciting adventure. It was fun sharing Samantha's texts with the gang in the salon: Victoria, Ann and Sandra, and the others, plus our clients, who are like friends. It was anticipating the next reveal, the next bit of news. I had not only discovered my DNA profile, as Arlene had made happen, but I had found Samantha wanting to connect with me. Out of that came the promise of potentially knowing my biological mother. Then, I pictured myself telling her that I was her 'dead baby' come back to life. This adventure was supposed to be filled with good news, but it wasn't. Wilma Faye's death was a sucker punch.

I prayed to God and asked Him to be my refuge and strength in the heartache that overwhelmed me and that I trusted Him through the pain I felt.

Samantha interrupted my prayer with a text. *We can make the assumption that you are the dead baby, but we don't know for sure.*

I'm pretty sure. I replied.

Maybe. Our DNA links us, that's for sure. She typed.

And, I'm related to a Mercados. I wasn't concerned. At this point, I knew for sure that I was the 'dead baby.'

She agreed. *Yes, and Wilma Faye was the only person from the family in Arkansas who's ever lived in Buffalo, New York.*

That was in 1969, the year I was born. I typed.

Samantha wrote back. *We'll need to have Glenn get a DNA test.*

Who's Glenn?

He would be your brother, if this pans out. He's Wilma Faye's son. I'll call him.

My brother.

Samantha messaged me later that she called Roberta, Glenn's wife, and told her about me. Roberta said that Glenn was getting off work soon, so Samantha gave her my phone number to give to Glenn.

After reading Samantha's text, I noticed another person on my list was quite active with the family tree, so I messaged her. Her name was Miranda, a woman who *ancestry.com* said we were connected with "extremely high confidence." I thought it was odd that these connections kept popping up.

She replied to my inquiry. *My maternal side is from Illinois, and my father's side from the southern part of New York. Where are your people from? That will help me figure out which side of our families connect.*

I typed back. *I was born in Kingston, NY.*

Oh, okay, then it's the Mercado side. You know, even though I can't prove it, I was told that my father had an affair when I was younger. As a result, I might have a half-sister somewhere. I don't think you're her, but it's possible that you are also related to her as well.

I studied the information. If her father was my uncle, then we'd be first cousins. *It looks like we match for first cousins.*

I think that's right. Is your mother named Wilma?

Yes, Wilma Faye is what the Arkansas side of the family calls her.

I remember my uncle had an ex-wife named Wilma, and they had a son named Glenn, but I didn't know anything about a daughter.

Apparently, very few people knew I existed. I replied: *I was adopted as a baby.*

Miranda told me that she had been working on her family tree for many years and had a lot of information compiled. She told me she had started writing down stories, gathering information and documenting our family from a young age. She said that she would listen to the stories told by our grandparents, great aunts, and great uncles during holidays and at other times the family gathered. When she got older, she would record them into notebooks to save for the future. Miranda said she had nearly a bookcase filled with family lore.

As I was reading through the history Miranda sent, my phone pinged making me jump. It was my brother Glenn. His message was short. *I want to talk to you.*

CHAPTER 5

WHEN THE LIGHTS DIM

"My grace is all you need.
My power works best in weakness."
~2 Corinthians 12:9 (NLT)

Past

Cary, North Carolina, Fall, 1984

Christi age 15

"Ow!" I yelled, watching blood ooze from a cut in my hand. I had been opening a moving box and sliced myself with a boxcutter.

"You okay?" Mom yelled from the kitchen.

"I cut myself," I retorted in monotone.

Mom rushed upstairs with a dishtowel and with one swift motion, mummified my hand, to prevent blood from dripping everywhere, and ushered me into the bathroom. She threw the red splotched towel to the side, and stuck my hand under a running faucet.

"That hurts!" I gave her a dirty look.

"Hush." She grabbed an emergency kit—*where did she get that?*—and laid out supplies on the counter. Mom, the nurse, was always prepared to administer first aid, which she did with hospital-like protocol using antiseptic practices that would make the Centers for Disease Control stand up and cheer.

We were back in North Carolina, the Tarheel state, in our home. Judy prepared to go off to college at the University of North Carolina at Chapel Hill, after a summer of touring Europe with a friend using their Eurail passes. It was her high school graduation present. While she was having the time of her life, I had to help mom move into our old house, which we had shuttered while in France. There were so many boxes to unpack that I thought it would never end. Our furniture had finally arrived and I didn't have to sleep on the floor any longer.

I also had bad teeth. The braces that the French dentist had put on years ago needed to come off so mom took me to an orthodontist. He took the jagged wires out of my mouth revealing dingy, gray teeth. I had about a zillon cavities that needed filling, too.

Daddy had stayed in France and began his new work routine: two weeks in France followed by two weeks in North Carolina, repeat. I was jealous and felt like my parents were unfairly punishing me. Daddy could enjoy Paris, with the restaurants and bars, and shopping and shows; all the things I missed so terribly. I didn't understand. If he spent equal time in both places, we could have easily just stayed in France, right? That way, I could have kept my friends and my school and my life. He was living it up, and we were back in the States, the place where I was, once again, the new kid at school.

Totally not fair.

They sent me to East Cary Junior High School and on the first day, I walked into class wearing an outfit I'd bought in Paris at La Défense: a pink and white pant-suit over a flowered blouse with black pumps and bobby socks. All of my clothes were Euro-style. It was what we wore in France and it felt comfortable and hip, like I could rule the world. Cyndi Lauper should look so good.

But, I should have known better. I should have taken a lesson from my past experiences. I'd been down this road before, and I should have known I was headed off a cliff. But, I was blissfully unaware because I was cocky now. I was a girl who'd lived in France, who smoked cigarettes and drank champagne, and took the train to Paris on my own. I was somebody now, so my ego was getting ahead of me. I had life experiences that my classmates in North Carolina could only dream about.

"Who does she think she is?" whispered a girl sitting at a desk behind mine.

"What is she wearing?" her friend hissed back, louder.

It was too familiar. Without looking around, I knew everyone in the room was staring at me. I could feel my

83

cheeks grow red and hot and I gritted my teeth. Not one person was dressed anywhere close to how I looked. I stood out in Cary, North Carolina just as I had in St. Cloud, France years prior, where I'd click-clacked my *Dallas* cowboy boots across the floor and swooshed a giant jean skirt into my tiny seat. This time, I'd taken my wardrobe cue from a French boutique and not an American mall.

If only I could beam myself back to Paris.

No such luck. These kids drank sodas not wine. Cigarettes were for their parents, and they went to the movies not the burlesque. They sported add-a-bead gold necklaces under Izod alligator shirts in bold reds, pinks and Kelly greens which some wore loosely, while other tucked their tails neatly into khaki pants or skirts with belts. They were a box of crayons seated in their desk rows. The boys had Members Only jackets. I stared down at their docksiders and penny loafers, wondering what kind of fresh preppy hell I was in, and pretended not to notice their comments.

Ironically, it was French class that I hated most. It was stupid that they made me take it, because I could speak French fairly fluently. But, I couldn't write it very well, so I failed the test that would get me out of the class. All students were required to take a foreign language course to move on to high school, so I got stuck in French class.

"*Bonjour!*" the teacher sang and the chatter died down.

"*Nous avons un nouvel étudiant,*" she continued, informing the students they had a new student. Her pronunciation was atrocious.

"*Bienvenue, Christina. Nous sommes heureux que vous soyez ici,*" she said, I believe telling me they were glad I was there, but who really knew because she was tripping over her tongue so badly. Plus, I highly doubted that anyone was glad I was there.

"*Merci, et c'est Christi,*" I thanked her, and gave her my preferred name. I thought that was rather mature of me.

"*Nous prenons des noms français, te nom c'est Christella,*" she said, mispronouncing half the words. Apparently the class assumed French names for their English ones. I was to be known as "Christella."

Lucky me.

The teacher blathered on and I was getting more upset by the minute. I already spoke French so I didn't need anyone teaching me any more of it, and certainly not this woman who would be laughed at in France for her accent. She obviously wasn't up for the task of teaching others.

Each time she mispronounced a word I grasped the sides of my desk tightly. This was insulting; to me, to the students and, frankly, to the French people.

"*Pourriez-vous s'il vous plaît écrire la phrase au tableau, Christina?*" She asked me to write a sentence on the board.

I could take it no more. It was beyond what anyone could endure.

"*Ce n'est pas 'see voo playyyy,' c'est 's'il vous plait,'*" I corrected her, stating her mispronunciation followed by the proper French enunciation.

Her lips tightened she didn't speak for a beat. I continued to stare at her, waiting for some acknowledgement. Aren't schools supposed to be places of learning? Maybe she was hip to learning how to speak French with a proper accent.

She wasn't.

So, there it was. My first day back at school in America was even worse than my first day of school in France. To my credit, I didn't run home and cry this time. I didn't beg my mother to take me to the store to get Izod shirts. I didn't care if anyone sat next to me at lunch, or came to my birthday party. I kept to myself mostly. In fact, I rarely spoke. Not in my other classes, and not ever again in French class. Not that the teacher called on me, because she didn't. Life was miserable and I tried to get through each day so I could go home. There, I could be a hermit in my room, smoke cigs out of the window, and lay on my bed listening to music. I felt so worthless. I had no drive to do anything.

But, as before, Mom noticed my misery and plotted a rescue. She always saved the day, which she did one Saturday. We went to Ashworth Drugs for lunch. The iconic downtown Cary drugstore was always crowded, especially on Saturdays, so we stood by the retail shelves, waiting for a space to open up. Mom kept her eye on the people sitting at the white counter which was dotted with green stools. We didn't want a booth. Mom said the full experience was always at the lunch counter.

When two stools became free, we sat down and ordered. I got a 9-inch hotdog and Mom ordered a grilled pimento cheese, a Southern classic. We both ordered fresh squeezed orangeade, their specialty.

Mom cleared her throat. "A magnet high school called Enloe is opening up. They need students."

"Huh?" I picked at a hangnail.

She put a hand on my shoulder. "Look, I know you're unhappy at East Cary."

"Yah, duh." I kept picking at the nail.

"So, I was thinking you might want to switch to Enloe."

I sighed. "I'm in junior high." *As if she didn't know.*

Junior high in those days was seventh through ninth grades, and high school was tenth through twelfth. My mother wasn't making sense. There was no way for me to go to high school.

Mom explained, "They're accepting ninth graders at Enloe."

"What?" I looked up. This was a big deal.

"Yes, ninth graders can go there. They're looking for ninth graders to attend. Do you want to transfer to Enloe?"

I didn't have to think about it for another second. I didn't even take a bit of the hot dog or a sip of the chocolate shake now sitting in front of me. I blurted out, "Yes!" She didn't have to twist my arm. I'd do anything to get away from that place with those people.

So, Mom enrolled me. I brushed the East Cary Junior High dust off my shoes—the black pumps with bobby socks— and started classes at Enloe High School.

It was there that I found my people.

We met on the smoking court. In high school, in those days, they gave us a smoking area because some of us smoked. We thought we were cool. Tobacco wasn't regulated much at the time, and even though there was an age limit on sales, retailers rarely paid attention to it. They sold cigarettes, chewing tobacco, called 'chaw', and Swisher Sweets to anyone who looked old enough at a glance and had money.

The smoking court was located directly outside the cafeteria. You could just walk out of lunch and go have a smoke. Most of the time we smoked just tobacco, but some kids smoked clove cigarettes that they rolled themselves, or occasionally someone would pull out a joint and we'd get stoned, carefully blowing the smoke away from the doors.

"Can I bum one?" A lanky boy with black, spiked hair nodded to the cigarette in my hand.

"Uh, sure." I handed him a cigarette, and started to give him my lighter, but he pulled one from a pocket of his black duster, and lit up, taking in a long drag.

"What's your name?"

"Christi."

"Hellooo, Christi," he said slowly, taking another drag and eyeing me up and down. "I'm Phil. Where're you from?"

Based on my outfit, I guess it was obvious I was not a local.

"France," I answered.

"You don't sound French."

"I'm not. That's where I'm from," I answered shortly. This guy wasn't going to rock me. I wasn't going to be playing whatever game he had in mind. I jutted out my chin and glared at him through squinted eyes. Smoke wafted around us.

He nodded and blew out a perfect smoke ring that hung in the air a second before drifting away into an infinity sign. Then he bent down toward me, his nose inches from my cheek, and asked, "Wanna go to a party?"

Well, what do you know? He did rock me.

After months of being a hermit and shutting myself away from everyone else, here was a knock at the door. I had gotten used to my solitude and wasn't prepared for this. It took me a beat to process what he'd just said and I wondered if I heard him correctly? Yes, I did. He asked if I wanted to go to a party, and I wanted to shout, "YES! Are you kidding me? YES!" But, I kept my cool. I was pretty proud of myself for that.

"Um, sure," I replied.

"It's down on Ashe," he explained, as if I knew where, or what, Ashe was. "You got wheels?"

"No."

"I got a ride. I'll pick you up."

And, that's how I found my people, in the punk rock and drug scene of the eighties on Ashe Avenue in Raleigh. That's where I 'came home' from France.

"Come'ere," Judy whispered to me.

It was quiet that evening. Mom was sewing in her bedroom, Sandy had moved to Florida, and Daddy wasn't home from work yet. A roast was in the oven, but dinner wouldn't be ready until Daddy was there. I rummaged in the pantry for something to eat. My sister Judy came up behind me, and pulled my arm, dragging me into the living room.

"You gotta see this," she whispered.

She sat down on the floor in front of the TV and pulled me down with her. Judy pressed play on the VCR. The volume had been turned low, but you could hear a woman moaning. Naked bodies entangled on the screen.

"It's a porn!" I couldn't believe it.

"Yeah, Daddy probably forgot it was in here," Judy said with a grin.

"He should've hidden this."

"Yeah, but he didn't."

We kept our voices low and watched for a while, pausing every few minutes to listen for Mom or the garage door to open. But the soft hum of Mom's sewing machine and silence from the garage assured our privacy. So we sat there for a few minutes watching a repair man and a milkman go down simultaneously on a housewife whose clothes instantly fell off. The next scene involved two women and a man stuffed into a bathroom stall.

"I'm hungry," I grumbled, as if Judy were preventing me from leaving. As if I couldn't just walk into the kitchen and eat. Something about sharing this dirty secret with her made me feel like I had to stay, to see it through. Like we were partners in this sordid secret.

"C'mon, Judy, I'm done. I'm gonna go get some chips."

"Oh, alright." Somehow she knew we were in this together, too. "First, I gotta rewind the tape to where it was."

"Why?"

"So, Daddy doesn't know we watched it, dummy. Don't you know anything?"

Obviously, I didn't. Judy was so much smarter than me. She rewound the tape to where she had first been watching it, which was earlier than when she showed it to me.

"Do you think Mom will know?" I was feeling a little weird about watching the porn tape.

"Not unless you *tell* her." Judy's tone was threatening.

"I won't, duh."

She turned off the VCR and TV and followed me back into the kitchen.

The next morning when I woke up, Daddy was leaving my room.

"Good morning, Tina, time to get up," he called as he walked out of my bedroom door.

My skin felt weird. It was hard to wake up, as usual, and I only wanted to keep sleeping. Daddy had left the door ajar and I could hear him in the kitchen brewing coffee. My PJ top was up around my neck so I pulled it down to cover my chest and rolled over to go back to sleep.

The music was blaring outside of a run-down, nearly condemned house on Ashe Avenue. We walked up some rickety wooden steps to the front door. Phil,

Priska, June and I were on the prowl and looking to score. Phil opened the door and we walked right in without knocking. The place was a mess with cans and bottles everywhere. A guy in the corner played an acoustic guitar, and a couple sat making out on the backseat of a what looked like Buick 98 that they were using as a couch.

I was in my element because I could just be me. I didn't have to be anyone's daughter or anyone's sister; I could just be myself. We planned to head over to Hillsborough Street, near the North Carolina State University campus, where the college bars were located. We all had fake IDs and we knew a place there that would let us in and serve us. At that time, the drinking age in North Carolina was 19, so even as high school students, we could get served pretty easily.

A skinny man with wavy blond hair and a knit cap emerged from the kitchen. He looked like Sean Penn's character, Jeff Spicoli, from *Fast Times at Ridgemont High*.

"Got any bud?" Phil asked.

"Yeah, dude, whacha want?" He sounded like Spicoli, too.

"Dime bag."

"Cool. Show me dinero."

Phil plucked a ten from his wallet and handed it to the man who disappeared into the kitchen again. He emerged with weed in a plastic bag and held it out.

"Thanks man," Phil said, snatching it and pocketing the stash.

As we turned and left, I saw that the couple was still making out on the repurposed car bench. The man in the corner started another song.

"It's gonna be a great Thursday night!" I yelled into the street.

"It's Friday," corrected Priska.

"I'm dying for a SoCo and Coke," June said. "Let's *go!*"

"Shit, yeah!"

We got into Phil's Camero, and he rolled a joint. We were ripped before we parked again, this time on a side street near the campus. Phil was cracking jokes, and we all laughed that laugh you get when you're really high and it comes out in little bursts, which makes you laugh harder.

We slid into a booth at a local pizza joint and ordered a pepperoni pie. Using our fake IDs, we ordered watered-down drinks, one round after another, and hung out until the place with the band opened up.

It wasn't a night out without a mosh pit.

The next thing I remember was an afternoon sun hitting the curtains hitting my bedroom. I stumbled down the hallway in sweats and looked in at Judy in her room. She was standing over her bed organizing a mountain of purchases piled on top of it, ready for her move to Chapel Hill.

I stared at the goods. "Wow, where do you get all this?"

"Really?" She stared at me blankly.

"Yeahhh," I said slowly, not sure what was going on.

"Are you serious? We all went together shopping for this. It was Tuesday. Don't you *remember*?" She sounded exasperated and frankly a little mad.

I wanted to say, no, I don't remember, tell me. But I didn't, because I knew that would be the wrong answer. Instead I muttered, "Yeah, oh, yeah, sure," and walked out the room.

Where was I on Tuesday? I had been over at June's. We were watching MTV and we'd been drinking her mom's white wine. We were sitting in her living room and she brought out some white pills that she called 'ludes. I remember taking one, and washing it down with the wine. Prince was throwing rocks into pond telling me to dream of a courtyard with an ocean of violets. I think they were in bloom. But what about those animals who struck curious poses? Did they feel the heat? I wasn't sure, but I was definitely feeling the 'lude. The colors of purple, blue, orange, red, all of them bright and vivid, like the preppy Izod shirts from junior high, flashed across the screen as we watched video after video into the afternoon.

Mom and Judy had picked me up. But we'd come right home, hadn't we? I couldn't remember going anywhere else. Yet, Judy said I'd been with them when they bought her dorm room supplies.

I had no memory of it. I had a total blackout.

"Hurry up, get outta the car!" Judy yelled at me.

"Keep your shirt on." I was in a mood.

We were at Shoney's, where we'd usually go to eat after Mass. Mom and Daddy were already inside the restaurant getting us a table.

I stumbled out of the car and weaved across the wet parking lot.

"Are you drunk?" Judy asked, grabbing my arm and glaring into my eyes.

"No," I spat back, and wrenched my arm away. I brushed past her through the door and stomped my combat boots on a large floor mat on my way inside. Despite being able to shop anywhere in the city, I preferred Army Surplus for my garb. I was wearing black boots and a blue dress with a black jacket. The dress was for my parents.

Mom and Daddy were seated at a table near the window and we joined them. After ordering lunch, Judy told us all about getting ready for college. She was set to start at Chapel Hill in a week and was excited about her new roommate and all the activities and sports in which she was about to excel. Mom and Daddy had bought her a townhouse in the college town.

I played with my food and stared out the window. Autumn trees in golds and reds reflected in the little puddles in the parking lot. They offered the only splash of color on a grey, overcast day. The sun was hiding behind a blanket of clouds and I wanted to be like the sun and hide under my blankets while everyone went about their day. I didn't want to be at church or lunch or anywhere with people.

When we were finished, Daddy paid the bill and while he signed the credit card receipt, I noticed that his hands were shaking. I looked up, and his forehead was wet with sweat. His shirt collar had wet marks along the top and he was shivering. I thought it looked like he was experiencing a sudden flu attack. Maybe he was getting sick.

The look on my mom's face confirmed that I wasn't imagining things.

"Alan, we have to get you home." The nurse in her was all business. Her lips were pressed tight, but she was evaluating him like a professional. For a second, I thought I caught a glimpse of something in Mom's eyes, like a look of alarm, but then it was gone.

"When we get there, I'll call Dr. Kinmont." She grabbed the keys from him, and guided him toward the door. He was unsteady, but managed to get into the passenger seat and we drove home.

Because of who my daddy was, Dr. Kinmont saw him that day. He agreed to meet them at the emergency room, where they spent the afternoon trying to figure out what was wrong.

As Daddy was getting checked over for whatever illness he might've had, I went to my room to smoke a cigarette and drink. I didn't see it as a problem at the time. It was my life, because drinking and taking drugs was normal to me. In the middle of my drug use, I went to school and hung out with people who were doing the same things I was doing, like sniffing rush/ poppers, smoking joints, dropping acid and popping pills. Therefore, all of it seemed to me just to be normal teen stuff.

There was this group of guys, and they were football players on the team, definitely not our crowd, but liked to party with us because we had drugs and alcohol. We went out into the woods, at this certain spot we'd go to when we could get some beer or bottles of liquor or whatever. It was there that I was taken advantage of. I was really, really drunk, and I knew exactly what was happening. It was one of those cases where a girl asks herself, "is this rape?" Because I didn't give consent, but I didn't push him away either. I was blasted out of my mind and couldn't push him off of me. It made me feel pretty stupid and worthless.

Afterwards, a friend of his tried to do the same to me, too, but by then I'd sobered up so I managed to push him away and join the larger group. I saw the guy who violated me at school the next week. He smirked at me in the hallway, and went on his way. I didn't expect anything more than that, because he was a big football star, and that's how they are. I saw myself as nothing. What did it matter? I wasn't worth much anyway.

Mom sat in a chair in the living room, with Judy and me on the couch. She had dark circles under red eyes. She looked like she hadn't slept all week.

"Girls, daddy is really sick."

"What does that mean?" Judy knew instantly the situation was bad and she wanted the real details.

"Daddy has a brain tumor." Mom's voice cracked at the word 'tumor'.

She went on to explain what that meant and what would happen. She was equal parts clinician and mom, navigating us through the medical jargon while remembering that this is our Daddy. She let us know that they were going to start the first round of chemotherapy and radiation in a few days.

I was scared. What was going to happen? But, Mom was in charge. She would take care of it. And, Daddy was, well, he was Daddy. He could do anything. He was omnipotent.

Despite my optimism, Daddy continued to decline. By, November, he was so sick that they had to admit him into the hospital. Mom pulled some strings to get him on the 7th Floor East at Rex Hospital, where she was stationed as a charge nurse. She switched her schedule to work nights so that she could be there with daddy.

Whatever parental supervision I had at the time, which wasn't much, completely disappeared. I could do whatever I wanted, whenever I wanted. The bonus was that everybody felt sorry for me. I didn't really have to try hard at school, or even at home. I took advantage of the situation and spent a lot of time on Ashe Avenue with my friends.

By Christmas, Daddy was really sick. He was thin and pale, and not himself. He had contracted shingles which killed his immune system. He had to take a leave of absence from work. No more trips to Paris. He still thought he could beat the cancer, though.

"Alan, you're dying." Her words hung in the air like rotten garbage that no one wanted to take out. I knew that Mom wanted him to know the reality of the situation.

My parents were sitting at the kitchen table and he just shook his head. He didn't actually think he was going to die. It was my mother who had to convince him. She had to put aside the role of a wife and act as a medical professional in order to help him understand that the disease had progressed beyond treatment.

She touched his arm and looked in his eyes, pleading for him to hear. "You're dying, Alan, you're not going to beat this."

"No, Amy, no…I'll get better."

"You're not going to get better, Alan, I've seen the records. You have to make peace."

I stood just outside the kitchen, in the shadows of the hallway, not sure if I should be there or not. My parents didn't seem to notice me, so I stayed as still as I could, pressing against the wall. I knew it was a private conversation, but I couldn't back away.

He stared down at his hands on the table. I could see the purple bruises, like splotchy tattoos, peeking out from the bandages. The IVs from the most recent treatment had left their mark.

"Alan, you've got to stop treatment because it's not helping. You won't get any better." She choked back a sob. "There's no point in enduring the side effects, because it's not going to make you well."

Mom understood the prognosis. But Daddy, the invincible leader at work, home and church, didn't see the shell he'd become. He still thought he was going to be fine.

The light above the kitchen table was on a dimmer, and it was at about half power. I thought that's what happens when someone is dying. The light keeps getting dimmer and dimmer until it's completely dark.

They went on talking for some time but he wasn't understanding what she was saying to him. Or, maybe he just didn't want to.

So I slipped back up to my room, and I wondered what was going to happen to us? Where would we end up when he's gone? I thought about God and the miracles He performs. Would He perform a miracle on my daddy? Should I pray?

In January, Daddy was thinner and his skin was gray. Hospice was called in. Daddy had no choice but to come to terms with his death, but he seemed confused. The world outside was cold and bleak, and our world inside the house was the same.

Hospice helped set up a hospital bed in the dining room, and they used a sling to get Daddy in and out of the bed. Our downstairs was always humming and active. People from the church came to sit vigil 24/7 and pray over Daddy. They would putter about and have hushed conversations. I escaped to my bedroom to get away from it all.

My friend Priska came over one afternoon. We all called her Priska, but she and I shared the same name, but she spelled Christy with a 'y'. I met her at the front door and we walked past Daddy in the bed with the old ladies praying over him, and my mom and a young priest in the kitchen drinking coffee. I got Priska up to my room, thankful we didn't have to interact with the church people on the way.

She threw her backpack on the bed and we sat on the floor.

"Did you get it?" I asked, wondering if she'd scored some pot.

"Nah, he was out."

"Bummer."

"What do you want to do?" she asked as she leaned back against the bed, her dark hair contrasting against the bright comforter.

"I guess we'll have to drink," I said exchanging my orange knitted sweater for a baggy sweatshirt, perfect for the task I had in mind.

Daddy kept his wine collection from France in the basement. It was cool and damp down there, and he stored the bottles on wooden racks. These were expensive ones that he had brought back with him on each trip. Before Daddy got sick, and while traveling back and forth from France, he'd accumulated a collection of fine wine. He had gotten a special license which allowed him to transport alcohol overseas.

I left Priska to pick out music from the stack of cassette tapes and snuck down to the basement. I grabbed a bottle and headed back upstairs, noting ironically to myself that given what was going on in our house, wine would never be missed. I walked past the gloomy scene and darted up to my bedroom. I had a corkscrew on my desk because this was not my first time in the cellar.

"Cheers!" said Priska.

"Cheers!" I said. And we drank the bottle down, listening to the Dead Kennedys. After we drained that bottle, I got another. And, then another.

While we were drinking that third bottle, I thought that it was fitting that I was in my room getting drunk and my Daddy was downstairs on his deathbed. So this was going to be my life: I was going to drink my life away, and I might just drink until I'm dead, too.

CHAPTER 6

A FRIEND OF BILL'S

You can enter God's Kingdom only through the
narrow gate. The highway to hell is broad, and its
gate is wide for the many who choose that way. But
the gateway to life is very narrow and the road is difficult, and only a few ever find it.

~Matthew 7:13-14 (NLT)

Past

Cary, North Carolina, February, 1985

Christi age 16

"*I* saw him take his last breath," Judy told me
afterwards.

Daddy died on February 1ˢᵗ. I couldn't imagine
seeing him die. Judy would have to live with that for
the rest of her life and I thought that was a horrible thing
to have to remember.

It was my first funeral and it was held at our church, St. Michael the Archangel. It was cold and windy, one of those days that felt like winter would never end. The rain from the weekend had stopped, but a gray sky hung over empty tree branches and brown lawns. It was depressing and miserable. I felt like the weather matched our hearts.

Inside the church, white satin cloths with gold thread draped over the altar table which held the shiny gold chalices and host saucers for communion. Daddy was to have a funeral Mass. Enormous flower arrangements with white lilies and chrysanthemums, nearly my height, flanked the candelabras filled with fresh tapers. The church had been cleaned and prepared with the dedication that matched how they felt about Daddy.

St. Michael's was the only Catholic church in Cary at the time. The original location was across the street from Cary High School on Maynard Road. I think every Catholic in the area showed up for Daddy's service. Add the IBM'ers, the New Yorkers, and his organizations and clubs, and that meant, as I found out later, that there weren't enough parking spots for everyone wanting to pay their respects. People were jammed into pews and the ushers put out chairs along the far walls for mourners. Daddy's funeral was a full-on Catholic production and it was standing room only.

Because Daddy went to college at the Vatican and served in the church, he became really important in the

Knights of Columbus. When I was little, I used to help him sell the giant Tootsie Rolls for the Knights. The candies were giant ones, the ones that took you days to eat and would sit on your dresser, sticky with spit, where you'd walk by and grab a bite whenever you felt like it.

Daddy and I would go to grocery stores to sell them. He would set up a table outside the entrance to a store and put out the money case. Behind us he'd stack all these boxes of Tootsie Rolls ready for sale. I think he used me as a sales technique to sell the candy. Who can resist a little girl? We would stand there for hours until the last one was sold. He hated going back with any leftovers and at the time I thought it was because he cared so much about the charity, but maybe it was also because he wanted to be the hero. Daddy always bought me one to pay me for my time. Things were simple back then because an extra large Tootsie Roll was all it took to make my day.

As the organist played a hymn softly, we were escorted through the front door of the sanctuary and up to the row reserved for our family. The sanctuary was warm compared to the winter day, and my fingers prickled in the heat as I twirled the white rose I'd been given. We crossed ourselves while bowing to the altar and took our seats. I was scrunched between mom and Sandy, whose husband Sonny was next to her with their kids. Judy sat on the other side of mom. Behind us sat Mom's sister, Aunt Nora, and her husband Merv, because Mom and Aunt Nora were really close.

I stared at the crucifix where Jesus' pain-stricken face stared up at God the Father and it seemed that Jesus suffered along with us.

A shuffling movement behind us made us turn to see the Knights of Columbus, regally dressed in brilliant satin capes and plumed hats as they took their places along each side of the aisle. Most of them wore red capes with white feathers in their hats, but one man wore a purple cape with a purple feather, and another had a green cape and a green feather. But no one was dressed in gold like Daddy would be. They stood still against the pew ends, facing the aisle with their swords at their sides.

The priest at the altar spoke reverently into the microphone, offering the introductory rite, and then indicated for us to stand. The organist started the prelude announcing the start of the first hymn. I could feel the chords pounding in my chest. We all sang *To Jesus Christ, Our Sovereign King* [1] as the other priests and pall bearers brought Daddy's coffin up the aisle. The coffin was draped in white and topped with a small arrangement of white roses, representing the purity of the Virgin Mary. As the processional passed, the Knights of Columbus, in turn, drew their swords, reaching them toward the ceiling in salute.

---

[1] Written in 1941 by Father Martin B. Hellriegel, a German-American pastor.

One of the priests sprinkled holy water around the altar as he made his way to one of the big chairs on the side. The casket was placed in the aisle in front of the altar and next to us as we finished the hymn. Mom wept, Sandy wept, Judy wept, and so I dabbed tissues at my eyes, knowing I should be weeping too but I wasn't. Crying wasn't something I liked to do in front of other people. So I went through the motions during the funeral: standing, sitting, and kneeling in all the right places. I dabbed my eyes but didn't shed a tear.

After the Mass, we followed the hearse in our limousine to the gravesite for the internment. Mom, Sandy, Sonny, their kids, and Judy and I fit easily into the large limo. Everyone else followed us in a procession in their own cars, their lights on and blinkers flashing. And some cops blocked intersections so we could get through.

Daddy's parents, Grandmother and Granddad Higgins, didn't need a limo because they hadn't traveled up from Florida. In fact, after Daddy died, we never saw them again. Sandy told me that Daddy had sent checks to them every month, but when he died, the checks stopped. And, when the checks stopped, they stopped calling.

At the cemetery off of Highway 70, we sat in folding chairs with velvet coverings under a canopy across from the coffin. The service was short, but I wasn't sure if it was short because that's how gravesite services are, or because it was so cold outside. At the end, we got up, and, in a processional line, we laid our roses on the casket and greeted the priests.

Afterwards, people mingled and talked in low voices.

"Who's that?" Judy asked me. She motioned with her chin toward a woman standing alone and at a distance from the crowd. The woman wore a black raincoat with pleats, black gloves, and a black hat with a netted veil. Her face was pale, and her jet black hair swooped back, maybe in a twist or a bun. The only color came from her bright, red lipstick.

"I dunno. Weird."

"She looks French," Judy said.

"How can you tell?"

"That coat, it's too, um, it's too, well…*French*."

"Yeah, I know what you mean," I said, remembering my clothes when we moved back from France. Not only styles of clothing, but the way clothes were made to fit people was different in Europe than in the States.

"Get over here," Sandy whispered, interrupting us and motioning us toward her and Mom.

I let the people hug me, and talk to me. Everyone said, "Your dad was so special. I'm so sorry." I guess it's something you're supposed to say, but it sounds really weird when you hear it over and over again. It's like when you repeat a word like a zillion times and it loses meaning. After a while, it just sounded like gibberish. They told me how they knew Daddy, whether from IBM, or New York, or church, or as an adjunct professor at North Carolina State University. They told me how great he was, and how lucky I was to have him for a dad. It was a blur of sympathies and pained expressions, and they were all well-meaning I'm sure, but I was cold and tired and I wanted to leave.

To my relief, the funeral director ushered us back into the warm limo. I looked around for the woman in the black coat and hat, but she was gone. We never saw her again and she never contacted us. She could have been colleague or a parishioner, or even a professor. She also could have been his mistress. Later, I had a weird thought and I wondered about Daddy living half the time with us and half the time in France. Did Daddy have another family over there? *Was she his other wife?*

I'll never know.

Sandy told me years later that the woman had asked to speak with Mom. She told my sister Sandy and my mom's friend Sandi Bailey that she had to tell Mom "something about Alan." But, before she had a chance for the conversation, the woman had left. Whether there was just too much commotion at the gravesite, or the woman lost her nerve, we'll never know. She was there, and then she wasn't.

That night, we lounged in sweats with my parents' close friends and their kids, and watched Bill Cosby's comedy routine movie, *Himself*. We laughed that cathartic laugh you get when the day was awful and you need to let off some steam. We ate popcorn and were all together in the living room, but without Daddy.

Sonny and Sandy became responsible for me, but with kids and jobs, they didn't have much time for monitoring my antics. Mom was still working nights as a nurse at Rex Hospital, and she was going to grief counseling. Judy was back at college at Chapel Hill. While everyone else was occupied, I got a secret mohawk. I had the stylist shave my head on the sides, but leave the top long and dyed jet black. Around my mom, I would brush my hair down to cover it up, but when I was out with friends, I thought I was cool with my mohawk, blending in with the punk scene in Raleigh.

One day, I forgot to cover up my haircut.

"What did you do to your hair!?" Mom yelled.

My hand flew up to the side of my scalp and my fingers brushed the stubble. *Gulp.* "Umm…"

She closed her eyes and took in a deep breath letting it out slowly. I stood and waited.

Finally, she opened her eyes and said, with a maybe exasperated tone, "Do you like it like that?"

"Yeah, I do."

"Okay."

And that was all she said about my mohawk.

Later that week, Mom and I went shopping at Crabtree Valley Mall. I was walking in front with my hair spiked up, wearing an army surplus outfit with military black boots. Mom was behind me with the bags. Out of the blue, two ladies stopped her, and one of them said, "Oh my goodness, did you see that girl?" They pointed at me.

My mother sighed. "Yes, that's my daughter."

The winter days blended one into the other and soon it was summer. I drifted in and out of blackouts, but of course, I didn't have a drinking problem. I drank because *I* was the problem.

One night, after many vodka tonics and a pill, I handed the keys of my car to Priska.

Hours later, when I came to, and still drunk, I found myself in my friend Nancy's apartment in Raleigh near NC State. I got up off the couch and looked around the apartment. Nancy was in her bed, but I couldn't find Priska, or my keys, anywhere.

"Nancy! Wake up!"

"Wha—what?"

"Get up, we have to find Priska!"

I explained to her what I thought was going on: that I'd given my keys to Priska and she was out there driving around somewhere, maybe crashed into a ditch or worse. Nancy grabbed her purse and keys, and we drove down to Cary trying to find her. The clock on the dash read 1:14 a.m.

After about an hour, without finding Priska or my car, we went back to Nancy's apartment. I sat on the couch and contemplated making another drink, when someone banged on the door. Nancy opened it and in rushed my mother. She had with her Bailey, a friend of the family. He was there to take me to the rectory.

I was still pretty out of it, so I grabbed my pack and got into the car with Bailey and mom. They drove me to our priest's house, where I stayed the night.

The next morning, the rectory housekeeper knocked on my door and told me to come downstairs. My mom, Bailey, and the priest sat in the parlor.

"Sit." My mother was terse.

I sat. My head was pounding and my mouth was like cotton, but I didn't speak. With the look on my mother's face, I knew it was better to be still.

"If I'd had a knife in my hand last night, I would have stabbed you, Christina, I swear to God!"

The priest shuffled in his chair uncomfortably, but remained silent because Mom was not to be interrupted. "I got a call from the police that my daughter had been in an accident. So, I rushed to the hospital and they took me back to the room where my daughter 'Christi' was being treated. Imagine my surprise when I found Priska lying in the hospital bed! Priska!"

"Ohh, her name's Christy, too."

"Yes, she's Christy, and they thought it was you because she was driving your car! Now, your car is totaled and Priska's in the hospital! Do you even want to know if she's okay?!"

"Of course, yes, is she okay?"

"They kept her overnight for observation. She was banged up, but will be fine. I had them contact her parents."

"That's good." I didn't know what else to say.

My mother was on a roll. "I sat by my husband's bedside and watched him die. *I watched him die, Christina.* And you're out drinking to all hours, taking God-knows-what-kind of drugs, and putting people's lives in danger...your *friends' lives.*" She took a deep breath and exhaled slowly. "This is causing me more pain than you can know."

I stared at her, but I wanted to look at the floor. I couldn't look away, though, because I knew she was right and I knew that I had to take whatever she said to me.

Mom looked at Bailey and the priest, then back at me. "This is the choice you have. You can either come with me right now, and I'm going to take you to a drug and alcohol treatment center. I don't know how long they'll keep you, and I don't know what they're going to do to you there. That's one option. The other option is this: I can take you home right now, and you can pack your bags and you will never come back home. Do you understand? Never."

I only had to think about it for a few seconds. I was still in high school. I didn't have a job. I didn't have skills to support myself. So, the smartest thing for me to do was to go to the treatment center.

Mom took me that day.

When I entered through the doorway to the patient wing, and the doors shut and locked behind me with a metal clanking sound, that was the scariest part of Charter Northridge Hospital. It was like going to prison. I was here to stay, and there was no way out. I was stuck there, and I didn't know for how long.

It was then that I decided they were going to get me, all of me. I brushed my hair up, revealing the shaved sides of my mohawk and strutted down the hall. I basically gave them the finger with my hair. This was me and they were going to have to deal with me.

The day Mom had put me into treatment, she told me that back when Daddy was dying, he apologized to her for leaving her to raise me alone. That what a pain in the ass I was. My dying father wasn't just sad to leave me, he was sad to leave Mom with the burden of raising me.

The hospital ended up saving my life. I stayed in their in-patient drug treatment center for three months. People in the AA program at our outside meetings would laugh at me and say, "Honey, I've spilled more beer on my tie than you've drunk in your lifetime." And, they were probably right. But I knew if I didn't stop then, I never would have stopped. I would have kept on drinking and drugging myself right into the grave.

'Live hard, die young' was my motto. I would have never seen my seventeenth birthday.

It was in treatment that I learned about the 12 Steps of Alcoholics Anonymous (AA) and Narcotics Anonymous (NA). They taught me about a "higher power" and putting my trust and faith in a god of my understanding. It was so different from my Catholic upbringing, that it took me a while to understand what it meant to rely on God and not myself. I'd been so self-sufficient and independent my entire life, it was odd to think of putting my faith in something other than myself.

William "Bill" Wilson co-founded the group Alcoholics Anonymous with physician Bob "Dr. Bob" Smith. They based it off a Christian organization which had helped him recover. They wanted to open their group to everyone while not promoting any certain religious or political view. Bill wrote the book, *Alcoholics Anonymous*, where he detailed the *12 Step Program* for recovery.

Wilson credits his faith and his program to a supernatural experience he had while lying in a hospital bed, where he'd been admitted for drinking. Deeply depressed, he cried out, "I'll do anything! Anything at all! If there be a God, let Him show Himself!" He immediately saw a bright light, and a feeling of ecstasy and peace washed over him. He never drank again. Wilson described the experience to his doctor, who said,

"Something's happened to you that I don't understand, but you had better hang on to it."

And, from that moment on, he did.

Because of the stigma attached to alcoholism, and AA's commitment to protecting individual's identity, members are known only by their first name, or first name with last letter. The familiar opening line everybody knows from the movies, "Hi, I'm Christi and I'm an alcoholic," is real. We are just first names with no judgments. If we ever encounter someone who is in trouble or having a difficult time, and we wonder if they've been sober before, we can ask them, "Are you a friend of Bill.'s?" or, "Are you a friend of Bill W.'s?" This refers the founder, Bill Wilson, and gives us a way to reach them without breaking program rules.

My treatment consisted of long weeks of personal and group therapy, AA meetings, and too much time staring at my bellybutton, pondering my own life. Mom would visit and call. Judy came by a couple of times, and Sandy always brought me cookies. I loved Sandy for those cookies!

At Charter Northridge, it was full of kids in trouble, and many came into treatment through 'The System,' one governmental social agency or another. And those were the saddest cases because no one ever came to visit them. They were all on their own. There was one kid, Mario, who had sweet brown eyes and even when he smiled, he looked sad. My mom wanted to take him home because she couldn't stand it that no one came to visit him. But, they wouldn't let her. Mario joined us when Mom came to visit me. When Sandy gave me cookies, I shared them with all the kids, but always gave Mario more cookies than anyone.

"Your Uncle Armon wants to see you," Mom announced during one of her phone calls.

"Who?" I knew that Mom had a sister, Aunt Nora. Who was this 'Uncle Armon?'

"He's my brother. He's visiting here and he wants to come see you."

"Mom, you never told me you had a brother!"

"Well, we had a falling out. I didn't see a need to burden you with that because I didn't know if we'd ever talk again." Mom and Uncle Armon had obviously mended fences.

"I can't believe that I have an uncle that you never told me about. This is crazy!"

"He and his wife want to see you. They're here in Cary and they're coming to the treatment center tomorrow."

"Anything else you're not telling me about?" I was annoyed.

"Well, if you have to know, you're not named after your grandmother, you're named after your grandfather's second wife."

"*Seriously?*"

"Yes. Do you want to know anything else?"

"No, I'm done, Mom, I don't want to know any more." I couldn't get off the phone fast enough. I didn't know what else she might tell me. Maybe about Daddy's second family in France? *I couldn't go there.*

Uncle Armon showed up the next day with Aunt Julie. Aunt Julie didn't talk much but spoke in Spanglish, which a lot of my family did in Florida. They were waiting for me in the common room. He had thick salt and pepper hair and dark eyelashes with hazel eyes. Julie looked like all the Cuban women of Ybor City. She wore her dyed red hair pulled up tightly into a bun, and a bright sundress in turquoise and coral, colors that reminded me of the building fronts and balconies of my grandfather's home town. She was the opposite of me, I thought, looking down at my stained gray sweats and worn flip flops, the uniform of treatment center teens.

"I haven't seen you since you were this tall," Uncle Armon said, holding his hand out about three feet from the floor.

"Oh." I tried to recognize his face, but I couldn't.

"It's okay if you don't remember. Your mom and I haven't seen each other in a looong time," he said, dragging out the o's in long as an 'aww.'

"I-I don't remember." There was no point in pretending.

He chuckled a little and coughed. "Amy, *your mama*, says you're doing alright in here. So, it's going okay for you?"

"It's going okay," I repeated. The thing was, it was going just 'okay'. I was getting bored with the routine of self-help and bellybutton staring.

"Maybe you're about done, eh?" He leaned back in his chair and cocked an eyebrow. He spoke in a thick, Cuban accent.

"I dunno."

"Look at you, you're strong. You're like your mama. She's strong, too."

I nodded.

Aunt Julie smiled at me, broadly with white teeth peeking through red lipstick. "Para you." She reached in her bag and pulled out what was obviously a book wrapped in blue paper with a yellow bow.

"Uh, thanks." I took the book, well, present, and opened it. It was a book about Ybor City.

"We inscribed it," Uncle Armon said, pointing to the book.

I opened it, and on the front page it read: *To Christina, Remember your roots. Love, Uncle Armon and Aunt Julie.* Turning the pages, I saw the book was filled with black and white photos of historic Ybor City, including a portrait of the founder, Vincente Martinez Ybor, and cigar factory workers. They sat in a large warehouse room, seated at long tables, with their heads bent, concentrating on their task. A man sat in the middle of the far wall on what looked like a tall lifeguard chair. The photo caption said he was reading the news, poetry and stories to keep the men occupied as they worked. Pages of photos and history of the cigar-making town filled the book. I could almost see the vibrant Cuban colors in the monochrome street shots.

I remembered my manners and looked up. "Thank you. This book is amazing." It wasn't amazing, but it definitely captured my interest.

"Glad you like it, Christina. Maybe you can come and visit us there, eh?"

I nodded. "Maybe." I wanted to go back to Ybor City and feel Abuelo's hand in mine as we walked along the streets. I wanted to eat Cubanos with him, and see all the pretty colors.

After Uncle Armon's visit, Mom showed up and busted me out of the facility. I left after three months in treatment and according to the official paperwork, "without medical advisement." They would probably have kept me as long as the insurance kept paying the bills, which they did forever back then, but Mom said I'd had enough, and she signed me out. They couldn't legally stop her, so they had to let me leave. I'm sure they were sad to see my insurance payments go, too.

Back at home, I chose to go to AA meetings and not NA (Narcotics Anonymous). NA was a relatively new entity, and I knew I needed the wisdom and knowledge that long timers in AA had to offer me. AA was really my life boat. The first meeting I chose was over by my old stomping grounds near Hillsborough St.

I walked into the meeting, located in a church basement filled with the smell of burnt coffee, and cigarette
smoke hanging like a blue haze in the air. A group of
guys were pouring coffee into Styrofoam cups, and one
of them looked up at me. He was wearing jeans and a
t-shirt that showed off his biceps and flat stomach. His
tousled blond hair brushed off to one side and his blue
eyes invited me over. My stomach did a flip-flop, and I
found myself standing in front of him unable to speak.
Thankfully, he did.

"Hey, there. I'm Mitch."

Chapter 7

The Dead Baby

Finally, brothers and sisters, whatever is true,
whatever is noble, whatever is right, whatever is pure,
whatever is lovely, whatever is admirable—
if anything is excellent or praiseworthy—
think about such things.
~*Philippians 4:8 (NIV)*

Present Day

Smithfield, North Carolina, Easter

" We don't know these people," my husband
John said, "and I think I should be on the
call with you."

The day before, my brother—*brother!*—texted me
that he wanted to talk to me. I had texted him back:
*Let's talk tomorrow. That way if we have questions, we
have time to think about them and what we want to say.*

I wanted time to gather my thoughts and get my
emotions in check. I wasn't sure if the news about me

was totally out of the blue, or if he knew his mom had given birth to another child. Or, maybe Wilma Faye had told him that she lost a baby. I wanted our call, a brother reunited with a long lost sister, to be purposeful, because I wasn't so sure I was ever going to talk to him again depending on his reaction. This might be it, this one phone call, this one chance to connect.

John and I were sitting in our living room in our home in Smithfield discussing my upcoming phone call with my biological brother, Glenn. Glenn had initially wanted me to call him late yesterday, but I put him off. It was all happening so fast, meeting Samantha, then learning about Wilma Faye and finding out she died. I wanted time to think about what I was going to say to Glenn, my biological brother. I was overwhelmed so my hands were shaking and I kept checking the tea in my glass. I wasn't drinking it, so I knew it couldn't be empty, but I kept checking and checking it like I was having some sort of OCD episode.

John grabbed my hands. "It will be okay, Christina." He was another person in my life, like my mom and my friend Victoria, that always called me by my full name, Christina. He stared into my eyes with those sparkling blue ones and spoke with a reassurance I could feel. "I'm going to be right there with you."

John was worried that Glenn might say or do something that would upset me. And, like I was wary with Samantha at first, he still wasn't sure if this was some sort of a scam or not. John had worked in IT, and since I'm technologically challenged—like when I was looking for my DNA results in the actual mailbox instead of an app, duh—he said he'd handle the logistics of getting multiple people on the phone with each other.

"I'll monitor the call as we're talking," John said. "That way, if things go sideways, I can just end it. And you'll never have to speak to him again."

And that was fine by me.

The phone call took place later that day, after church and dinner. It was Easter. That hit me as ironic since everyone in Arkansas had thought I died and here I was risen from the dead, just like Christ rose from the dead. Easter is a day of being risen, so when I say that I rose from the dead I don't mean that in a blasphemous way but in a very reverent way. As Christians we are risen with Christ.

On our way to church, we'd listened to the Easter hymn, *Christ the Lord is Risen Today*. Our church played contemporary music, and since John wanted some traditional he pulled up a playlist on his phone. The familiar strains gave me a sense of peace as we traveled the narrow Carolina country highways to our church.

Love's redeeming work is done, Alleluia!
Fought the fight, the battle won, Alleluia!
Death in vain forbids His rise, Alleluia!
Christ hath opened paradise, Alleluia!

Soar we now where Christ hath led, Alleluia!
Foll'wing our exalted Head, Alleluia!
Made like Him, like Him we rise, Alleluia!
Ours the cross, the grave, the skies, Alleluia![2]

After a praise-filled church service at Focus Church in Raleigh, we went over to John's parents' house for Easter dinner. Pa, John's father, also named John but who everyone called "Pa," had made the masterpiece of a turkey. He basted it in butter, orange and spices and the aroma in the house was heavenly. He also mad sweet ham with a glaze he made from brown sugar, mustard and spices. He was the chef in the house and Easter dinner was in his hands. He'd made Yukon Gold potatoes, which he baked in the oven by wrapping them in wet paper towels and sealing them in aluminum foil. He served those with lots of butter, sour cream and chives. The "sin salad" was made with pistachio pudding, crushed pineapple, whipped topping, cherries and mini marshmallows. We had a big bowl of buttered sweet corn that had been "put up" from the summer growing season. When you "put up" food that means that it's been preserved by canning, drying or freezing. Pa's corn had been frozen and he thawed it and cooked

---

[2] Charles Wesley, the co-founder of the Methodist Church, wrote *Christ the Lord Is Risen Today* in 1739. It was initially titled *Hymn for Easter Day*. He based it on an older anonymous Bohemian hymn titled *Jesus Christ is Risen Today*.

it with butter, tasting as fresh as it had in the summer. Same with mason jars of tomatoes, from the past summer's garden tasted ripe and sweet for our Easter table. Our meal also included yeast rolls and a fresh salad.

We had a proper prayer of thanksgiving for Christ's ultimate gift of Himself before we dug into the bowls and platters. Pa, John's mom Martha, his sister Teresa, John and I filled our plates to brimming while I filled everyone in on my life-altering events of the last 48 hours. I still couldn't believe so much had happened in such a short amount of time. I told them about finding out my DNA results, discovering the family in Arkansas, and learning that I had a biological brother, Glenn, in Virginia. It sounded like I made up the story.

After dinner, while Teresa and Pa cleaned the kitchen, Martha, disabled from Parkinson's Disease, went to sit in her recliner in the living room to watch *The Gaither Gospel Hour*. Dessert would have to wait until later, because we were stuffed.

John and I walked down the hall to the green bedroom to make the call to Glenn. We had thought of going outside, but the pollen was pretty bad. Even though it was a warm day, the pine pollen, which coats everything in the South in an ugly layer of yellow-green dust each Spring, covered all the furniture on the back porch. So, instead of enjoying the warm day outside, we went into the bedroom.

John sat in the one wingback chair, and I sat on the quilted bedspread propping a pillow behind me on the headboard. John checked our internet connection, or whatever it was that he did, and told me that we were set to go.

I texted Glenn. *I'm ready to talk, if you are.*

He answered right away. *Sure.*

My heart was fluttering as John made the call.

"Hi, this is Glenn."

"And, I'm Roberta, Glenn's wife." A woman's voice chimed in.

"I'm Christi, and John's here, too." John didn't speak, but he gave me a reassuring look.

There was some silence after the introductions. It was so awkward us four being in on a phone call together.

I broke the silence, "So, um, it seems we're related."

Glenn chuckled. "It looks like it. Samantha said you showed up on the DNA test as my sister."

"Were you surprised?"

"A little, yeah. See, Mom had said a few times that she had a daughter that was still 'out there' somewhere. But I really didn't know if it was true."

"I guess I'm *that* daughter."

"Yeah. Samantha emailed us a picture of you. You look like her. And, you know what's weird? You sound like her, too."

That had to be creepy that I sounded like his dead mother. I wasn't sure how to comment.

Glenn added, "My mother, or I guess, *our* mother, died of a brain tumor. Two years ago. It was really hard, you know, losing her. William, um, did you know that I have a half-brother? His name's William? Well, William and I were really close to her." Glenn paused. "And, now she's gone."

"William, your brother. *My* brother. This family keeps growing. I can't believe there are so many of you."

"There's just the two of us."

"Well, yeah, but you've got 10 aunts and uncles."

"Fourteen actually. My—uh, our dad has four brothers."

"You know, I was thinking about contacting *our* dad." It felt weird to say that.

"Mike can be a pretty rough guy."

I wondered what he meant by a "rough guy."

Glenn continued before I could ask. "Mike Mercado is my dad. He's not going to believe this. It's gonna come out of left field for him. I think it would be better if I told him."

"So, I shouldn't contact him?"

"No, not a good idea. Don't say anything to him, and don't talk to William, either. Not until I get a DNA test. Then, we'll know for sure, and then I can tell them. It's better coming from me. I know you're my sister, but I think more proof for them is better. No sense in making a big deal outta something if it doesn't pan out."

I didn't think it would matter because I was pretty sure I was the dead baby, but he wanted to get the DNA test done and I thought why not let him get his own set of results? I also wanted to honor the fact he wanted to be the one to break the news to our dad, after all, I was the newcomer. I would wait for Glenn to get the DNA test done, and then he could contact *our* father.

Weeks later, while waiting for Glenn to take the DNA test, I was scrolling around on Facebook on my home computer and realized it had been a while since I checked in with Samantha. So, I clicked over to see Samantha's profile. I saw a picture of her mother, Karen, the one who confirmed that Wilma Faye had lived in upstate New York. I clicked on Karen's picture and brought up her profile. I may be the most unsavvy tech person in the Triangle, but I knew how to find people on Facebook.

As far as I knew, Karen was the only other person in Arkansas who knew about me, so on a whim, I messaged her. *I know you know who I am. I'm contacting you because I wanted to get more information about the family.*

Karen replied later that morning. *We just got out of church service. Give me a call.*

She'd left her number, but instead of calling her, I gave her mine. I wanted her to call me. I felt so exhausted by these interactions, I couldn't keep driving everything. I couldn't be the only one working to make a connection.

She didn't call me, and I thought, well, that's okay then, it's her choice to call or not. I grabbed a sponge and some cleaner and went into the bathroom.

Looking in the mirror, there's no surprise I have Spanish heritage. It's all there in my face. The features I thought might be Cuban or Greek, are really Puerto Rican. I can see it so plainly, even if I don't think I look that much like Wilma Faye.

Growing up, my mom told me I was born in Kingston Hospital in New York state. Five years ago, when I needed to get a passport to travel, I contacted Ulster County in New York to get a certified copy of my original birth certificate. I sent them the money with the birth information and waited. In a few weeks, they wrote me back. Instead of sending me a copy of the certificate, they sent back my check, uncashed, and told me that they had no record of me. I wasn't born in Kingston Hospital. Which was shocking, because if I wasn't born there, where was I born?

My mom had always said it was Kingston Hospital. But, I guess she only assumed that I was born there because they were living in Kingston at that time they adopted me. My birth certificate had no information on it. I mean, nothing. If you looked at my birth certificate, there was literally nothing on it. No names, no details, not even a time of birth. It only stated that a baby girl was born in January 1969 in New York state. I always thought it looked like something my daddy's secretary typed up.

I was placed in foster care from the day of my birth until I was nine months old. That's when my parents, Amy and Alan, adopted me. I have a picture of me in a crib in foster care, sitting on the mattress and looking up. My mom received it when they adopted me. *Adopt a kid, get a free photo!*

My whole life, I wrote down my birthplace as Kingston, NY. I was sure that I was born to famous parents, of course. We kids of adoption come up with our own ideas about our biological parents and invent the stories that fill in our gaps. My parents kept their identities hidden because I was their secret love child, just like the Diana Ross and the Supremes song. It was the Seventies, so current events guided my fantasy of who my biological parents were. Cher, the famous pop star, and a NASA astronaut, a man who surely walked on the moon, were my real parents. They had me and left me in the hospital so they could go back to their celebrity lifestyles. That's how I figured it happened.

The only document that says anything about me was a paper from Child Services. I found it years ago, stored in a box with other old papers, in my mom's attic. The state had blocked out all the contact information, which left another big blank in my history. I knew basically nothing about my birth until this DNA business opened up a big can of worms.

My phone pinged that I'd received a message. It wasn't Karen, but Miranda, my cousin on the Mercado side, who unearthed tons of information on our family tree.

I wanted to let you know that I am completely estranged from the family. It's all because of my parents. Long story short, my father kidnapped my daughter in 2005. They fraudulently obtained paperwork stating she was their ward. It took many court dates and court orders, some television appearances, and a stint on Oprah, to prove that they were not his legal guardians before I got her back. When they had her, they abused her physically, emotionally and sexually.

What in the heck? What she said didn't make sense to me. Was she really on Oprah's TV show?

I do not know if Uncle Mike or anyone else knew what was going on, but I decided not to take a chance that they were part of the plot to destroy my life. I had to distance myself from my family and I set up blockades so they couldn't get to me. I am willing to share whatever information I have about our family with you, but I ask that you don't disclose or share any information about me and my immediate family with anyone else. It's important that you don't share anything I've told you because they might use it against me.

I stopped reading there. If this were a phone call, I'd have to hang up. Thankfully, it was just a message. Either Miranda had been taken advantage of by her family, and I might know a little bit about that, or she was completely off her rocker. I wasn't sure what to think, so I swiped out of the program and went back to cleaning. All these new connections were turning out to be difficult situations.

As I was wiping a spatter of toothpaste off the counter, my phone rang. I grabbed it out of my pocket and practically dropped it on the floor.

"Hi, Christi! This is your Aunt Karen, and I want to apologize. We have terrible reception at the faith center, and I had to wait until we started driving to call you. You're on speaker. Samantha's here, and I have Diane in the backseat. Diane is my sister."

"Hi, Karen. It's, um, wow, kind of weird to talk to you."

"I know. Say, I spoke to my brother Leon. He's the pastor at our church. And, we just had a family meeting with everyone and talked about how Wilma Faye might have a daughter in North Carolina. It was a shocked room, to be sure."

I wish I had been a fly on the wall in that room.

Karen said she knew about me, the dead baby. Like the others, she had been told that the baby had died. By everyone's accounts, Wilma Faye was so distraught about losing her child that they believed she had mental lapse. She would say things like, "I think Michael did something, I think the baby is still alive." Or, "Michael paid off the doctors." The family chalked it up to grief. The way Wilma Faye described it to her family, and the things she said over the years, made it sound like she wasn't aware of any adoption.

Wilma Faye and Michael weren't married when they had me. Hardly anyone in Arkansas knew that, but I think that Karen did and maybe Wilma Faye's mom. When she was young, Karen had lived with them for a time, too, and she was very close to Wilma Faye. She also said that four years after I was born, they had Glenn, then four years after that they divorced. Their divorce might have had something to do with Michael having an affair, but whatever the reason, according to the Arkansas family, Wilma Faye and Michael weren't friends after that.

I wondered about that. Did her anger and grief manifest as blaming him for giving me up for adoption? Is that why she always told her family that she believed her daughter was alive and that Michael had 'arranged something?'

You hear about these stories all the time. In fact, my client and good friend Janice told me about a book she read called *The Baby Thief*[3]. It was about a woman named Georgia Tann who ran an orphanage and turned

---

[3] Raymond, Barbara Bisantz, *The Baby Thief: The Untold Story of Georgia Tann, the Baby Seller Who Corrupted Adoption* (New York: Union Square Press, 2008).

a profit by selling children and babies to couples who wanted children. I wondered if that was what Michael did. What if he didn't want a baby, so he had them put Wilma Faye to sleep, then they took the baby from her? He could have worked it out with his connections because he was in medical school. He might have been able to pull it off because he could have known someone who knew how to "handle the situation." There was no sense in wondering about it further because whether or not Wilma Faye knew what Michael had done is something that she carried to her grave.

"Had Wilma Faye known about you," continued Karen, "she never would have given you up for adoption. It hurts my heart so much that Wilma Faye never had the opportunity to know you."

"It hurts my heart, too." And that was the truth, maybe…

John had gotten home and found me in the bathroom on my cell. I whispered into his ear, "Arkansas family." He nodded and we stood there in the bathroom.

"Glenn was in his forties before he got married, said Karen, "and he's never had kids. I think Wilma Faye babied her boys. Maybe because she lost you, she tried to make things better by babying her sons."

She went on to say that Glenn hadn't kept a regular job until recently, and he never had a career. My half-brother William never had a job. He's sort of a loner and played video games. Listening to Karen describe the boys, I think that Wilma Faye might be to blame for their slow launch.

As Karen and I spoke with each other, it was really odd because it was like I'd known her my whole life. We were talking and laughing like old friends.

"We all think the chances are pretty high that you are Wilma Faye's lost daughter," said Karen.

"I think I am," I replied, feeling hopeful that she believed what I felt to be true.

"You sound like her, you know," Karen offered.

"That's what Glenn said."

"You do. Here's the deal, let's wait for Glenn's DNA test to confirm everything. That way, we're totally sure."

And, my heart sank. This was so defeating. I kept getting pushback on being "the dead baby" and everyone needing proof. First Samantha, then Glenn, and now Karen.

Feeling emboldened, I said, "Karen, if you're so worried about whether I'm related or not, you could get the DNA test yourself. I've already done a DNA test, there's nothing more I can do."

I explained to her that a DNA test showing connection between aunt to niece would be stronger confirmation than one connecting first cousins. So her DNA test would have value. She was silent for a moment and then said she'd think about it. We ended the call with her promise that she would at least consider whether or not to do a DNA test herself. She added that she also wanted to see Glenn's.

I turned to John. "What is going on with these people?"

He patted my shoulders. "This is a shock to them, so, of course they want proof. They shouldn't need it, but they do. It's clear to me that you're Wilma Faye's daughter."

I nodded. "I believe I am."

"What do you want to do?"

I was beyond frustrated. I didn't ask for any of this to come into my life. I had so much else going on, that this was a really unnecessary complication.

I prayed out loud with John beside me. *Lord, why did you bring this family into my life? What is the purpose of all of this stress? I never asked for them, I never asked for any of this. And, yet, here I am. What can I do? Help me, please!*

I felt an immediate calm. God answered my prayer by providing me with His peace. I didn't need to be worried about what my newfound family did or didn't do. I decided to not even 'go there' anymore, because I thought maybe they were feeling threatened by me. Everyone seemed to want ironclad proof of my relation. And, I thought, even if we get Glenn's DNA test results, then what? Will that be the conclusive proof they want?

Maybe yes, maybe no.

I didn't know any of these people, and I've lived all my life up until this point without them in it. So, I asked myself, what would happen if I ended the search now? Nothing. I could let them go, and life would continue as it did before. Everything would be fine. Whatever will happen with happen, I thought, rather in a Doris Day, *Que Será, Será* manner. I couldn't waste any more energy on this, and I didn't need them, because I already had a family. I didn't want more drama in my life, because my life had already been too full of drama.

"Well? What do you want to do?" John was still studying me.

"God's given me peace. I'm going to let it go. No wait, that's wrong. I'm going to let *them* go."

CHAPTER 8

MY SECOND BIRTHDAY

So be on your guard, not asleep like the others.
Stay alert and be clearheaded. Night is the time when
people sleep and drinkers get drunk. But let us who
live in the light be clearheaded, protected by the
armor of faith and love, and wearing as our helmet
the confidence of our salvation.
~1 Thessalonians 5:6-8 (NLT)

Past

Cary, North Carolina, 1986

Christi age 17

*M*itch lived in a single wide mobile home on his property off of Highway 64 just on the outskirts of Apex, a sleepy bedroom town south of Cary. The five-acre lot was tangled grove of native tree and shrubs broken up by a graded gravel driveway. Mitch's mother owned the property and had bought the trailer for him because he was such a mess. He was separated from, but still married to, his wife Linda; a complication that I ignored.

It was early in the morning, when we awoke to the sound of tires crunching on the rock drive. A vehicle circled the trailer and came to a stop out front. I knelt on the bed and pulled the blinds back to get a look out of the window. "It's my mom."

The car skidded to a stop, and I could hear Mom getting out and slamming the car door shut. Her feet pounded up the rickety wooden steps that weren't quite attached to the trailer. She announced her arrival by banging on the glass storm door, each thud hitting my gut.

I fell back into bed and pulled the worn comforter up around my neck. I wanted to pretend we weren't home, but Mitch had already gotten up and yanked on his jeans, tucking his billfold in his back pocket, out of habit, I assumed. He arched an eyebrow at me and slicked back his hair with one palm. I thought pretty fine looking in the morning. His face offered a mixture of resignation and alarm. "You know, I want to jump out of that window about now," he said, pointing to the one opposite where he'd seen my mom, "and get the hell out of here."

But he didn't. Instead, he opened the door to let her in while I got dressed. She sat down at the small kitchen table and pushed aside last evening's dishes.

Mitch brewed coffee and I pulled out a metal chair, the one with the missing plastic on its foot, and it squeaked across linoleum. It was an unpleasant sound anytime, but more so first thing in the morning. I plopped down to face Mom.

She sighed, whistling out a long, loud whoosh of air against her teeth. I would say that it was for dramatic effect, but that wasn't Mom's style. She didn't do it for theatrics; she was really that exasperated. Her face was tired and there was too much skin around her eyes. Had she always had those wrinkles? I couldn't remember. I wanted to massage my fingers over her face and smooth out the lines bunching there, those folds of skin that made her look so many years older than she was.

She looked me in the eye and stated slowly, but firmly, "I need you to come home."

We talked for awhile, and drank the coffee, but it didn't matter what else was said. What mattered was that she wanted me home. Since I was still a minor, and I had a healthy amount of respect for her, I packed up my duffle. Mitch put my bag into the trunk of my car, the one Mom had bought for me. It was a newer white Mustang with a blue interior and a growling engine. I loved that car. It was my "hey, you graduated from treatment!" car. Mitch gave me a kiss through the driver's window, and I followed Mom home.

Months before, when Mom had checked me out of the Chatham Northridge Hospital for drug and alcohol treatment, she withdrew me from Enloe High School, as well. She said it wasn't going to turn out well for me there. My old friends with the same habits and same party haunts would be a lure to the life that I needed to leave behind. I can't say I was upset because school was never my thing. I had nearly flunked out the Spring semester because I'd been partying so hard and neglecting my studies. The only reason I didn't fail was because they gave me "pass" grades for all of my classes, since my dad had died. Then, I'd missed the start of Fall semester due to treatment, so catching up was clearly not an option. Mom went down to the school and filled out paperwork to legally take me out of school. I was set free.

My mom was living in the absolute freaking chaos that I had brought into her life. Not only did she just lose a husband and still worked the nightshift at Rex Hospital, but she had one daughter, Judy, who was having a bit of trouble in college, and another daughter, me, who she had to remove from both drug treatment and high school, not to mention try to figure out some kind of future for this wayward child. I don't know how my mom was holding it together, but she did. Sandy, of course, was married with small kids and earning another degree. She would say jokingly, "What about me?" because Judy and I got all the attention. But, Sandy, as the firstborn, was perfect, so she totally filled in the gap and helped Mom cope with everything on her plate. Sandy said that she and Mom had a lot of long discussions about what to do with Judy and me.

Judy's situation was fairly easy to resolve. With the help from an understanding school guidance counselor, and more semester hours, for which Mom paid, they devised a path for her to graduate from UNC Chapel Hill with only spending one additional year in college.

On the other hand, I was a bit harder to set straight. I was kind of like Humpty Dumpty, with all the pieces laid out at the foot of a wall from where I'd just fallen. Those pieces didn't easily fit back together. What do you do with a Recovering alcoholic, former drug addicted high school dropout? Well, besides taking her out of her 28-year-old married boyfriend's trailer on New Year's Day? I'm not sure. I wasn't helping Mom or Sandy find a solution. It was like I was doing everything I could to make life more difficult. There was a part of me that felt like no matter what I did, even without the booze and drugs, it caused my mom heartache. So, I went to AA meetings, drank coffee and smoked. I tried to fill my life with something.

The answer showed up unexpectedly in mid-January, a few weeks after my 17th birthday, when my mother met a man named Mark Mitchell, one of the brothers from Mitchell's Hairstyling Academy. The brothers Mitchell, along with their father, owned the local beauty school over at South Hills. During this chance encounter, either designed by fate or God

Himself, she had shared with him a little bit of what was going on in her life. Mark was a Christian, and so he asked Mom to pray with him and his wife. Now, this completely threw my mom a curve ball. Catholics usually don't pray with other people that aren't Catholics, at least that's been my family's experience, so she was definitely entering a place of faith to pray with this new acquaintance who wouldn't know the Stations of the Cross from the stations on the radio. But, it was during that prayer that my mom received an answer to my situation. God spoke to her and told her to listen to Mark.

"Amy," Mark said, "I have an idea. Why don't you send Christi to our academy?"

"She's not even in high school."

"True. And, normally, we only accept students with high school diplomas, but, I'll tell you what, if she can get her GED, I'll see to it that she gets in."

Mom came home from work that morning full of energy and found me at the kitchen table eating a bowl of cereal. She gave me a broad smile that I hadn't seen in a while and told me about her encounter with Mark Mitchell.

"So, you'll need to get your GED, and Mark will see to it you get into the academy." She was bouncing from side to side on her white work sneakers.

"Uh, okay." I didn't know what else to say, as I was kind of stunned. I had no idea if I could get my GED or not, but Mom seemed really excited about it, so I thought I might as well go along with the plan.

"Listen," she said, finally sitting down. "It's my job as your mother to make sure that I set you up. You know, so that you can go on to have success in your life."

"I get it." I think I understood.

She continued, "What you do with this is totally up to you, but I will pay for you to go to this school and get your certificate."

"Wow, okay, thanks." I wasn't sure this was going to work, but I did appreciate her trying.

"The rest is up to you."

"Okay." I felt like she took a large pack off her back and handed it to me. It was as if she'd been carrying around my stuff for so long and it was a burden, and now she was giving it to me. It was my turn to carry my own load.

And that's how I ended up getting my GED and going to Mitchell's Hairstyling Academy.

A few weeks later, my mother came over to get me from Mitch's again. She sat at the kitchen table in the trailer, again, with Mitch brewing coffee, again, and me waiting in the uncomfortable silence for her to give the marching orders.

Instead, she turned to Mitch and said, "I think, at this point, you don't want to see me come over here anymore. Heck, *I* don't want to come over here anymore. So, let's be done with all this. Here's the deal: I will pay your electric bill if Christi can live here while she's in hairstyling school, and I'll pay for her school. Are you okay with that?"

He nodded in agreement. And with that, I moved permanently into Mitch's trailer the following weekend.

As I was packing up my clothes from Mom's house, she came in and sat on the bed to gave me a final piece of advice, a serious look on her face. "Remember this, Christi, you always need to keep your own checking account. Having access to your own money is important for any woman. And, if that guy, or any guy, isn't good to you, I want you to wait until the dead of night, take a heavy frying pan and hit him over the head with it, and get the heck out of there."

"Okay, Mom." I agreed even though I didn't think she was joking.

"Mitch, you need to get a divorce." Those were the first words out of my mouth when I got back to his place, with the trunk of my Mustang filled with my clothes and other stuff. If I was going to live there with him, he needed to be single. He agreed to start the process. I was seventeen, and he was twelve years older than me, but I couldn't see myself shacking up with a married man, even if he was separated. I still had a little integrity.

This was God directing my life, and I didn't know it. I remembered those hypocrites in the church, and I didn't want to be one of them. I didn't want to live a lie and pretend that everything was fine.

During hair school, I got a terrible case of mono which landed me in the hospital, and then laid me up in bed for a few weeks. So, that delayed my graduation. I had never been so sick in my life. It cost my mom some money, because she had to pay for extra semesters of tuition, but a few years later, I finally graduated and got my certificate. I was 19 years old and I felt like I finally had made it.

My first job was at Color My World on North Glenwood Avenue in the building (that later became an Adam and Eve sex shop). I was in charge of facials at the salon and ran my own schedule of seeing clients and offering products. I loved it. I was working, making decent money, and it didn't cost Mitch and I much to get by. He was working gigs as a subcontractor, and he was quite good. His artistry and skill were desired by the up-and-coming young professionals who were part of the tech boom in Research Triangle Park. They made enough money to spend on upgrading their older homes on prime real estate in Cary and Raleigh.

Our lifestyle was perfect, working a lot, eating out or getting take out, and spending nights watching TV or, at least for me, meeting up with friends. We attended AA meetings every day, together or separately, and I never really felt like I wanted a drink or to use. It wasn't who I was anymore. I also knew that if I was drinking or using that would be an issue since I was living with someone who was sober.

It's interesting to me that the "higher power" of Alcoholics Anonymous, or who I believed to be the God I grew up with, spoke to me. He put it on my heart so that I saw my addictive personality, and that I had no other choice but to stay sober. I celebrated August 18th as my second birthday—my sobriety date—when I finally entered the hospital and stopped drinking and drugging. The next day, and for all the days after, I woke up without wondering what I did the night before.

When Mitch and I met, I was only days out of rehab. I was smitten. He was handsome, and sure of himself, and twelve years older than me. But, he was just as much of a wreck as I was. Neither one of us had any place in having a relationship with another person, both being newly sober, but there we were. They suggest you wait at least a year in total sobriety before getting into a relationship. I didn't listen and I didn't want to listen. I believe that neither of us knew how to do life if we didn't have someone else. That was the reality of our life together: we needed each other to stay sober. The kitchen silverware drawer, which was more of a junk drawer, held Mitch's eight white chips. When you start out in AA, they give you a white chip to keep in your wallet, to remind you that you're doing the twelves steps. Most people keep them with their credit cards and money, so you see it if you're thinking about drinking. Each of those chips represented eight slips and eight fresh starts for Mitch.

Because I had Mitch in my life, it was a reason to stay sober. The only reason he was going to be in my life was if I was going to be sober, so it helped keep me sober.

One late morning, I stopped by his mom's house on my way to work. She lived in Cary in an old bungalow near downtown. There was a woman in the kitchen. It was Linda, Mitch's ex. His mom introduced us, and I offered the excuse that I had a client and I had to go. I couldn't get out of there fast enough.

The next day, I received a phone call. I was at home on my day off, and Mitch was working. I figured it was him, asking about dinner plans. But, it wasn't. It was Linda.

"I thought we could meet, Christi. You free this week?"

We agreed to meet for pizza after work the following day.

Inside the restaurant was dark, but it wasn't crowded. The hostess took me to a booth by the window, and I slid onto the vinyl seat to sit opposite my boyfriend's ex-wife. She was already there. The hostess asked what I wanted to drink and I ordered sweet tea.

Linda was about ten years older than me and had short, dark brown hair. She wore it spiked on top with a

153

shiny barrette on the side in the shape of a butterfly. She introduced herself and I told her to call me "Christi."

The waitress came and introduced herself as Betty, as she set down my tea and a Coke for Linda, which she must've already ordered. Betty pulled out a paper pad and pencil from her black apron. "What'll you have, hons?" After a quick exchange of the stereotypical female "I don't care's," we settled on a mushroom and sausage pizza.

Linda filled in the quiet space after Betty left. "I know this is awkward. It is for both of us, right?

"You could say that." I took a sip of my tea to give my hands something to do.

"I wanted to tell you about my marriage. With Mitch, what it was like. I think you should know what happened and how, um, how we split."

I sipped more tea, and nodded. I couldn't imagine what she wanted to tell me.

"You know that Mitch drank a lot and used drugs when we were married and living together, yes?"

"Yeah, I know. But, he's sober now." I took another sip.

"He wasn't for a long time. And, every time he got drunk or used drugs he was angry. Sometimes violently so. He never remembered any of the bad stuff. He used to get so wasted he'd have blackouts."

"So did I."

Linda looked surprised.

I nodded. "Yeah, there were times I woke up and I couldn't remember the night before." I told her about my own addiction, and about drinking and drugging in high school. I explained how I drank wine in my bedroom at 16 while my dad lay dying downstairs. I told her about the night I nearly killed my good friend, Priska, and how my mother gave me an ultimatum of either getting kicked out the house or going to rehab. I don't know why I felt it was important to tell her. I think I wanted her to know that Mitch wasn't the only screw up. I could handle his past because I had one, too.

The waitress delivered hot pizza in a pan which she placed on a metal pizza stand. I used the spatula to serve myself a steaming slice. Linda did the same.

"We're both sober now, so it's good," I assured her.

She nodded, lifting the slice to her mouth. "Ow, hot." She laughed and dropped the pizza to her plate, and she picked up a knife and fork to eat.

I removed the silverware from its napkin and the fork slipped out of my hands onto the floor with a clickety clack. I should've known that was going to happen. I fumbled the hot slice in my hands and blew on it. I took a small bite, stinging the roof of my mouth with cheese. I gulped the rest of my sweet tea.

Linda was watching me as she lifted her fork to her mouth, but she didn't say anything.

"Linda, all of us in the program, we all have our stories. It's why we're in the program."

"I know. Look, I was part of Mitch's stories, I was there when it happened. I just want you to be aware of how bad it got with him."

Linda explained that she became a member of Al-Anon, the group that offers support for relatives and friends of alcoholics, regardless of whether the alcoholic admits they have a drinking problem or seeks help for the problem.

"I don't see how any of this makes a difference. He's sober now."

Linda sighed. "Did you know about the time he held me and his mother hostage?"

"What? Really?" The sugar and caffeine from the sweet tea was making my heart do a jog. This seemed like quite the exaggeration.

"Yeah, he got so blotto that he trapped us in the house. He pointed a gun to my head."

"I can't imagine that." *Mitch?*

"It's true. The SWAT team came in and arrested him. Cary had just gotten a SWAT team and Mitch was pretty much their first 'customer.'" She made quotation marks with her fingers when she said 'customer.' "He was threatening my life, and he didn't even remember it the next day. That's how 'out of it' he was."

I flashed back to some of my own escapades. No one called the SWAT team on me. "I guess it's good he's sober now."

"He's dangerous, Christi."

156

"He *was* dangerous. He was drunk and using. There's a difference."

"No, there's not. That's who he is. They called in a hostage negotiator. The only reason the situation ended well was because Mitch had passed out in the yard. That's when they arrested him. He did sixty days in jail."

"I did some pretty bad stuff in my using days, too, but I'm sober now. So is Mitch. It makes a difference. You don't understand because you haven't seen him get sober. He's in control, and he doesn't use. He's normal. Sobriety makes a huge difference." The sweet tea gave me a boost and I was practically preaching the virtues of Mitch.

"I saw him go in and out of treatment many times, Christi."

I thought about all those chips in the drawer, but I didn't have anything to say. We ate in silence for few moments and Linda switched topics. She asked me about my job and we made small talk as we finished our dinner, then she paid the check. Outside on the side-walk, we parted with an awkward half handshake, half hug, and I got back into my car and headed back to the trailer, back to Mitch.

People who aren't in the program don't get it, I thought.

Six months later, going about my routine at work and seeing clients, I received a call. It was Mitch.

Through a thick tongue he slurred, "I want you to know that I'm drunk as a skunk."

I hung up and started crying, in public, which was totally out of character for me. I was so scared and mad. *How could he do this to himself? How could he do this to us?*

Stephanie, the woman who owned the store ran over. "Are you okay? What's wrong?"

I sobbed, "He's drinking!"

She didn't know anything about me or Mitch being in the program.

"It's alright, it happens. These things happen." The look of pity mixed with confusion on her face didn't match my reality.

I stared into her confused face and stated with exasperation, "He's *drinking*."

She hugged me. "It's okay, Christi, men do that. He'll sober up."

She didn't understand. She couldn't possibly understand. Being an alcoholic wasn't something you brought up to your boss. She didn't understand what it meant when an alcoholic was back on the bottle. She didn't understand the battle he'd just lost because she didn't know about the war we were fighting.

I felt alone and isolated and I didn't know what to do. I thought about who could help me get my stuff out of Mitch's place. I couldn't be there when he got home. I wracked my brain for who I could call. Mom was sleeping off her nightshift. Judy had moved to New York City to work as a sales rep. Sandy was at work. So, I pulled out my address book and planner from my purse. Out fell my poker chip, my sobriety chip, that I'd gotten in my first AA meeting. I thought it was ironic that it tumbled to the floor, kind of like Mitch tumbling off a cliff by going on a drinking binge.

I picked up the white chip, and as I fingered it, I remembered Hank, a really kind man in the program who didn't live too far from us. He had told me that if I ever needed anything, all I had to do was call him. He had scribbled his number in my book. I flipped to the page with his writing on it, block letters in blue ink, and quickly dialed his number. I told him what had happened and that I needed to go to the trailer and get some stuff, but I didn't want to go there alone. He said he'd meet me there.

I got home and was relieved to find that Mitch wasn't there, but Hank was. He was standing by his truck, in the driveway but near the road with his truck facing the road as if ready to leave.

I pulled in and rolled down the window. "Thanks, Hank."

He was a big man, much larger than Mitch and I felt comfortable having him there. But I needed to get out of there fast before Mitch got home.

Hank smiled down at me. "No problem. Why don't you pull up to the house and turn around, that way you can exit as soon as you're packed."

"Will do."

Hank waited outside the door while I went in. I grabbed a couple of duffle bags from the closet and started throwing my clothes and toiletries in them. There was a gun on the bedside table, so I took it and put it into the back of the closet, hiding it under some towels I plucked from the bathroom. I hoped he wouldn't be able to find it because drinking and drugging don't mix with guns.

My retainer box was empty, so I searched my own bedside table, but I couldn't find it. I ran my hand under the pillow and between the sheets. Down on the floor I looked under the bed. Nothing. I ran to the bathroom. *Where is it?*

"You coming, Christi?" Hank called from outside, a slight edge to his voice. He could take on Mitch, but I doubted he wanted a confrontation.

"Yeah, yeah, just looking for something," I yelled back.

I could hear the tick-tick-tick of the battery operated clock on the wall of the bath. *Hurry, Christi, hurry.*

I searched the medicine cabinet and the shelves over the toilet, but no retainer. I heard an engine. *Panic.* I ran to the window, but it was just a neighbor driving by. *Thank God.* I had to get out of there.

I gave up looking for my retainer and zipped up my duffle bags. Walking through the kitchen, one duffle swung over an arm and the other in my left hand. I spied my retainer on the kitchen counter next to the coffee pot. I reached out with my right hand, but it got me off balance and I ended up tumbling to the floor.

"Christi? You okay?" Hank was at the stormdoor looking in through the glass. He came in and helped me up. I popped the retainer in my pocket and he grabbed both duffle bags.

"Let's go! He pushed me out the door. "Follow me to my house and we'll figure it out from there."

Hank threw the duffle bags in my trunk and I fumbled for the keys as I got in. My hands were shaking so badly that I couldn't get the key inserted into the ignition. My breaths were coming in short waves. Hank had already started his truck and was pulling out of the drive. Out of the corner of my eye, I saw Mitch's truck turning down the road from the highway. I took a deep breath and finally plunged the key and turned it. The Mustang roared to life. With a clunk I threw it into gear and jammed the accelerator, spraying rock as I gunned onto the road. I flew past Mitch traveling the other way, and got onto the highway, barely missing a semi as I followed Hank.

Of course, Mitch called me the next day at work and told me he was so sorry. He begged me to come home, saying he couldn't do it without me. And, after a few days, I did.

That first time, I left him for only a couple days while I stayed at my friend Maureen's. This pattern went on for almost a year, jumping between living with Maureen and Mitch. He would go to meetings, and then he would fall off the wagon. I would take his weapons that he had in the house, guns and knives or whatever, and I would hide them, hoping that when he was drunk he wouldn't be able to find them.

Somewhere along the way, I realized that I couldn't be responsible for somebody else's sobriety or the choices that they made. I had my own life to live. At times that would be with Mitch, and at times it would be away from Mitch. I lived my life dancing around Mitch's drinking and drug use.

"Take what you need and leave the rest," the AA leader would say about the money in the money bucket we passed around at our meetings. You would put a few dollars in, or if you needed some, you'd take a few out.

I sat at a table in Melba's Country Kitchen where our AA meetings were held. This was our home group. The restaurant was on Chatham Street and we attended that meeting because it was closer than the one in Raleigh. The restaurant closed early, and allowed us to use the entire back room. They provided us coffee for a small fee. Usually, AA meetings take place in a church, but the members of this group joked that they were so sinful that if they walked into a church they'd catch on fire. Plus, many members had bad experiences with organized religion.

I got off work and went to meet Mitch at the AA meeting. I picked up my coffee mug with my left hand and found a table. My right hand was numb, probably from work, so I was trying to do everything with my left hand. Mitch shuffled in late and my table had filled up so he sat at a table in front of mine.

About halfway through the meeting, Mitch got up and left. He didn't look at me, and he didn't tell me where he was going. And I thought to myself that he was going to go use. That was the vibe I got from him.

I was stupid enough that when I got home, I still held out a glimmer of hope that maybe Mitch hadn't left to drink. I had a military green duffel bag that I'd stuffed full of my clothes and my cosmetics. I even packed the book Uncle Armand and Aunt Julia had given me on the history of Ybor City. I didn't want to leave, not until I could see Mitch to see if he'd been using or not. So, I sat at the kitchen table, my packed duffle on the floor next to me and waited for him.

If he's not using, then I don't need to leave, but if he is, then I need to get out of here fast.

It was hours later. I was still waiting with my packed duffle. Time had passed but I wasn't aware of it because I was in some sort of anxiety stupor. Mitch pulled into the driveway and skidded to a stop. He practically fell out of the truck and stumbled up the stairs. I wanted to cry because I knew he was drunk, but I also knew I needed to get myself out of that trailer. I reached for my duffle to make a dash for the door, but my fingers were asleep from sitting in one place for too long. I couldn't pick up the bag.

Mitch staggered in the front door while I was standing in the kitchen and shaking my hands to get the blood flowing again. I prepared myself for what he might do. But, to my amazement, he didn't even look at me. He staggered across the room and threw himself down on the couch where he passed out. With relief and tingling fingers, I picked up my duffle and left the trailer.

I drove to Maureen's house, like I normally did when I left Mitch. Maureen was an older woman who I knew and loved. She lived off of Trinity Road and smoked like a chimney on fire. I was there for a few days before Mitch called me and said he wanted to meet me. I told him that I would meet him, but only at a public place, so we went to Waffle House. By then I'd been in sobriety long enough it made me realize the progress I would lose if I started using again or kept living with someone who was. So, I told him that I would not be going back home with him. I would meet him at meetings. I said that he'd have to attend meetings and he'd have to remain sober. It was then that my sobriety became more about me than about him. I think

God planned it that way, that I would see his using and understand I can't pin my sobriety on someone else. I had to own it.

For nearly a year, I stayed at Maureen's and Mitch did his best to perform. I wanted to believe him because I loved him, even through it all. But, through all those months, I realized I didn't know anything about having successful relationship and neither did he.

I'd been volunteering with Chatham Northridge Hospital, and my job was taking teenagers to AA and NA meetings outside the hospital. When I was a patient there, I remember volunteers would take us out for meetings, and I wanted to repay the favor. They would let me drive the large, white van and shuttle the teens to meetings.

Other times, I would volunteer to run AA meetings in the hospital for the teens who couldn't leave. Eventually, I set up hair cutting area there in the quiet room where I would cut their hair. A lot of the kids in treatment were in the foster system and didn't have the means to buy extra services. So, I cut their hair for free. It was another way I felt I could help.

After I'd been volunteering there for a few months, Sophia, the nurse manager, pulled me aside. I was a little nervous, wondering if I'd done something wrong.

"Is everything okay?" I asked her.

She laughed. "Of course, silly. Say, I've got some flexibility in my budget, and I was wondering if you'd be interested in working here full time?"

"Full time?"

"Yes, I need someone to help out Sharon and me with the paperwork and insurance. You'd be my assistant as a CD technician."

I jumped at the chance at being a chemical dependency technician. I'd been feeling so comfortable volunteering with fellow addicts, people who would know what to say if I got a call from my drunk boyfriend.

I'd be working under Sophia, helping her run the hospital and keep the paperwork in check. I'd also be available to help Sharon, our insurance guru, who always wore a sparkly barrette in her wavy dark hair. Though it was apparent that she didn't need much of my help.

I gave my notice to Color My World and started working at the treatment center the following week. I dove into my job at the hospital and loved it. I was nineteen years old working a dream job with my people. People who were 'friends of Bill.'

CHAPTER 9

LIFE SENTENCE, NO PAROLE

Trust in the Lord with all your heart, do not depend
on your own understanding. Seek his will in all
you do, and he will show you which path to take.
~*Proverbs 3:5-6 (NLT)*

Past

Cary, North Carolina. 1990

Christi, young adult

*M*itch and I got married on Cinco de Mayo,
because when two recovering alcoholics get
married, they get married on a drinking day, right?

We had lived on-and-off together for nearly five
years by now, and it was time to get married. I was
twenty-one years old and Mitch was thirty-three. Our
wedding took place in Cary, at Greenwood Forest

Baptist Church. Mitch and I couldn't get married in a Catholic church because he had been divorced, so we got married where we had recently been going to our 12-step meetings. Neither of us were affiliated with a church, and Mitch had this idea that God was the Father, but Jesus was just a carpenter.

My brother in law-Sonnie, Sandy's husband, walked me down the aisle since he was really the only guy in our family at the time. He and Sandy had looked after me when Daddy died and Mom was trying to hold it together, so I felt that he was the one who should do it.

Besides what was left of my family, and Mitch's mother and sister, we had around seventy people at our wedding, which were mostly our AA friends because they were like our family, the people that we could count on.

I wore a Spanish style dress, with graceful lace detail. I wasn't sure if it should be white, considering I had lived with my soon-to-be husband, but Mom said I should get the dress I wanted, since I wouldn't be doing this again. I had three bridesmaids, two who were my 'friends of Bill,' and my sister Judy, who I put in long, peach dresses with matching shoes.

We went to Okracoke Island for our honeymoon and drove our beige Ford Pinto to the coast. We left a trail of black smoke, like a black wedding veil, behind us on the two-lane highway that was lined by cotton and tobacco fields. We had to pay to have our junker worked on, so we could make the trip, yet still ended up driving with the 'check engine' light on all the way to our hotel on the ocean.

Back at home after all the festivities, we returned to 'life as normal,' which meant: work, AA meetings, smoking, and drinking coffee. I was at Chatham Northridge Hospital full time working for Sophia and helping her run the center.

Working with teenage addicts is terrific, *for about ten minutes*. While I loved volunteering there for a few hours each week and getting back into a place where people understood addiction, working with the teens was another story. I'd be walking down the hallway, thinking about things at home or some paperwork I needed to file, and then *boom!* I'd get sucker punched by a brat in attack mode. I get it, I was there because I used to be that teen, with all the anger and resentment and wanting to lash out at anyone for anything or nothing. But, I wasn't that girl in a mohawk and army boots anymore. I was an adult now, and I wore business casual outfits and had bills to pay. I lived outside of the bubble these kids thought was the entire world. Their only job was staying sober and spending their days contemplating the lint in their own bellybuttons. On that last day, with the goodbye hugs and cake—*there's always cake for everyone's 'last day', right?* I walked out with tears in my eyes because I knew I could never go back. It was time for me to move on to the next chapter of my life.

I applied for a temporary job at IBM in RTP, where my daddy had worked. They put me to work on the Azalea Line, building computer boards, and I had dreams of following in Daddy's footsteps and becoming an IBM-lifer. But the economy had other plans. IBM, or Big Blue as it's known, after decades of growth, floundered just as I was set to start my career there. So, a short year later, when my contract ended, they let me go.

After I'd been sent packing, I sat at home trying to figure out my next move. I slept in, and stayed up late watching reruns and old movies on TV. I wore the same sweats three or four days in a row, and I might have showered on a given day, or I might've not. If I were in my drinking and drugging days, the weeks would have passed in a blur, but instead they kind of dragged on as a perpetually dull yawn, taking me and my dirty sweats with them.

One morning at breakfast, at what I *think* was breakfast, but it might have been in the afternoon, Mitch and I were sitting at the kitchen table in the trailer. I was drinking coffee and he was eating leftover lasagna, which because of his odd diet really didn't narrow down the time of day for me. It was raining and the rain ran down the window in a stream, because the gutters were clogged. Mitch didn't work construction in the rain, so he was in sweats, too. I was feeling antsy, thinking that

I really had to get back to work and contribute to the bills that were piling up. Lighting another cigarette, I asked Mitch through a puff of smoke, "So, what am I gonna do now?"

"Maybe you should do the thing you were trained to do," he answered, with what I noted was more than a touch of irony.

Duh.

So, I took a shower, changed into some clean clothes, and started the task of renewing my cosmetology license. It took about three months to weed through the process, but I finally was able to work.

My first job back in the hair world was working for the mother-daughter team of Gina and Flo Kidd. Both were stylists and owned two salons, one in downtown Cary at Ashworth Village called the Hair Gallery, and one over off of Kildaire Farm Rd. called Klassy Kuts. They set up my station in the latter salon and I started seeing clients.

Working for the Kidds was my first experience dealing with Christian people who lived for the Lord everyday. It was so much different than my own experience, performing rituals like doing stations of the cross in the car on the way to Mass, reciting the rosary and other memorized prayers, or taking communion by the hand of a priest. The Kidds packed up their religion from the comfortable cushions of a church pew and took it

171

into the real world. Clients, 'friends of friends' and even store clerks were not safe from the Kidds' outreach.

The first time we'd all gone out to lunch together, the Kidds asked our waitress what she needed in the way of prayer that day. I wasn't upset at them for asking, as it was probably what good people should do, but I was also wondering why we couldn't just order our food because the eggplant parmigiana looked pretty tasty to me. The waitress told them she was having issues with circulation from diabetes, so they asked if they could lay hands on her head to pray for healing. She bowed her head reverently, and nodded. Then, the Kidds stood up from the table and stood on either side of her. I kept looking at my menu, because I wasn't sure if I was supposed to stand, too. I didn't really feel comfortable standing and praying over someone in public. The Kidds placed their hands on her head, and I realized maybe this was something I should do, too, to cover her head as well. But it was too late for that, as they'd already begun to pray. So instead, I did the only thing I knew how to do when someone was praying: I folded my hands and bowed my head. Flo spoke aloud in a commanding voice, invoking the Holy Spirit and asking for healing and protection. When it was over, the waitresses eyes glistened and she thanked them. I had this funny feeling down deep that I'd just taken part in a reverent ceremony.

Gina and Flo also spoke in tongues, which freaked me out a bit when they did it, because I'd never heard anyone do that before. It sounded like a really weird foreign language, like maybe some lost tribe on a remote island. To hear them made me nervous, but also a little curious because it was so strange, and I knew there was something to it.

The Kidds were totally comfortable in all things related to Jesus and would talk about Him with everyone. They stood and prayed aloud in public places and they weren't part of some exclusive religious group, they invited everyone into a relationship with Jesus. It was so different from my own upbringing where we were part of an exclusive club, the "IBM Catholic Group" and every Sunday at Mass we looked up to the same carved wood crucifix at the altar. The Kidds showed me a way to God that I never experienced before.

One day, we needed some supplies at Klassy Kuts, and so I drove over to Hair Gallery to get some. When I got there, I walked into the shop and introduced myself. I've never had a problem entering a room of strangers and feeling right at home. I feel like people are going to take me for what I am, so there's no point in being afraid or trying to impress anyone.

"Hi, I'm Christi from Klassy," I announced. "Flo sent me over for some supplies."

"I'm Sandra, hon," said an auburn-haired woman in a thick, Southern accent, her blue eyes sparkling in the salon lights. She had dimples that danced when she smiled.

We chatted for a bit and were soon talking like old friends. She had been born and raised in Burlington, North Carolina, and had been doing hair in the Triangle for about 10 years. During our conversation, I noticed a purple plastic bowl at her station and pointed to it. "What's *that*?"

She lit up. "Ooh, y'all gonna looove this!"

Sandra showed me a new technique using tubes of hair color. The contents could be mixed together in a bowl and then painted onto the hair with a brush. It was like putting frosting on your client's hair. She showed me how it was done on one of her clients.

"It's so much easier than those darn bottles," she said with a laugh. The bottles of liquid color were messy and would normally splatter. This paste was revolutionary. The company was Matrix, and I browsed through their catalogue of colors and products thinking that this was something I needed to know more about.

The pamphlets told the story of how Matrix was born. Matrix was a company that was owned by Arnold and Sydell Miller, whose first company, Ardell, sold false eyelash kits to stylists. That endeavor morphed into creating a line of haircare products called Matrix Essentials, and an expensive, but foolproof permanent wave called Synerfusion. Arnold had not planned on entering the hair color business, but when he started receiving calls from colorists across the country who complained that they couldn't get the same dark browns and vivid reds, he thought it might be a right move. The FDA had banned certain dyes, and the coloring companies changed their formulas without alerting the clientele. Arnold jumped in to solve the problem. He had heard about the SoColor company in Italy that had corrected hair colors years before, using the newer, less toxic dyes. So, he flew to Italy and bought the SoColor to distribute in the States under the name of Matrix.

Handing me the sales rep's card, Sandra implored me, "Give'er a call, hon!"

"Definitely," I assured her.

Not long after that, Gina and Flo sold their salons, and the new owner closed the Kildaire Farms location and concentrated on the shop downtown. Things changed with the new ownership, and not for the better, so I decided to leave.

Monica, a friend of mine from AA, told me that she was moving to Jamaica and her booth at Hair Loft would be free. She promised me that it was a great place to work. So, after Monica flew down to the Caribbean, I packed up my supplies and took over her booth down the street.

"Matrix is coming soon," Ann reminded me. Ann Hillard owned the Hair Loft and was a stand up gal. She made my transition to her salon seamless. She was a typical ditzy blonde, but everyone loved her.

"I'm almost ready," I replied, setting out the supplies I'd need: bowl, brush, foil, drape, as well as extra combs—they always seemed to find their way to the floor.

Matrix was coming to interview me. The company offered classes on cuts, perms, updos, weaving or highlights, well, anything really, and they would pay stylists, like me, to give the classes. They rented out meeting rooms in local hotels across the region, recruiting local college kids to be hair models in exchange for getting their hair done. I really wanted this opportunity because I could get paid to teach skills.

The bell chimed at the front door. "I'm Sam," announced the woman who burst through the entrance like a racehorse out of the gate. She wore a dark pantsuit with a bright orange shirt with matching plastic earrings. In one hand she clasped a black leather bag, as her heels clicked against the floor, and glanced around the room as if expecting it to be filled with people. It was Ann and me at the moment. She stopped abruptly, extending her right hand. "You must be Christi."

"I am," I stated, walking up to her outstretched hand. "Nice to meet you." Behind her stood a petite, mousy brown haired girl. She'd been invisible in Sam's wake. She was wearing faded jeans and a Rolling Stone's logo t-shirt with its red lips and tongue sticking out, and couldn't have been older than seventeen.

Sam motioned to the girl without turning around, "This is Melinda, and you're going to give her a new look."

I took a deep breath and exhaled slowly. "Melinda, I'm Christi. Have a seat." I patted the top of my salon chair.

Melinda sat down and I threw a cape over her and lifted her hair up to clasp the back. I pointed at the empty station next to mine. "Make yourself at home, Sam."

Sam sat her things on the empty station counter and watched me intently as she maneuvered into the swivel chair.

"What would you like me to do?" I asked. I looked in the mirror at Melinda, and then over at Sam, and then back in the mirror, and then over at Sam again. I wasn't sure who was going to tell me what to do. Melinda looked at me, and then at Sam, and then back at me, and then at Sam. It was as if Melinda and I were watching a bizarre tennis match between the challenger in the mirror and the champion in the chair next to us. Who would win?

After a very awkward silence, which I thought was going to go on forever, because I was kind of thinking, 'come on lady, we're sitting here waiting for you, jerking our heads back and forth.' Sam finally answered, "Give her something that looks like Cindy Crawford."

And my heart lurched. Everyone wanted to look like Cindy Crawford, but really, very few people do. This girl in my chair, while cute, didn't look anything like the famous super model. I looked down at Melinda's hair, and thought that I'd have to be careful. Too much pouf she'd look like a 60's go-go girl; too little, and she'd look like a wet Shih Tzu. I ran my fingers through her limp, brown hair. She'd need framing highlights, shaping cut, and drying under the hood with big rollers. I could probably get this thing to do what it needed.

"Okay!" I said, smiling at Melinda, with much more enthusiasm than I felt, "Let's get you transformed!"

I gave her highlights, shampooed them out, and cut away at her long locks, knowing full well, even if I could get the style to work out, it certainly would not make her pretty but plain face look like a super model.

I found out Melinda was a high school student and wanted to be a nurse like her mom. I was excited, because of my mom being a nurse, too, so we chatted like old friends about the life of daughters of nurses, and all things pertaining to nursing. Melinda and I really hit it off, despite me being so much older, and I wanted desperately to make sure her hair came out well for her. I tried to include Sam in the conversation, but she stayed coolly professional. This was an interview, after all. Sam busied herself by watching my every move and writing notes in a binder, with a flamboyant twist of her wrist, using a black Mont Blanc pen.

I only dropped three combs on the floor while cutting, so that was pretty good. But, I managed to let two brushes slip through my fingers, so that wasn't so good, because I had to borrow another brush from Ann.

"There we go!" I said, upon finishing, and stepped back to admire the work. It actually looked pretty on her, and I was surprised.

"Very nice. Well done," Sam said.

Melinda beamed. "I *love* it!"

"Alright then, we'll get you set up for your classes." Sam handed me some papers. "Fill these out and bring them with you."

They enrolled me into a class taught by Matrix professional instructors. They would teach a portion, then we'd practice, and then we were tested. This went on for three days. Finally, at the end, I passed the classes, and I was in.

I fell into a good routine of working at Ann's and having my Matrix gigs on the side. But, then, one day Ann came in and announced that she was closing the shop. Her ex-husband, who was doing her books, had never paid her taxes. Not a single dime. Since, the IRS doesn't look kindly on people who don't pay taxes, she was forced to close. She handed the keys of the shop to her investors.

After consoling Ann, and knowing I didn't want to work for her bankrollers, I approached Tucker. Tucker and I were the only other stylists working at Ann's salon.

"So, what are you going to do?" I asked. The question was just a conversation-starter, because I already knew the answer.

"Christi, I'm going to open my own salon."

"I know, and I'm going with you," I blurted out, not giving him an option. "And, I have a pretty good idea where you're headed."

He cocked an eyebrow and rocked his head, but not one gelled spike of hair moved. "Yeah?"

"Yeah, you're going to rent that space at Ashworth, just down from the Kidd's old salon."

"Girl, *how* did you know?"

"Because, I know that spot's been empty for about a year, and it's the perfect place for us to go." I had already planned it out in my head.

It was like God had kept the space vacant just for us. Tucker got the lease on the property, and he and I worked together remodeling and updating the Ashworth salon, putting in new stations and chairs and updating the fixtures.

Ashworth Village was a small strip mall next to the infamous Ashworth Drugs, which serves the best hotdogs in town. It was the place where Mom and I would sit at their counter for lunch because at a 'lunch counter restaurant,' according to Mom, you should sit at the counter. I stuck with their hotdogs because they were the best, and Mom would only eat a pimento cheese sandwich, which I never understood. It's a Southern thing.

Tucker had one condition of my working with him. He made me promise him that I would never let him hire his friend Stuart. Stuart had a bit of a drug problem and brought suitcases of drama with him wherever he went. I promised Tucker I would hold him to it, and we put the finishing touches on the space and stocked our booths.

For a celebratory dinner, I met Mom at the Irregardless Café in Raleigh, a place that I think got better after they were closed down for a year due to a kitchen fire. We were finishing up plates of roast chicken and vegetables fresh from the Farmer's Market. The former vegetarian restaurant had recently expanded their customer base by adding chicken and fish to their menu.

As we finished our meals, the waiter brought the check.

Mom smiled at me. "I'm glad things are going well, honey."

"I know, Mom, it's just great." I pulled out my checkbook and placed it on the table.

She reached her hand out to stop me. "No, it's my treat."

"Oh, I'm not--but, yeah, thanks." I pointed at the checkbook with my pen. "It's just that I'm headed to the store after this."

"Why are you filling it out now?" Mom asked, handing the waiter the bill with her credit card.

"It just takes too long at the register. People are always impatient behind me."

"Don't I know about impatient people!" That was a nurse talking. "I'm heading to the restroom, back in a jiff."

When she came back I was almost done filling out the check. I left the dollar amount blank until I hit the register.

"You're still writing?"

"Ugh. You know how *bad* my handwriting is!" I laughed.

She laughed, too, "Oh, I know. You could be a doctor." Mom turned her attention to the bill the waiter had left in her absence and she figured out the tip and signed the receipt. We left the restaurant and hugged outside. "I'll see you next week, honey," she said, planting a soft kiss on my ear.

"You got it." I walked down the sidewalk to my car.

"Christi!" Mom's voice was sharp.

I turned to see what was wrong. "What is it?"

"Your gait, er, the way you're walking. When did you start walking like that?"

"What?" She was making no sense. She didn't even have wine at dinner.

"Your gait is funny."

"Ha. Ha. What am I, a horse?"

"No, something's *off.*"

"You do realize, Mom, that I've been standing all frickin' day, right? You might know something about that."

"Oh, don't tell *me* about standing on the job!" she snorted.

"Yeah, yeah. I'll go home and put my feet up. Have a great shift. Love you!"

"Love you, too, honey!"

The following weekend, Matrix had a show. We were at a hotel in High Point and I drove a rental car the hour or so over there while mine was in a shop. I'd had a minor fender-bender in Raleigh, ramming into the back of a minivan. Having a car in the shop was the most inconvenient thing. I hated having to figure out where the lights and the windshield washers were in a different vehicle.

A Matrix coordinator met me at the lobby door. "We're running behind and I'm putting you in charge of signage," she informed me breathlessly. She thrust a marker, paper and tape at me so unexpectedly that I had to put down my bags to grab them.

Stashing my own stuff in the back, I canvassed the building, writing out and putting up the signs that directed models to their rooms and attendees to the class area. I put them up all over the building and then went to prep.

"What's that?" The coordinator was pointing at one of my signs.

"I'm sorry?" I asked, not understanding why she seemed so irritated.

"It looks like a *third* grader wrote it. We can't use this!" She ripped it off the wall. "I'm going to have to do all of these over. Where's the stuff?"

I opened my mouth to answer, but closed it, as she lurched for the supplies I'd left on a table nearby. She rewrote and replaced every sign I'd just put up. I was embarrassed, but also confused. I didn't understand why they had to be so perfect. Wasn't the point to direct people to the right place?

At the chair, my fingers didn't seem to work properly, and I couldn't get foil on my model's hair, so a fellow stylist helped me. "Thanks," I told her, "I'm all thumbs today."

The next day was even worse. I veered my fresh-from-the-shop Mustang into an oncoming truck. I was driving a stick shift and somehow I couldn't get my feet to move fast enough to get to the clutch, brake and steer at the same time. I went *bam!* I drove right into the truck's grill and it made that sickening metal pop that sounded like gunshot. I must've blacked out because the next thing I remember was the EMS team loading me into an ambulance. They took me to the nearest hospital, which was Western Wake in Cary, not Rex where Mom worked, so I was upset about that. And, so was she.

She came to oversee my treatment, talking shop with the other nurses in the ER, and directed my care to her liking. I eventually received several stitches and some bandages, but nothing was broken. After I was cleared of a concussion and concluded I wasn't impaired through substance use, they finally released me with paperwork. Mom spoke with the doctor as I signed all the exit paperwork. Then, she pulled up the car to the front door and they wheeled me out in a wheelchair. I thought she was going to take me home, but instead she told me I needed to go see her trusted practitioner, who also happened to be a neurologist, Dr. Barouse. And, because 'Nurse Amy' was in charge, off to Dr. Barouse we went.

Dr. Barouse was a small Indian woman with a thick, Indian accent. The first thing she did was to give me what I call "the drunk test." That's the test where you have to close your eyes and touch the tip of your nose with your finger. I was having trouble finding my nose when my eyes were shut, but I knew it wasn't due to a bump on the head from the accident, because I'd just been cleared by the emergency room physician. And, it wasn't due to impairment, because I had *not* been drinking. Next, she told me to stand with my feet flat on the floor and lift my right toes toward my chin, while keeping my heel on the ground. My foot would not respond, and I realized that I was unable to lift my foot. It was the oddest feeling. I didn't know that I couldn't lift it. It was as if I wasn't able to raise my arm and never noticed. *How could I not notice?*

Dr. Barouse scheduled me for an MRI, which I was able to do the next day.

I went back to work afterwards, and Tucker was seeing his client Penny, who had multiple sclerosis (MS). Penny walked with a cane, and she took one look at me and said in a raspy voice, "You look like you got hit by a bus."

"Christi crashed head-on into a truck, I kid you not!" Tucker was always overly dramatic.

"And, the truck bit back." Penny, the wise-cracker, propped her cane on Tucker's counter and worked her way into the black seat in his station.

I watched her as she navigated into the chair, lifting her leg with her good hand, while the other arm hung by her side. "Penny, can I ask you a question?"

"What's up?"

"Can you tell me how you found out you have MS?"

She had a look of surprise. I guess it wasn't a question she expected. "*Why?*"

I told her about seeing Dr. Barouse, and having problems with dropping things and that mom said I was walking weird. I told her about not being able to manage the clutch and the brake, and then how I couldn't touch my nose or lift my foot in Dr. Barouse's office.

Penny listened and nodded sympathetically. "You think you might have MS?"

"I dunno, I might. I had an MRI."

"Well, I'll tell you, Christi, I've had some of the same symptoms as you describe, but others as well. I wouldn't jump the gun on it, just wait until your doctor gets back with you about the MRI, and then take it from there."

Her words were comforting, but I wasn't sure if I was relieved that our symptoms didn't exactly match up, or nervous because some of them did.

During my next break, I ran to my mother's house, which was only a few miles away in Cary. I knew there I'd find the one thing that would help: a library of medical reference books. She was sleeping, so I unlocked the front door with my key, and snuck into the Farmington Woods house where I'd grown up. I made my way down a small flight of stairs to the sunken living room, with its dark paneled walls and sliding glass door to the backyard, and plucked two books off the shelf. I plopped down on the couch and fingered through one of the books to the section on MS.

I looked over symptoms. One stated, "The patient may exhibit Lhermitte's sign, a feeling of an electrical current down their spine, radiating through the patient's trunk and limbs."

I dropped my head forward. *Buzz.* I felt the familiar current shoot all the way from my neck to my rear and out to my arms and legs. *That's not normal?* I'd had that feeling since I was a little girl. I thought everyone had it.

I continued reading down the list and checked off the symptoms of MS: *yes, yes, yes.* Fatigue, vertigo, weakness, dropping things, numbness in extremities, lack of coordination, and so on. Every symptom seemed to click.

"I thought I heard something." Mom was standing on the stairs.

I jumped. "Ah! You scared me!"

"No, you scared me!" Mom came into the living room, tying a belt around her peach terry cloth robe she'd obviously just pulled on. "What are you doing, honey?"

I held up the thick book in my shaking hands. "I think I might have MS."

"Ohhh." She sat down beside me on the couch and patted my leg. "Sweetie, we don't really know, yet, do we? Let's just wait for the MRI results, okay? No need to jump to conclusions."

The nurse in her didn't want me to get ahead of the diagnosis. She didn't want me to be afraid. *Or were the fears her own?* I was scheduled to meet with Dr. Friedman, a neurologist and a friend of my mom's, in a few weeks. He was going to read my MRI and go over the results with me. Placing the books back on the shelf, I promised her that I would stop researching and wait for Dr. Friedman's assessment.

But, we can't really stop our minds from thinking about something can we? We can't just turn off the switch. As I thought back on the things I'd been ignoring, putting pieces together, so many things pointed to a problem. Over the past couple of years, I'd been eating and brushing my teeth with my left hand, despite being right-handed, due to lack of coordination. I filled out my checks in advance of grocery shopping because it took me so long at the register that people in line behind me would make some not-so-quiet comments about how slow I was. I'd gotten into two separate car crashes because I couldn't work the clutch and I was having problems steering. I couldn't walk long distances and would drive around parking lots several times searching for the closest spot. That electrical current I'd always felt down my spine wasn't something other people felt. To my dismay but also relief, Matrix never called me back after the sign disaster. *Sign disaster?* That was fitting. There were signs I missed because of my not wanting to see them.

I needed those MRI results, because I needed to know what was going on. Something wasn't right.

Mom called me, waking me up as she got off her late-night shift.

"I've got good news, honey."

"Yeah?"

"I finally pulled Dr. Freidman aside last night on my shift and made him look at your MRI. He said it's not a brain tumor, but, yes, given your symptoms, you might have MS."

"That's not good news, Mom."

"It's not a brain tumor," she said sternly.

For her, I guess it was good news. She'd lost her husband to a brain tumor and it was a quick but painful death and she was by his side the entire time. So, yes, to her, MS was better than a brain tumor.

But I don't want to be sick at all.

When I finally got an appointment with Dr. Friedman's office, I went with my mom, not Mitch. Mom was in charge of these things. Like Dr. Barouse, he made me do the drunk test. And, walk down the hall. At this point, I paid attention to how I was walking and I noticed that I dragged my right foot. I wondered when I had started doing that.

After a few more exercises, Mom and I sat in chairs opposite Dr. Friedman. He frowned at me. "I do believe you have MS and that you are in the middle of a serious exacerbation. I need you to go to the hospital for treatment."

"When?" I asked, rummaging in my purse for my planner and a pen.

"Now."

"But, I can't today. I have clients this afternoon and tomorrow, so I need to—"

"I need you to go right *this minute*."

My eyes began to tear and he handed me a tissue box. Mom put her arm around me.

"I know," he said in a soothing tone, "you don't have time for this right now, do you?

190

I shook my head. You're right, I thought, I don't have time for this, as I dabbed the tears coming out of my eyes. I'm 24 years old. I'm a newlywed. I've got plans for the future. I have my whole life in front of me.

"You're going to get through this," Mom chimed in. "You'll be okay, and after your treatment, I'll take you shopping."

Shopping cures all ills.

They kept me in the hospital for a week for that first treatment. I was hooked up to an IV that pumped me full of steroids. I blew up like a balloon, my legs and arms were thick and swollen, and I was so uncomfortable. The worst part was that all my food tasted like metal. I tried eating everything to find something that tasted halfway decent. Mom brought me doughnuts and cheeseburgers, but they were disgusting. Then, she brought me pretzels, cheese doodles, and chips, but those were just crunchy metal. She tried chocolate and an assortment of candies. Out of those I found something that tasted very un-metal like: strawberry Starburst chews. They were the only thing that tasted good to me. I must've eaten a hundred of them, which I'm sure further rotted my teeth, still discolored and worn thin from the braces having been left on too long.

At the hospital, they tested me for everything: HIV, Lou Gehrig's Disease, STD's, different kinds of cancer, or whatever they thought it might be. It wasn't any of those things. Test after test came back negative, and with some of them, I was pretty relieved. By default, because they didn't have a test for it, other than seeing multiple lesions on my brain during a scan, I was diagnosed with MS.

Multiple sclerosis, known as MS, is a disease in which the immune system eats away at the myelin sheath, the protective covering of nerves. The resulting nerve damage disrupts communication between the brain and the body. MS causes many different symptoms, including vision loss, pain, fatigue, and impaired coordination. The symptoms, severity, and duration can vary from person to person, and in my case, a severe lack of coordination, which was the basis for my catalog of excuses.

I realized I'd been in denial. I said I was "tired of standing on my feet all day," when I was really unable to walk without a limp. I told myself I was eating 'European style' with my fork in my left hand, but it was because my right hand was unpredictable. I brushed off the clumsiness, when I'd drop a comb or spill a drink, as fatigue. I wrote my checks before entering the supermarket because it took me so long to write. I traded in my stick shift for an automatic because I couldn't operate the pedals, change gears and steer all at the same time. As I accommodated more and more of my habits, my excuses became more and more outrageous. I'd been blind to what was going on. As Mitch said, "No one trades in a Mustang for a Chrysler."

The MS diagnosis made me confront the elephant in the room: accommodations were necessary to my daily life.

I summoned up my courage to ask Dr. Friedman the question to which I really didn't want to hear the answer. I was once again sitting in his office, on the other side of a very large and imposing polished wood desk. Frames filled with impressive degrees and gold seals with flourished signatures lined the dark green walls. The room smelled of cinnamon potpourri and medicinal cleaner.

"So, Doc, how long do I have before I'm in a wheelchair?" I held my breath, waiting for the answer.

He took off his readers and looked at me with gentle, gray eyes. "It might be about ten or fifteen years."

My heart sank. I did the math and it meant I would be crippled by my mid thirties.

"Or longer," Dr. Friedman added with a note of hope. "It depends on the steroids and physical therapy, but you're young and strong and you could have some positive results to therapies."

The only treatment was awful steroids, so I did not see much hope. Weeks ago, I had a lifetime in front of me and now it was reduced to only a few years. I went from planning a future, to living day by day, just like they tell you in A.A., which was ironic.

"We'll be seeing a lot of each other," he stated.

That didn't sound good. I wanted to pray to God in this mess, to help me to trust Him to guide me, but I wasn't even sure what to pray. I knew that I desperately needed to trust a higher power. Living life as a Recovering alcoholic meant surrendering my will and life to something more than myself daily, but this was something different. This was a life sentence. How do you pray about that?

So, I prayed the Serenity Prayer: "God, grant me the serenity to accept the things I cannot change, the courage to change the things I can, and the wisdom to know the difference."

Afterwards, I felt stronger. I felt like I could handle whatever was going to happen. I knew it was a futile diagnosis, but I also knew that I could do it, that God would be there with me somehow. Only, I didn't know what that would entail.

I let out a big breath and told Dr. Friedman, "Well, I guess I need a Bucket List."

CHAPTER 10

HITTING A BRICK WALL

And the peace of God, which transcends all
understanding, will guard your hearts and
your minds in Christ Jesus.
~Philippians 4:7

Present Day

Cary, North Carolina, Spring

"*Y*ou're giving up on them?" Victoria asked.
"I have to," I said. "I need to step back and ask,
'what do I really want?' They give me pushback. I've
been waiting and waiting, but Glenn's done nothing."

Victoria tapped on her phone, probably setting a
timer for her client's highlights. "What do you mean?"

"He hasn't taken the DNA test, yet."

"What does it matter? You already know you're the
baby." She held up her hands and bobbed her head in
a knowing manner.

"Yes, I know that, but *they* should know that I'm the baby. They keep wanting more proof. But the site says we're related, so they shouldn't need Glenn's DNA."

It was Tuesday and the salon was hopping. Chairs were filled and lively chatter drowned out the Christian rock station I'd set on the system when I'd opened. Victoria's client was busy on her phone and mine hadn't arrived yet.

Victoria continued, "Christina, you can't give up on them. They're your family."

"They're not my family! I already have a family!" I spat back, maybe a little too harshly.

"Truuue." Victoria was too good of a friend to be shaken.

"Well, okay, we're related. But, they're not my family, I have a family."

"So, maybe they're only blood relations, then?"

"Yes," I stated with finality. Then, I remembered how easily Karen and I had talked, like we were old friends. On our phone call, we clicked and it was so natural. "Well...yes and no. They're more than DNA, but I don't know exactly *what* they are."

Sandra spun around from behind me. She'd been listening in. "They're y'all's family, it's only that they're y'all's *more* family," she drawled. Sandra was from Burlington, a native North Carolinian, something rare in Cary. Nothing is more important to a country Southern girl than 'family.' I accepted her bias.

Victoria nodded. "Yes, *more family*, that's it. They're like a bonus family, like highlights with your full color."

I laughed. "Well, that's one way to put it."

Yah was in the salon today and she didn't miss her opportunity to add her opinion. "Here is somet'ing you are going to do," she stated, in her Nigerian accent. Victoria put her hands on her hips, and Sandra grabbed a towel to wipe her hands, but we all gave Yah our attention. She would have to put her two cents in eventually, so we went ahead and gave her the floor.

"You," Yah said, pointing at me, "will text that Glenn boy and find out when he's getting that test. Ee? Yes? Then, you need to text that Karen and, um, what's her name?"

"Samantha," I offered.

"That Samantha," she continued, "and bring into you. Ha bụ ezinụlọ, they are family."

"Yes, they are family of sorts for me," I agreed.

"Text them now."

There was no use arguing with Yah, so while everyone went back to their chairs, I pinged Samantha. It was easier to message her, probably because she was younger and used to talking through texts. And, I wasn't up for contacting Glenn, yet.

Samantha, what are you doing?

Hey, cuz. Cindy wants to friend you on fb. Can I give her your deets?

Who's Cindy? I asked.

197

Cindy is our cousin.

I noticed that she said "our." Now, I would say 'our' because I'm sure I'm 'the baby.' But, here was Samantha saying it. Then, I realized, that was the thing that was driving me crazy. Everyone kept connecting me to them with family inclusive pronouns using phrases like, "our mother," "your mother, " or "your brother." Yet, they kept saying they wouldn't believe I'm the baby until they got proof. It was crazy-making. Did they believe I was the baby or wasn't? I felt like they needed to make a choice and stick with it.

I texted her. *Sure, go ahead*. What did I care at this point?

Samantha typed back. *K, gotta run bye*.

I went back to work. Later that day, Samantha texted me again. *I hope it's okay I gave some of the cousins your information??*

Yeah, sure.

I had grossly underestimated the number of Arkansas relatives who wanted to get in touch with me. The next day, while sitting at my home computer on my day off, I received over a dozen friend requests from cousins, aunts and uncles. My Facebook friend list exploded with new family members. Cousin Cindy and I con- nected, and Diane, too, who had been in the backseat of the car when Karen and I first talked. Hooking up with this extended family felt a little weird, especially considering we were all waiting for Glenn's DNA test.

A few days later, I texted Samantha to let her know I'd been in contact with many of the family relations through Facebook. She filled me in on some family history.

She told me that my newfound grandmother had died two weeks before we connected. So, I missed meeting her, too.

Wilma Faye had ten siblings, and countless nieces and nephews. Some of her siblings were too young at the time of my birth, so they didn't know she'd been pregnant. The older ones knew that she'd been pregnant, but they were told that she'd lost the baby. Samantha said that most everyone in the family still lives in Arkansas. My uncle Leon is the pastor of a local church where many of them worship together, and most of them volunteer or have full time jobs there. Karen is youth leader, and cousin Cindy's dad plays guitar. Other members of the family work for the local government or schools. The family frequently spends time with each other, eating dinners together and the like, since they all live nearby. Some of them haven't travelled outside of the state in their lives, and some of them haven't even been outside of their county.

I was freaking out a little bit because there were a lot of them and they were very close. I didn't grow up in a large family, or one that was really tight like that. I've always had to protect myself and take care of myself most of my life, which has made me intensely independent. My safety net was always *me, myself and I*. To think that I was connected to this close knit, big family in Arkansas was exciting in a way.

Could I be a part of all this?

During the time that Wilma Faye had been pregnant with me, Samantha told me that her grandma, Wilma Faye's mother, had been pregnant, too, and had given birth to Karen. That must've been odd for Wilma Faye. She watched her little sister grow up, knowing that she had a daughter the same age. Every first for Karen, would be a first, too, for her baby, the baby she would never hold again. The first solid food, first steps, first day of school, first crush, first time driving…a whole lifetime of firsts that she saw her sister taking, but she didn't get to see her own baby girl, *me*, take.

I wondered if, when Wilma Faye watched Karen, Wilma Faye thought about me. As Karen giggled, blew out birthday candles, or danced to a silly song, would Wilma Faye wonder if I were doing the same? Did she think of me as she hugged and kissed her little sister Karen?

My sister Sandy has a daughter and a son, both of whom are brilliant like she is, but one of them ended up in prison, and now Sandy's raising her grandsons. I think she's looking at this is opportunity to get it right. So, when I started thinking of my sister Sandy, and I saw her trying to have her "redo" with her grandsons,

I thought of Wilma Faye. I wondered if Wilma Faye had a "redo."

I found out eventually that Wilma Faye never did live in Arkansas again, but I could envision her talking to her mother on the phone about Karen, or visiting for a wedding, a funeral, or a holiday. And, there would be Karen running around, my age, doing things I would have been doing with Wilma Faye, if she had still been my mother. But I, Wilma Faye's baby, wasn't there. I was with my adopted family: my mom and daddy, and my sisters. I wasn't in Arkansas, not physically, but for Wilma Faye, I was probably there in Karen's shadow. I might even have been the 'ghost in the room' in Arkansas.

But, I'm not the "ghost." I'm the baby. I was tired of being treated like my feelings didn't matter.

I texted Glenn. *Are you going to do a DNA test or not?*

He messaged back. *I already know you're my sister, so I don't think I need to.*

My heart sank when he said that because we'd all been waiting for his test. He even asked me not to contact our dad or half-brother until he'd had the DNA test and could tell the himself. I thought to myself, this isn't right. I honored his wishes by not contacting our father Michael or half-brother William, but he didn't follow through on the test. So, where did that leave me?

I needed to step back for a minute and take stock. It didn't make any sense. I prayed for direction. Frankly,

I didn't ask for this to be in my life, because I didn't even know there was a family to find. As far as I had been told, I was left at the hospital as a baby (as Cher's and the astronaut's love child, of course). I really didn't think that there would be anybody interested in connecting with me. It wasn't my plan. I only wanted to know my ethnicity. I didn't want anything else, and I didn't think that finding my birth family was possible, as it had never even crossed my mind, and yet here they were.

I wanted to text Glenn or call him, but I couldn't. The words would not come out. I wanted to call Karen or text Samantha. Or even message cousin Cindy. Cousin Cindy and I had gotten close since connecting on Facebook. But, every time I went to connect with her or anyone, I didn't know what to say. Instead, text messages came out of my eyes in the form of tears. But, I knew they weren't tears, they were unspoken words. I shut myself in the bathroom, so that no one would see the words running down my face.

After I took a hot shower, and went to make lunch, Samantha texted me.

Glenn texted my mom. He saw your new Facebook connections from Arkansas. He said he had a problem with her talking to you.

So, Glenn didn't like Karen talking to me? I texted back. *I don't think that's any of his business.*

Since he was the one that dropped the ball on getting his DNA test, I wondered why he now had a problem with Karen and me connecting. I called Karen to try to figure out what was going on because this was really weird behavior.

She was open with me about the situation. "Christi, he has a problem with any of us here in Arkansas talking with you. And, there's something else I think you should know that might explain why."

Uh-oh.

"When Wilma Faye died, William, your half-brother was living with her. It was left to the boys, William and Glenn, to plan her funeral. Well, long story short, the boys weren't doing their job, you know, making funeral arrangements, things like that. So, Frank, William's father, called me."

"Why would he call you? Weren't you in Arkansas and they were in Virginia where she was living?"

"Yes, but Wilma Faye and I were close. Frank trusted me to get it done. And, that's when things went south. Glenn thought I was butting in where I didn't belong. I'll tell you what, though, if I hadn't stepped up and made the plans, I don't know what would have happened because Glenn and William weren't doing it."

"So, he was angry with you for planning Wilma Faye's funeral?"

"Yeah, he thought I shouldn't be involved. He thought I flew up there to take control and try to get her money."

"Did she have money?"

"Some, but not much. The family and I didn't get any money, please believe me on that. You have to understand that Glenn has a lot of anger toward me, and everyone in Arkansas."

"For planning a funeral?"

"Frank, William's father, called me to come and help with the funereal because he wasn't married to her. He felt he didn't have the legal right to make any of the decisions. He said that her two sons couldn't get their *stuff* together—although he used a different term—and take of the situation, so he hoped I would come and take charge."

I was confused. "I thought Frank was Wilma Faye's second husband?"

Karen explained. "No. She was his mistress."

"Wait, what?"

"Yeah, she was his mistress. You see, Frank is married to another woman and has a family. Wilma Faye was, well, the *kept woman*, I think that's the term. He bought her a very large house, like a mansion, and helped her live a really nice lifestyle. Frank was William's dad, but he was *definitely not* Wilma Faye's husband."

This was turning into a soap opera, I thought, but said instead, "Well, that's awkward."

"Mm, yeah. But he did love her."

"I guess that's something." And, it was. Still, it was shocking to discover that Wilma Faye was the 'other woman'. "So, when she died, Frank, who had a wife and family, called you to help with the arrangements?"

"Frank knew he could count on me. That really ticked off Glenn, you know, the fact that we came up and sort of handled everything. We only did so because it wasn't getting done."

Karen went on to explain that Glenn felt the Arkansas family had come up to take Wilma Faye's valuables. Karen admitted that they had taken a few mementos and for that, Glenn told them that they weren't real Christians. He was also mad because they referred to her as 'Wilma Faye' and not 'Faye,' as she preferred to be called. Wilma Faye wasn't fond of her first name, and went by her middle name. Karen said that Wilma Faye had another sister named Fay who lived in Arkansas, so the family called them by different names to prevent confusion. With eleven children in the family, it was easy to get mixed up.

Glenn was also angry because he claimed that he and Roberta weren't allowed to sit in the front row at the funeral. It was his assumption that the family wouldn't let them sit there. Karen had another version of events. She said that he and his wife had shown up late to the funeral, and the family, including William, had already been seated up front. The funeral director had to scramble to seat them as near the front as possible.

I realized that Glenn's problems with the Arkansas family started long before I came on the scene.

Karen had to go, but promised to talk more later.

That afternoon, I got a message from Samantha. *Glenn sent me hate mail because I'm in contact with you.*

I wondered why Glenn cared so much about who I contacted. It wasn't right. Glenn didn't follow through with getting the DNA test, but was upset that the family in Arkansas connected with me. It wasn't his business to be upset. It's a free country and I could talk to anyone I wanted.

Not only the Arkansas family, but he took issue with me connecting with our dad and our half-brother, too. Glenn had all these reasons why I shouldn't contact our dad. He said, "dad is rough," and, "don't worry, I can handle him." But he hadn't done anything. He hadn't done the test, or contacted our dad to tell him about me. I think he was stalling.

This made me really angry, so I messaged Glenn. *I tried to honor your wishes, but you're leaving me with no choice. Think about it from my perspective, as the dead child. I want to contact our dad.*

I got back a message not from Glenn, but from his wife Roberta.

She got right to the point. *Are you going to constantly go on and on and on about this dead baby thing?*

To me, that was out of bounds. *Yes, because I'm the dead baby. You know, I don't need to go out of my way to talk to someone who's going to offend me.*

Why do you hate us?

That was out of left field. I thought about it for a while. It dawned on me that they must look at me as a threat. I know I didn't want anything, but they couldn't know that. I knew I didn't want any property, money or anything of value. I wanted…well, I wasn't sure what I wanted. Connection? Belonging? This wasn't anything I had planned when I spit thousands of times into that darn vial. I only wanted to find out my heritage, but what I got was a guest starring role in a soap opera.

I replied to Roberta's text. *I don't hate you. I hope someday we can have a relationship.* And, I really meant it.

I also realized then that Glenn was probably never going to get a DNA test. And, if he wasn't going to do that, then he probably wasn't ever going to tell his dad about me. Which really made me mad. This was my dad, too. I was born first, actually, and if anyone had a right, certainly a firstborn child would. No, I wasn't going to wait for Glenn to act, and I wasn't going to sit on the sidelines quietly. That's not my style. I knew then what I needed to do. I planned to go around Glenn and contact my biological dad, Michael, myself, no matter how 'rough' he was.

And, so I did.

Chapter 11

Bucket List

Jesus replied, "You don't understand now what I am
doing, but someday you will."
~John 13:7 (NLT)

Past

Apex, North Carolina. 1993-2000

Christi, adult

As I laid back in the hospital bed watching a time-worn rerun, the IV dripping into my veins, Dr. Friedman walked into the room to check on me.

"How are we doing today?" He asked, giving me a wink and grabbing my chart.

"Horrible," I spat at him. I was in a mood.

His eyes darted up from the pages, and he walked over and sat on the edge of the bed. "What's wrong?"

"I'm done. This is the last time I'm coming into the hospital. I can't do this anymore."

"I hear that you're frustrated."

"Nice try, Doc, but I've been through rehab and worked in therapy, so I know the tactic. I don't need to 'be heard,' I need *this*," I waved my untethered hand in a circular motion around the room, "to go away." The steroids had made me fat and angry.

"Okay. Okay." He flipped through the pages, looking at the test results, vital signs and notes left there by the nurses. "There's a new delivery method that could make your dosages mobile."

"Like how?"

"See, we'll give you a semi-permanent port in your arm, like this here." He pointed to the IV needle stuck in my arm. "You can take home bags of the steroids that you can then self-administer."

And, just like that, I was free! I wasn't tethered to a hospital bed, with the random night checks from overly intrusive nurses and the exotic choice between eye-bleeding daytime television or brain-numbing mag-azine articles about whether women should ask men out on dates.

The first attempt at giving me an IV system failed because the tall pole with casters they gave me to take home knocked against everything in the trailer. I kept breaking stuff not because I was dropping it, but because that darn pole hit everything. There was barely any room in the trailer to begin with because of Mitch's stuff everywhere. He had boxes and piles of things on the floor, and also on the tables and chairs we never used. The pole was like having a clumsy aunt come to stay. It bumped into the already precarious towers of junk and would send half of the pile flying off. Which really annoyed me, and not only because the steroids made my mood foul, but due to the fact that I had to bend down, pick up, and restack whatever had been strewn about. I was about to lose it and told them, yet again, that I was 'done'.

So, they offered me a different delivery system: a duffle bag. The bag itself was thick and black, about the size of a small gym bag. It had a nylon strap with a cushioned pad that fit over my shoulder, and allowed me to move around freely while getting my drip. The bag and I went everywhere together, so I named the IV bag Shadow, because it was always there, just me and my Shadow. (I know that I wasn't very creative with names.) Together, we went to the salon, AA meetings, the grocery store, my living room couch, restaurants, or anywhere else I wanted to go.

What I didn't realize is that I'd swapped one chain for another. It was tiring carrying Shadow around all day during the days when I received my treatments. My body ballooned and I was so irritated at everyone that I wanted to stab people with my arsenal of combs. But I didn't, of course. I smoked cigarettes and drank coffee that tasted like liquid metal from the steroids and muttered under my breath. It was hard getting the treatments and living with the effects of what the drug was doing to me. I know it was helping abate my MS symptoms, so I didn't really have a case to complain, but the steroids made life hard. When I got the steroid treatments, I could walk almost normally and use my hands without problems for about two or three weeks out of a month.

At one of my appointments, Dr. Friedman told me about a new drug on the market. Biogen, a pharmaceutical manufacturing plant in Research Triangle Park (RTP), had developed and won approval for an MS drug, called Avonex, an interferon beta-1a. The medication was developed to slow the progression of MS. Unfortunately, so many people wanted the medicine, that they decided to hold a computer-generated lottery to dispense it. Dr. Friedman told me I would be an ideal candidate to get the drug, so, with my permission, he entered my name into the lottery.

While waiting to see if they would accept me into the trial, I went to work on my Bucket List, because time was ticking. The wheelchair at the end of the decade called my name and I needed to enjoy life while I could still move my body. I was running out of time, and even though I walked with a cane and stumbled about a lot, I wasn't ready to sit down. Not yet. The steroids only allowed me to live a little bit more normally, but they weren't a cure.

One thing I needed to do was to get my finances under control. I'd been shopping like crazy, because Mom taught me the mantra well: *shopping cures all ills*. For her it did because she had a lot of cash to live on, but not me. I had to address the fact that my wallet was light, my credit cards were maxed, and my bills were piling up, like massively. There was a giant mountain of them, like one of those Tibetan mountains that have never been climbed. That's how many bills I had.

I also had the nagging fear that my insurance company would drop me. I had private insurance because I was a business owner. If I cost the insurance company too much, they might see me as a liability and want me out of their system. I knew I was costing them too much because MS is not a cheap disease to treat. I had to figure out a Plan B in case my insurance company let me go. As a sneaky tactic, I decided to drop them first. My plan was to have Mitch get us corporate insurance. I told Mitch that he needed to get a job, a real job, with real benefits, like group insurance. He wasn't happy about it, but since he was also on my private insurance, he knew if I got dropped, he would get dropped, too. So begrudgingly I knew, Mitch left his subcontractor construction projects and got a job working for the Town of Cary. It was a huge pay decrease, but solid benefits, which is what we both needed.

Because I'm an optimist, which my mother said was the one thing getting me through the MS treatments, I decided to see the positive. When you have ten years or so left of mobility to live, you have a choice. You can choose to sulk about in the short time you have left, or you can choose to be positive and enjoy that time. I decided that my life wasn't going to be about my limitations, but about my possibilities. I had MS, but I was determined that MS was not going to have me. If I only had a decade or so before my mobility was gone, I had to get to the task of living.

I wanted to get more grounded, to feel more at peace with myself and my life, what of it I had left. Something was missing and I thought, well, it might be church. I had stopped going to church after Daddy died. The last time I went was to his funeral Mass, and I hadn't stepped a foot inside a church since. In recovery, I had faith that God helped me stay sober, and Mitch and I shared the faith in a 'higher power'. At our wedding, we had a pastor officiate, and we recited The Lord's Prayer, but that was the extent of Mitch's church going, especially since Jesus was just a carpenter to him. So I knew if I wanted to get back to church, it was something I'd have to do on my own. And, that decision to go back to church led me to another Bucket List item.

Early on a Sunday morning in August, I attended a church in downtown Raleigh. The church was a multi-story, red brick building that peeked out above the flat industrial buildings and trees. Raleigh's landscape was thick foliage, even in the city proper. Except for the blocks containing federal and state offices, a court-house, and a few tall buildings that might be called 'skyscrapers,' the city was made up of old buildings, apartments, and houses carved into what was basically a forest. Raleigh is known as the City of Oaks, and there are probably well over a dozen different types of oak trees in the central part of the state. In Moore Square, a park in the center of Raleigh, they put up a giant copper acorn sculpture a few years before. Every New Year's Eve since—*not that I'm celebrating much*—they hook the acorn onto a crane, lift it high in the air, and then drop it down at midnight during Raleigh's First Night celebration.

I parked on the street in front of the old church, and walked along the sidewalk to the main entrance. On the corner rose a bell tower that looked like it belonged in London and should hold the Queen's jewels. It had ornate arcs in stone colored concrete, and four brick turrets, each capped with a little green metal Hershey's kiss. The main spire, also of green metal, pointed straight to Heaven. From the belfry, a hymn floated out through Sunday's empty city streets to welcome worshipers.

The church was a cool sanctuary from the summer morning humidity, and I slipped into a pew near the back. I was alone, but I didn't feel lonely because that's not how I'm wired. I placed my purse beside me and took in the setting of rows of wooden pews and an altar with a cross above the lectern, but no crucifix. The service was structured differently than my Catholic church, but I felt a connection there that I hadn't felt in a long time, like meeting up with an old friend.

During the service, a woman with shoulder-length brown hair and a flowered dress sang a hymn. Her voice was like a bell, ringing the words out with clarity and precision. And, that's when it hit me: I wanted to be like her and move people in the same way she moved me with her voice. After the service, I jostled my way through the departing crowd to make my way up front to meet her. She was chatting with a couple of other people, but I didn't want to lose the moment, so I touched her arm. She turned and gave me a warm smile.

"Hi, I'm Christi," I blurted out.

"Hi, Christi, I'm Debbie Bennett."

"You have the most beautiful voice I've heard. You sound like an angel."

"Well, um, thank you," she blustered. I think she wasn't used to people complimenting her on her voice. I learned later this was wrong. Debbie, it turned out, was not only the soloist at the church, but the lead as a Rosemary Clooney-like vocalist for the Raleigh big band group called the Casablanca Orchestra.

"I know this is strange, Debbie, but I want to sing like you. Do you know anyone who gives voice lessons?"

"Yes, I do know someone. That someone is me."

"*You* give lessons?"

"Yep."

And, I started taking voice lessons from an angel.

I had plowed through my Bucket List by going back to church and taking singing lessons. I also wanted to open my own salon.

The right side of my body took on a life of its own and made my hand turn limp when I needed to cut hair. It made my foot stay in place so I would have to drag it behind when walked. The MS was wreaking havoc on my body and I looked like I had a stroke, because of how pronounced it was on my right side.

I knew I wouldn't be able to continue working at the chair with my MS, but I thought I could at least provide a place for others to work if I owned my own salon. I could earn income from the rented booths, keeping food on the table and paying for my treatments. I didn't want to take out a loan and have others own what was mine, so if I was going to own my own business, I needed my own cash. I thought of my friend Ann, left with nothing after her ex-husband didn't pay the taxes. I didn't want to end up with anything like that, and then having investors run my shop. My pride kept me from wanting help. I had to do this on my own.

First, I needed to pay off all of my bills, that Tibetan mountain, and then I would need to save cash like crazy. So, I worked extra hours and saw clients whenever I could. Mitch and I barely saw each other, as I kept busy with AA meetings, doctor appointments, and clients.

One day, I showed up for work with Shadow slung over my shoulder, and a familiar, old voice called out to me in a fake Jersey accent, "Hello, Gorgeous!" It wasn't Michelle Pfeiffer from *Married to the Mob*, it was Stuart.

I stared at him with my mouth open. *What was he doing here?*

Tucker had made me promise him that I wouldn't let him hire his former lover, Stuart, who had a drug problem. And here was Stuart, giving a client a blowout, with a syrupy grin on his face, greeting me with a cheesy movie line.

I stomped over to Tucker, grabbed his shirt sleeve and pulled him into the stockroom. "You are renting to *him*?" My hand was shaking in anger as I pointed to Stuart with my other hand, still firmly gripping his sleeve.

Tucker pushed my hand down from his shirt, and pleaded, "He was desperate, girl, he really needs the money. And, you know, he's not using as much as he used to."

"Not as MUCH?" I was breathing heavily out of my nose, practically snorting like a bull. I was trying to hold in my rage. Drugs nearly brought me down. They bring everyone down. It was only a matter of time before Stuart would be brought down, too, and I didn't want to be in the aftermath of that chaos.

"Really, darling, he's barely using. Hardly anything. Look, he's working!"

We had a very intense back-and-forth exchange. I scolded Tucker, and Tucker defended Stuart, over and over, until I'd finally had enough. We would never see eye-to-eye on this.

"I'm out," I stated. There was nothing more to say.

I couldn't take the danger of an addict, still using, working next to me. And, on top of that, the drama of ex-lovers working together. I'd had enough with addicts and drama. I finished out the day and cancelled my appointments for rest of the week. I went home to figure out what to do next, hoping for some peace and quiet, but Mitch was in one of his moods.

"What's the matter with you?" I threw out the words even as I knew it was only adding gasoline to his flame, but I was too upset to care.

"You know, just shut the hell up!" He was pissed and went on a tirade. He yelled and cursed.

I ignored him until a picture frame whizzed by my head and crashed against the wall. "Hey!" I yelled. "That almost hit me!"

And, he continued yelling and swearing at me. So, I turned my back on him and opened the fridge. I needed dinner and I thought maybe he'd calm down once he got it out of his system. I figured being quiet might be the best way to go. I pulled out some plastic containers of leftovers and set them on the counter. I didn't know whether to get out two plates or one, but decided he probably needed to eat, too, so even though he was still really angry about something. I took down two plates from the cabinet. I filled the plates and heated them up, one at a time in the microwave. Then I took them to the table, shoving my stuff aside.

"Well, here's dinner, then," I said, flatly. And, when I looked up, that's when I noticed the gun.

My making dinner, instead of giving him some space to get it out of his system had instead set him off. Mitch lowered the gun and fired it. The bullet struck the beautiful, new couch I just had bought. I was more upset about him making a bullet hole in the couch than I was about him shooting off a gun in the trailer. I don't know why, but I was really mad about him messing up my new couch. The gun didn't scare me, but it probably should have. I have often wondered why we ignore certain clues in our lifetime. I still married him.

It was a cold afternoon when I got a call from Dr. Friedman's office. It was his receptionist and she sounded excited. "Christi, your name has been selected!"

"What?" I had no idea what she was talking about.

"You've won the drug lottery. You are one of the first people to try the new MS drug. Congratulations!"

I yelled out loud to an empty trailer, "I WON THE LOTTERY!" I fist pumped the air and whooped. I thought that this was probably the best day of my life. I patted the IV bag sitting next to me on the couch, "Bye, bye, Shadow! Nice knowin' ya."

The nurse told me that I would need a letter from my insurance company to get into a trial to receive the medication. Even though I'd won the lottery, there were so many phone calls to make, and tons of paperwork to fill out. It was a tedious process with a lot time spent 'on hold' with horrendous music piped through the receiver. One of the calls was to my insurance carrier and they assured me that they would send an approval letter.

I rented a booth from Gloria Reed at Reed's Hair Design because Gloria was a friend from hair school and invited me to rent a space. Victoria and Yolanda worked there, too, so it was great working with them.

A woman named Phyllis Jewell came in to get her hair cut. She quickly became a regular client. She told me that she ended up at Reed's because the Lord told her that she was to share the Good News of the Lord with someone that was working there. She said it apparently was me.

"There's only one question I have to ask you, dear," she asked me on that first visit, "do you know the Lord?"

I wasn't sure how to answer that question. Did I know the Lord? Well, I guessed that I did. I didn't go to Mass and I wasn't a good Catholic, but AA had steered me to relying on a 'higher power' so I knew that somehow, what some call 'God' was helping me overcome my addictive tendencies.

I told her honestly, "I don't know how to answer that question, Phyllis."

"Tell me what you know."

And, I told her my story. Of growing up Catholic and reciting the prayers. Of standing in the cathedral in Paris and hating the congregation, and walking away from religion, but then finding out that I needed something bigger than myself with AA. And, now, here I was dealing with MS, and looking at maybe ten years of mobility left of my life. Phyllis listened to it all with the most loving eyes I had ever seen.

When she came in for her appointments, which often ended in us going out to lunch afterwards, she and I would talk about the Lord. She described a God that I never knew. She would tell me things about the Lord that I hadn't heard before in my Catholic upbringing. And, something amazing: God wanted a personal relationship with me. A relationship? That was a new idea. What did that even mean?

"God is there for you, just talk to Him," she encouraged.

Like the Kidd's, Phyllis gave me a lot to think about with God.

To save money for my own salon, I plowed into work the same as I had at Tuckers, seeing as many clients as possible. I would work, eat, smoke, and go to AA meetings. Mitch worked at the town, and took jobs on the side, but we never pooled our money. I took care of some bills and he paid others. I never wanted him to have access to my business account because of the temptation. The amount I was saving to start my own business would certainly bankroll a massive drinking and drug spree.

At the salon, Victoria, and another stylist Yolanda, and I became inseparable. We went out for dinners and lunches outside of work, and inside the salon we made every day a gab fest. The best part of my day was heading into work to see them. I couldn't wait to share with them that I'd been accepted into the drug lottery. When I told them, they cheered for me and I felt really elated. Things were totally looking up. Happy and feeling well, my lips started flapping. I let it slip about the time that Mitch had shot the couch.

The smiles on their faces disappeared and they stared at me.

Yolanda was first to break the silence. "So, this guy is shooting off a gun *in your home* and you're still living there?"

Victoria motioned to Yolanda. "Yeah, that." Her eyebrows raised and finger wagging over in my direction. "Why are you still there?"

They both looked at me like I was nuts.

"He wanted to shock me. He wanted my attention, that's all. That's just how he is, he didn't mean any harm." I believed it, too.

I had learned that I had to say nice things about Mitch to justify me staying with him. I would say all the good things he did to make up for the bad stuff he'd done. He wrote me a note once, and it said, "Have I ever told you how much I love you?" And, I put that note in my wallet so that I would see it every time I reached in there, so that I would remember it when his actions weren't so loving. I kept it right next to my sobriety coin.

I always hated those girls in bad relationships who convince themselves everything's okay because they "loooove him." But, that wasn't my relationship with Mitch. Mitch was different. When he did things, I could firmly say, "That's just how he is," because, as far as I was concerned, I had a handle on my situation. I spent a lot of time justifying and apologizing for his behavior.

Victoria and I moved our booth rental business to a more modern, upscale salon. About a year after we established our businesses, I heard about a salon for sale in Cary. The owners had upfitted the space for their daughter to run, but she wasn't interested or didn't have the skills to run the salon, so she'd moved on to something else. I approached them and asked how much, which it turns out, was more than I could pay. I was bummed because it was in a great location.

I prayed to God to make a way for me, and He must've been working behind the scenes, because the owners contacted me a few weeks later. They asked me how much I could pay, and I gave them a price. They said they needed to think about it and I thought it must be out of my reach again. But then the next day they called me back and agreed to the sale. They sold it to me for exactly the amount I had in savings.

I'm not too good with the creative side of things, other than salon decorating, so I was having trouble coming up with a name. I finally decided on 'Salon 329'. Later, when a client asked me the meaning behind the name, I told her, well, it's our address number. That's about the most creative I could get.

Some of my friends rented booths from me—friends like Kathy and my partner-in-crime, Victoria. It was like being home again. We got the salon up and running, and things were humming along. Life was good. In no time, my five-station salon was full.

I was sitting at the kitchen table opening mail one morning, when I saw an envelope from the insurance company. *The letter!* I tore into it excitedly unfolding the official looking paper. I scanned the first paragraph, but instead of approving the drug trial, they told me that they had made an error and that they shouldn't have paid for my MS treatments. Like, not one dime since the beginning of my treatments years earlier. I dropped the letter on the table.

This can't be happening.

The room was spinning and I couldn't catch my breath. It seemed as if all the air had been sucked out of the trailer. I swiped my face with my sweatshirt sleeve, and tried to take in a long breath to calm myself, but I only made little shallow gasps. My fingers fumbled with my cigarette pack and I pulled out a stick. I lit the end with shaking hands and drew in a short drag. I sat there sniffling and smoking for a while, until I got up the nerve to pick up the letter.

It went on to explain that they had already contacted the hospitals and my doctors directing them refund payments made on my behalf. Instead of getting a letter approving me for the MS drug trial, I would be responsible for the full billing amounts of all of my treatments to the hospitals and doctors. That amounted to tens of thousands of dollars. I laid my head down on the table in the tiny trailer, where I sat alone, a cigarette hanging on my lips with tears flowing down my face. I owed more money than I could make in one, maybe two years.

On top of that devastation, without permission from the insurance company, I couldn't get into the drug trial. I might not even be able to get treatment at all and the MS would run rampant. I could be disabled before I could repay. I wanted to move away from my life. This is not what I signed up for.

The next morning seemed better, though not brighter. I went back to work with the same ferocity as before when I worked to get rid of the bills and save for my own space. Now, I was working to pay off my medical bills.

I think the thing that gave me the ability to do it was that I literally had no where else to go. I had to pay off the bills because I couldn't get lost in alcohol or drugs, as I knew that would kill me faster than the MS. I couldn't run home to mommy, because my home was the trailer with Mitch. I was a grown woman with grown-up problems, and there was nothing to do but solve it on my own.

It would take me years to pay off the medical debt, but I kept at it. Every month, I owed a little less, and a little less. If life had taught me any lesson so far, it was that perseverance with any task will help you reach your goal. Don't give up: never stop. So, I didn't. I worked and made payments, and went to AA meetings. I relied on my AA friends to keep me on track.

Mom came to my rescue, again, not to get me out of debt, but to help me with the medical trial. She worked in tandem with Dr. Friedman and his staff, and resolved the situation with Biogen so I could join the drug trial. I don't know how she did it, but she always has had her special brand of magic. I didn't have to give up my lottery win.

My friend Sharon from Northridge Charter Hospital, the woman who always wore sparkly barrettes in her hair, and who I'd worked with in the treatment center was an insurance guru. She had a special touch dealing with hesitant insurance companies. I asked her to help me with the insurance portion. She was able to contact my insurance company. She not only got me on a payment plan to repay what I owed, they reduced the amount I owed by a small percentage. It wasn't much, considering how much I owed them, but it was something. I was so grateful for Sharon's help dealing with insurance.

They started me on the drug, Avonex, within a month. And it made such a difference in my life. I could walk and stand for longer periods of time, and I had better motor control, which meant less dropping and replacing broken drinking glasses and plates. More importantly, I was IV-free. Since I was once again fairly mobile, I decided to get involved with the MS society and take part im the MS walk in Raleigh. Mitch was clean again, and he became obsessed with exercise and running. So, when I said I wanted to form a walking team, he was all for it.

Our first MS Walk was the Umstead Park 5K. I walked with a cane because even with the new medicine, I still couldn't walk properly. I hobbled along okay for the first half of the walk. Mitch went ahead of me and ran all the way to the finish line. After completing it, he came back around to where I was to walk with me. At that point, I was exhausted. The cane was helping, but my leg felt like lead. I was going at a snail's pace. The last mile, hot tears streamed down my face. I wasn't yet thirty, but I was staggering a few miles like an old woman.

Mitch came up beside me and tried to take my arm, but I shoved him off. I didn't want help, not from him, other people, or even God. I wanted to do it for myself. When I finally crossed the finish line, they were already tearing down the booths.

In the moment I felt defeated, because it took me so long to cross the finish line, but later, I realized that I had finished the race. The fact I made it to the end was encouraging. I did it. I finished the race. So, I thought, why not more?

I entered us into every walk or race I could find. I dove into volunteering with the MS Society. We'd spend our evenings with me walking and Mitch running, and our weekends at the MS races. At one event, I was interviewed by the local paper, The Cary News, for my work with the MS Society. The walks, events, and people I'd been meeting through the MS Society buoyed my spirits. It felt good to be part of something honorable.

One day, while Mitch repaired the wooden steps leading to our trailer, and I sat in the grass on a lawn chair, he called out, "Hey, it would be great to get a bike team together for MS!" He was really getting into biking and wanted to push himself physically, which was a plus in my book. I knew it was helping keep him sober and I wanted to be supportive.

"Sure!" I called out from my chair. I was sorting some of his construction nails. I knew I couldn't bike myself, but anything for the cause. The MS Society had become a part of my life and I wanted to do everything I could to help promote treatment and research.

"I want to ride the New Bern MS 150."

"I'm so jealous! I want to do it with you." I was so excited for him, but there was nothing I wanted more than to be able to move my body like I could before MS, before I needed a cane to walk. Funny how we take things for granted.

The local MS Society held their big ride at different venues such as Oriental, New Bern, and other North Carolina towns. It was a huge fundraiser for them. So, that year, Mitch and I drove to the coast, to the town of Oriental, and he rode the MS 150 while I volunteered at a booth and cheered on the bikers.

There were a couple of bike teams at the race with maybe 5 or 10 cyclists per team. Mitch didn't join a team, but I loved watching them gather together before the races in their matching shirts, all working together, prepping for the race. After my first year of volunteering with Mitch riding the big bike race, I thought we should start our own bike team. It would give me more to do than 'man a booth' at the race. I could spend the year creating the team and scheduling practices. Mitch agreed, and so I did some research to find out how to form a bike team.

My friend Kim owned a women's sporting apparel shop near my new salon. She thought forming a team was a great idea, too. "You know what?" she said, "I can get enough sponsors together for you to pay for all the jerseys. That sound good to you?"

"Heck, yeah."

"How many jerseys do you think you'll need?" she asked.

"I dunno. Teams are usually about five to ten people."

And, so she went to work, getting the sponsors and having a friend design the jerseys. Our team was named the MS-ING LINKS.

Amanda Lamb, a well-known reporter with WRAL, the local TV station, had seen the story on me in the Cary News and contacted me. We spoke for a bit and I told her how I was forming a bike team. Amanda was really interested in my new bike team and said she would love to do a story about the team and me. She said, "Say, how about this? We'll bring a group of people down for the MS 150, and we'll be on your team."

I was stoked. Amanda joined us at the MS 150 and brought her colleagues. They rode with our team and it was very exciting because they brought a news crew with them and filmed the race. That year, we had 32 people on our team. Kim had to screen print a lot of extra jerseys. We raised a ton of money for the MS Society, thanks to the news coverage and our large team.

Between races, our team would practice on Saturdays and one weekday night each week. I attended the practice rides to support Mitch and the team, but I got so jealous. They were having the time of their lives riding while I sat in a camp chair, with my cane propped up next to me, and cheered them on. It was depressing, I wanted to pedal into the wind and ride like they were. That camp chair might as well have been a wheelchair.

Things at home continued going well because Mitch concentrated so much on biking and running that he didn't have the energy to fall off the wagon or get depressed and angry. I think he was able to get outside of his own head enough to look around. He noticed my pouting about not being able to ride, so he did something for me.

Mitch surprised me with an ancient tandem Schwinn bicycle from the 1970s. It was clunky, heavy, rusty and old, but it was a tandem bike, and a tandem bike meant I could ride!

"That way, when you can't peddle," he explained, "I'll be peddling for the both of us."

Mitch rode in front to steer and guide us, and I sat in back and peddled as I was able, or coasted when I needed. I felt the wind in my hair and I got to be with the group on our practice rides. It was really a thoughtful gift.

The tandem gave me freedom and allowed me to ride with the team and I really loved that, but it had one issue and it was kind of a big issue. The bike would sometimes blow a tire. The tires couldn't take the summer heat on the road and when one would blow, it went, "POW!" really loudly. Not kidding, it sounded like a gun shot. It made us all jump. On top of that, once the tire blew, we had to figure out how to get it home, because the bike weighed about 45 pounds. Team members would take turns volunteering to help us lug it home. I was having the time of my life because I was free, but I don't think everyone was as happy as me.

Kim pulled me aside one day. "Christi, I love the fact that you can ride," she said, "but the blown tires are taking a bit of a toll, you know? *On all of us*."

She was being kind, because I think they'd more than hit the limit with the random gun shots. I'm sure that they also resented leaving their practice ride to help us drag the behemoth home. To save the team, I had to say 'goodbye' to the tandem. But, those were some great days.

The tandem, it turned out, had been a good transition for me as a biker. With all those rides on the tandem, I got my strength up for riding on my own. The team suggested that I get a mountain bike, with wider tires to keep me safer on the road. Mitch bought me a mountain bike, with big, rounded tires and a sturdy but light frame. I could finally ride along with them. But, since I was a heavy smoker, I couldn't make it up hills very easily. I kept huffing and puffing, and it took me longer than everyone else to finish the practice route.

Once I got up to full strength on the mountain bike, I graduated to a road bike. It was smooth and sleek and awesome. I got stronger and my balance got better. Soon, I was obsessed with biking and my friends' circle expanded beyond AA to the people on my bike team.

As a business owner and self-proprietor, I could work when I wanted, so I booked appointments in the afternoons and evenings, and saved the mornings for my rides. I had finally paid off all of my medical debt and I was feeling lighter because of it. I was at my peak physically, as I hadn't been in years. I was riding like mad and felt most at home atop my bike. I started keeping track of how far I rode in a year, and I was easily hitting 5,000 miles.

By then, I had been taking a different drug called Copaxone, and it really made a difference in my physical ability. My neurologist, Dr. Freidman, had taken me on the ABC's of MS therapy, starting with Avonex, Betaseron, and finally Copaxone. With this newest one, I had to mix the medicine myself to make a subcutaneous injection. I wasn't going to give myself an injection, because I hate shots. Mitch or Mom had to give it to me. I guess being related to a nurse and a drug addict had its payoffs.

I wrote a letter to the company that made Copaxone and told them what a difference being able to take the medicine has made in my life. I told them I hadn't had a bad attack since I'd been taking the drug, and I was getting stronger and able to bike in races. I told them, "you should sponsor my bike team!"

To my surprise, they answered my letter with a phone call. They were encouraged by my results, so they set up a meeting with their local pharma representative, Derek DeGroot, at the Bahama Breeze restaurant on Wake Forest Road in Raleigh. I showed up with all of my photo albums filled with years of pictures and news clippings from my MS walking and bike teams.

After we ordered lunch, Derek looked through my albums, turning the pages slowly. He commented on the shots, and asked some questions about where one was taken, or how many did you have on your team there, pointing to certain pictures. I was touched by how interested he was in my MS fundraising.

When he closed the last book, he looked at me and said, "Well, I have a couple of things to say, things my bosses told me to say to you."

His bosses? "I hope it's not bad," I said with a half laugh, trying not to sound as concerned as I felt.

He smiled, "No, it's not. They told me to tell you that absolutely we're going to sponsor your bike team. So, we're taking care of that."

"Thank you, thank you!" That was a huge deal to get a big sponsor. I could have kissed him, but didn't of course, because that would have been inappropriate.

"Sure thing. But, listen, they wanted me to ask if you would come work with us as an Advocate."

"What?" *A job?*

He explained that an Advocate was a parttime position traveling the country and speaking to doctors, healthcare professionals and patients about my experiences with Copaxone.

And that was the start of my parttime career working for Teva Neuroscience, one of the largest pharmaceutical manufacturers at the time. Teva flew me all over the country. I went to New York City, Chicago, Los Angeles, Sacramento, Seattle, Miami, Atlanta, Pittsburg, well, just about everywhere. At the conferences, some large conventions and some smaller meetings, we'd have sessions with the marketing teams and connect with healthcare providers and patients. I had an opportunity to meet other Advocates, too, people like me who had been helped by Copaxone. Sometimes, Teva would send me phone numbers of patients, and I would call them and talk to them about my experience. I also learned very quickly how to talk in front of a large audience. The time I'd spent in AA helped out big time because in telling my substance abuse story in AA, I learned how to tell any story.

I used the three elements in story telling from AA, which were:

1. **What was it like before:** My life with MS was full of accidents, clumsiness, and difficulty walking. When I was taking steroids, the symptoms would abate, but the side effects were horrible. It didn't last, either. I would feel good for a couple of weeks, but as the steroids wore off, I'd end back where I was before where I had to walk with a cane. I was depressed.

2. **What happened during:** I tried other medications, and some would work for a time, then stop working. Life on the drug Copaxone gave me the most notable and long term changes. Copaxone allowed me to ride a bike, and join my cycling team as a full member.

3. **What is it like now:** I am able to bike for many miles, racking up about 5,000 miles in a year. I am physically active without MS symptoms getting in my way of doing practically anything I want. I am able to function fully in daily life.

And, that's what I told thousands of people as I toured the country and talked about my experience with Copaxone.

"Let's have a baby," Mitch said, one night, out of the blue.

"What?"

For years after my diagnosis, Dr. Friedman would tell me that I shouldn't get pregnant. He said it could exacerbate my MS symptoms. I didn't know if I wanted to have a child with Mitch. I knew he had anger and addiction issues, and I wasn't sure if I wanted him being a dad to my kid. He also wasn't a social person, so I knew everything would fall on me. If we had a kid, I'd be the one doing everything. I would feed it, bathe it, change its diapers, and everything. I'd take the kid to daycare, to school, to the doctor, to soccer practice, or wherever. I would basically be a single mom, but with a husband; a single married mom.

Once I started thinking about it, though, I decided I might want to have a baby. There was something inside me that was probably my maternal instinct. I could see myself as a mom. And, I think I wanted a baby. The only problem was that I had to stop taking Copaxone because it might damage the baby. That was hard, because I would have to give up biking, but since it was only for a time, I thought it was worth it.

We tried to conceive, but month after month it never happened. I was having a hard time getting pregnant. So, I went to my doctor, who referred me to an OBGYN. After some tests, they decided to flush my fallopian tubes. That did the trick and I finally got pregnant. I felt elated, even if I was a little sick to my stomach most days.

At twelve weeks, I started to have some ongoing pain, so I called the OBGYN office. I was in my 30s, so they thought it was because I was an older mom and they weren't too concerned. I didn't know if I should be worried or not because I'd never been pregnant before.

I was cleaning the salon on a Monday, our day off, because I've always done my own cleaning. It saved money and I enjoyed the results when I did it myself. I felt something wet run down my leg, and I ran to the bathroom. I was bleeding, dripping blood, and I realized that it was a lot of blood. I was terrified. I grabbed my cell phone. It was small, like a block of soap, and it was still so new and strange to use. I called my mother, who had moved to Smithfield, a town outside of the Triangle and I told her what was happening.

"CALL AN AMBULANCE!" She yelled.

"No, no, I'm going to get in my car, it's down the way." So I cleaned up, and drove to Rex, where my OBGYN was located. Mom met me there.

"I'm here, honey." She grabbed my hand and squeezed.

They told me that I was having a miscarriage. After some tests and an ultrasound, the 'on call' doctor told me to go home and wait to lose the baby.

That made no sense to me. "I'm supposed to wait to have a miscarriage?"

Mom said, "I'm going home with you, you need to be on bedrest, you need to sit and not do anything. Not one thing!"

How can this even be possible? I looked at her and asked, "What am I waiting for? I can't move, and not moving is crazy. I can't sit forever." My slow MS walk to the wheelchair always lay out in front of me. I never felt like I could sit still. But what to do? Where do you go while you're waiting for a miscarriage?

It was near the holidays and I had planned to take all six of my hairstylists out to dinner for our Christmas celebration at a fancy restaurant. I knew I needed a new dress for the occasion and since 'shopping cures all ills,' I thought, why not?

Outside of the hospital, I told Mom, "I need a new dress, so I'm going to TJ Maxx."

She replied, "No."

I stood firm. "Yes."

"Okay, but I'm going with you. If you start to feel dizzy or strange…or *anything*, we're calling an ambulance immediately!"

"Fine," I agreed, deciding *that* would never happen. We wouldn't need an ambulance. Mom was overreacting.

So, we headed off to TJ Maxx where I rummaged through the dresses, looking at bigger sizes than normal due to my weight gain. My phone rang, and I fumbled with it because it was brand new technology and weird to have this block of plastic in my purse.

Victoria's voice shouted out, "WHERE are you?!"

"Um, I'm at TJ Maxx," I replied, concerned I was missing a client's appointment.

"You're not supposed to be there! Your doctor's trying to get in touch with you and you need to call her immediately!"

"Okay, okay!" I pressed the 'end call' button and pressed the speed dial for my OBGYN, where they put me on hold while they got the doctor.

"Christi," she said, coming on the line. "I looked over what they sent me from the hospital, and I need you to meet me at the hospital *right now*. We need to get you in for a 3-D ultrasound. Something's not right."

"I know, I'm having a miscarriage." It hadn't sunk in yet.

"No, this is something serious. You might need immediate surgery. I'll meet you there."

It turns out that I was having an ectopic pregnancy, and the fetus was attached to the fallopian tube causing internal bleeding. In a flash, I went from having a miscarriage to experiencing a life-threatening situation where I might bleed to death.

I called Mitch and left a message, "Mitch, I have a situation. I'm going to the hospital for emergency surgery, but don't meet me there, Mom is with me."

I found out later that he had called his mom and she told him, "Mitch you *have* to go to the hospital." That was a great thing she did for me, because I'm sure he would've followed my advice to stay away because my mom, my protector, was on top of it. He didn't handle stress well, and I didn't want to have to be the one to take on his issues. I had enough of my own.

He showed up as I was getting prepped. They did the surgery and removed the fetus, and they were able to stop the bleeding, but they had to sever one of my fallopian tubes because it was the only way to keep me alive. They said my chances of having another child were very slim. Basically, that meant I would probably never get pregnant again. It changes something about you as a woman. Anyone who's gone through breast cancer, or hysterectomy, or removed any part of themselves that make them a female, it changes them in a major way. You aren't the same. It's like you have something taken away from you that's precious. I would never be a mom.

On top of that, I felt guilty that I had killed the baby.

CHAPTER 12

TELLING A SECRET

Watch out for false prophets, who come to you in
sheep's clothing but inwardly are voracious wolves.
~Matthew 7:15 (NLT)

Past

Apex, North Carolina, 2002

Christi, adult

I had settled into the new normal, life without children in my future. I was thinking that it was probably okay that we weren't having kids, given the fact
were both recovering alcoholics and I had and a wheelchair waiting for me down the line. Being DINKS (dual
income, no kids) would mean more money for bike
tours and other adventures, while I still could, that is.

I didn't want to stay cooped up at home, so Mitch
and I did a lot of outdoor activities. We became interested in kayaking, and through that activity we met a

whole group of friends for camping and paddling. I was as physically strong as I'd ever been before, and being outdoors, on the water in the daylight, brought me peace.

One issue that seemed to come up was that the groups of friends we had always seemed to enjoy hanging out with me, but not Mitch. He caused stress and wasn't fun to be around and he always resented me for that. Yet, we still went on kayaking weekends with the group.

But as good as kayaking was, it never topped my love of biking. I had become intensely competitive about biking and one of my goals was to take a bike ride across Cuba. The United States had opened up travel to Cuba for tour groups, and I thought I could get some of MS bikers together for a trip. I wanted to visit my grandparents homeland and experience the island from the saddle of my bike. I plotted out a few different routes by consulting guide books, mostly written by Canadians. Since Canada never had the restrictions on travel the US did, citizens from up North had been traveling to Cuba for quite awhile. I was able to find a bunch of guidebooks on the country. I wanted to ride alongside the brightly painted, old fashioned cars, feel the powder white sand under my feet, and tour caves, sugar plantations, and coffee bars. But what else? *The food*. I looked forward to scarfing down roadside restaurant variations of fricasé de pollo (chicken stew), ropa vieja (shredded beef with spices) and plantains, or picadillo (ground beef with onions and peppers) served with rice and beans, dishes that were unique to Cuba, and had been served on my family's table in Ybor City. I loved eating different cuisine, and often joked that I had to bike to support my eating habit.

I spent my days running the salon and seeing clients, while dreaming of Cuba at night. Each evening, I would get out my map of the country island, and trace routes using my handwritten "x's" marking the attractions, rooms for rent, or camping sites, and try to figure out which way would be the best. I wanted a long tour, so I could chalk up the biking miles, but I also wanted to experience Cuban culture.

To keep in shape for this adventure, I would take a long ride every morning. I was riding along the highway one day, when a blast of a car's horn startled me. Somehow I had veered into the middle of the road. I had no idea how I got there, or what was going on. The car whizzed past me as I steered my bike into the right lane, and then came to a skidding stop on the rocky shoulder. My heart was racing from the scare. I looked around me, trying to get my bearings and figure out what had happened. Things didn't look normal around me, but I couldn't figure out why and I started to have pain in my left eye. Maybe it was the adrenaline. I shook off the scare and pedaled home to get ready for work.

Once inside the salon, I was having trouble navigating the cabinet where we stored supplies. I couldn't seem to figure out which containers were which, they all looked alike.

"Christina, what's going on?" asked Victoria.

"I don't know. I don't know what's wrong." I felt confused and wasn't sure what was happening. The world looked blurry and weird.

"Is your MS flaring up? Here, take a seat." She pulled out a chair from the table and helped me sit.

"Something's not right."

"Christina, look at me. Can you see me?"

"Yes, out of my right eye. I can't see much out of my left eye, only gray and green." My heart was racing and I felt panicked. "Oh, my God, I'm blind!"

"Shh, it's okay. I'll call my ophthalmologist and you can see him."

Because I couldn't see well, I called Mitch to give me a ride to the doctor's office. Mitch was mad that I made him leave work in the middle of the day to shuttle me around.

Victoria's ophthalmologist had an office in an older house in the tiny downtown section of Apex, the town where we lived, but our trailer was out in the country. A flight of stairs led down to what felt like a dungeon and smelled of mildew. It creeped me out to walk down the stairs, so I grabbed hard onto the railing with one hand and steadied myself with my cane in the other. The dark, closed-in area accentuated my blindness.

The doctor gave me an automated perimetry test, where I placed my chin in a stand, fixed my eye, first left then right, on an object in the middle, and I had to punch the button every time I saw a light flash. It would flash anywhere on the field in front of me and give the doctor an idea of where I could see and where I couldn't. Apparently, I didn't do very well.

"I believe you have something called Optic Neuritis, which is temporary."

"So, I could regain my sight?"

"Yes, Optic Neuritis is almost always transitory. It's an inflammation of your optic nerve that causes blurred vision, or even blindness. Patients with MS can develop this condition. I'm sending you to UNC Hospital for further evaluation."

If Mitch was annoyed that he had to take me to come get me in Cary and take me to Apex, he was really irritated he had to drive me all the way to Chapel Hill. And, maybe a little scared, I imagined.

I called my neurologist Dr. Friedman on my cell and told him that I was walking into UNC for evaluation.

"Why are you going to UNC?" he asked.

"Well, maybe because I'm blind!"

"Christi, I don't have permissions at UNC, so when they take you back, *do not*, under any circumstances, let them admit you."

"Okay."

"I mean it. Do not let them admit you. After they evaluate you, call me."

They put me in an emergency room bed, smeared my face with jelly and gave me an ultrasound. Since UNC is a teaching hospital, I had a group of med students surrounding my bed observing the procedure. One by one, each of them took turns giving me an ultrasound. By the time they all had a swipe at me, I had jelly running down my face and neck. My face hurt from all the rubbing.

The head physician said, "We'll need to admit you."

Mitch, who had been quietly stewing in a chair in the corner, stood up and yelled, "No! Our doc told us not to admit her. We have to call him when you give us the results."

I don't think the doctor was particularly pleased with that outburst, but he said rather coolly, "We'll need to do an automated perimetry test, as well."

I thought, well, I had one of those in Apex, but I kept my mouth shut. At least he didn't kick out Mitch or admit me to the hospital.

A nurse came in, and he put me in a wheelchair and took me to the elevator. Mitch followed close by. I couldn't see him, but I knew he was there. The nurse wheeled me down a long hallway and into a dark room where I took the test again.

I thought that I should be seeing something, so I scrunched my eyes and started hitting the clicker randomly.

"Oh, my gosh." Mitch was standing behind me.

"What?" I kept scrunching and clicking.

"Oh, my gosh," he said again.

"What?!" Now he was making me mad.

"You really *are* blind!"

"Duh, I know, that's why we're here!" By then, I was completely blind in my left eye and I almost wanted to laugh it was so comical.

They sent the results to Dr. Friedman, who wanted us to come over right away. He gave me a prescription for steroids. I hate steroids.

My new insurance wouldn't pay for my IV bag, so there was no "shadow" for me. They insisted that I go into their designated medical offices for treatment. Once they got me hooked up, and the nurse would walk away, I would adjust the drip to a faster rate. I was mad that I couldn't have a bag, and I wanted to get out of there as fast as I could. I had been on steroids for years, so I knew what rate I could handle.

Luckily, Aimee, a friend of mine from elementary school was one of the nurses that worked there. The other nurses would get mad at me for increasing the drip, and change it back, but not Aimee. She was there one time when one of the nurses complained about my behavior, and she stuck up for me.

She told them, "Look, we know she's going to adjust it. She knows how much she can tolerate, so let's just let her do it."

And, after that, they left my drip alone and let me set the speed.

Mitch had to drive me in for treatments then drive me home. He wasn't as mad about it because he knew I really couldn't see.

I was panicked being blind because I realized how vulnerable I was. I had to rely on others to take care of me, which was hard because I'm so self-sufficient. While blind, I had a lot of time to think and use my other senses. My sense of hearing and touch became more prominent. I heard the cars stream by on the highway and wondered why I hadn't heard them before. My favorite soft blanket had pilled with use, and I wondered how I didn't know my blanket had all these little bumps on it. I could glide my fingers on it, and the bumps seemed so big. Being blind gave me a new perspective on my world. I felt like Saul/Paul on the road to Damascus.

In the Bible, God blinded Saul who was on his way to Damascus to persecute Christians, God did that to give Saul some private time with God. God used that time to show him who had complete power, and it wasn't Saul. God showed Saul that He had a plan for his life. After the three days of blindness, Saul got his eyesight back, and the world was completely different.

God prompted Saul, later called Paul, to do God's work, so instead of persecuting Christians, Paul converted people to be Christians. In fact, Paul went on to write a lot of the New Testament and start churches all over the ancient world, converting thousands to Christianity.

God gets our attention in various ways, and I wondered if God wasn't doing something with me. God's gift to Saul was blindness, but was God giving me a gift of blindness, too?

I prayed some prayers from my childhood, but they seemed flat and stale. I remember that Phyllis Jewell had told me to talk to God. "Just talk to Him," she'd said. *Well, okay.* I gave it try and it felt strange, like I was talking to myself. It was sort of like the first time a kid rides a bike, it was awkward and unnatural. I wasn't sure I'd get the hang of it and not entirely sure that this was for me.

After thinking about it for some time, I decided that maybe I just needed to ask a question, because telling God what was going on seemed a little redundant. If He's God, then He should know what's going on. So I braved a question out loud, "God, what are you doing in this?" The trailer was empty and quiet. No disembodied voice shook the roof and called my name. I guess that's what I expected, the God of the Old Testament sending out a booming voice from the clouds. But, no such luck. Maybe it takes practice.

After about three weeks of blindness—not Saul's three days, I noted—I started to regain my vision. It was slow, but I could start to see shapes, and then actual objects. A while later, I gained enough vision that I could drive again, and book my clients. It felt good to be back in the salon and going places again.

One of those days, the weather was miserable and the rain came in waves, flooding the parking lot and lashing against the big picture windows. But inside the salon, it was bright and lively, as always. Nearly all the chairs were full, and hairdryers buzzed and chatter filled the air, which smelled like a combination of perm solution and lavender.

"I used to come home from school," my client Nina was telling me, "and I would grab two Twinkies and run to the TV to watch reruns of the *Petticoat Junction*."

We were talking about our childhood memories as I cut her hair.

I laughed. "I remember that show. The girls were swimming in the water tower or something like that."

"Yeah, that was it. *Petticoat Junction*. Oh, and did you watch *Bonanza* and *Beverly Hillbillies*?"

"Oh, I loved the *Beverly Hillbillies*," I said as some childhood memories came back to me in snippets. I remembered sitting in front of TV with Judy and she'd found Daddy's porno. Now, thinking about those images of the writhing bodies, I felt shameful. I should have known better than to watch it.

"Did you, Christi?" Nina startled me.

"Wh-what?"

"Did you get to stay up late in the summertime or did your parents make you go to be when it was light outside? I hated that. The sun was still up, why should I have to go to bed?"

"Yeah, uh, no. I had a hard time staying awake at night. I always wanted to go to sleep. I think I was a morning person."

"Oh, no, not me. I hid under the covers with a flashlight and read books all night."

An image flashed in my head. I'm in my bed, there's a man over me, pulling my nightshirt up and exposing my chest...

I'm telling a secret.

The thought was so sudden and so intense I didn't understand it. *What secret? Why would I think that?*

"...and that's why I let my own kids stay up late. I didn't want them to feel like they have to hide reading from me." Nina fluffed her hair. "Oh, Christi, this cut is perfect, thanks!"

"Uh, sure, Nina, anytime," I said, startled back into our conversation as I took the cape off Nina and she got up. We walked to the register to check out, and all I could think about was that secret.

It happened a few times after that. Flashes of things I wasn't sure were memories or what they were. I knew the man was Daddy, that it was wrong, and it filled me with such shame. I didn't know if I was making it up, or if it really happened.

In the early 1990s, when TV talk shows were wildly popular, hosts like Maury Povich and Phil Donahue brought on abuse victims and psychologists to talk about retrieved memories. The victims said they had recently restored memories of their parents performing sexual abuse or satanic rituals on them. Some psychologists said that dishonest therapists led their clients into making false accusations against their parents by filling their heads with fake memories, which they called False Memory Syndrome. Other psychologists said that the abuse was real, and using Retrieved Memory Therapy, they were helping unlock secrets the brain had hidden away for a client's self-protection. They had unearthed real memories which were lying dormant.

Each time I remembered something about Daddy, I thought about those abuse allegations on those shows. Were they fabricated or not? I had the same problem. Were my memories real or fake? Sometimes, I would think that it couldn't possibly have happened the way I was imagining. I thought I must not be remembering things right. Other times, it seemed so real.

My daddy was always angry with me, because I was such a "pain in the ass" as a kid. He would get so mad at me that veins would stick out of his forehead. Like, when I threw up my lima beans, or refused to answer a question, or simply do what he said. Each time, those veins would stick out, because he couldn't control my behavior. He couldn't control me.

Some of the memories I had seemed inappropriate. I called Judy and asked her if we could meet for dinner. I wanted to see what she remembered. She told me to come over that night because she was making pasta.

I went to my sister Judy's house, and she heaped pasta with meat sauce on plates, with Caesar salad in bowls. She pulled a loaf of sourdough out of the oven and tore off a chunk. Her daughter Hampton took a plate of pasta and disappeared into her bedroom. We sat down at the table to eat at the kitchen table.

"Judy, do you remember Daddy getting really mad at me?" I asked, spreading butter over the hot bread.

"Oh, yes," she said, "you could make him so angry."

"Do you remember the lima beans?"

"That he wouldn't let you leave the table until you ate them all?"

"Yeah, did that happen?"

"Oh, yeah, you were being so stubborn, and he always hated it when you got stubborn. Don't you remember, when he'd get angry you could see the vein popping out at his temple?"

"So, I didn't make that up." I said, more of a statement than a question.

"No, he would get seriously angry at you. A lot."

"What about other stuff. Was he, I mean, did he make you...um, feel uncomfortable?"

Judy took a deep breath and put down her fork. "I told Mom. I told her that I didn't like the way that Daddy kissed me. And, when Mom confronted Daddy, he said, 'Oh, she's just being a 'big girl' and she doesn't like her daddy hugging and kissing on her.' And, Mom bought it. She *bought it*."

My stomach lurched. "Mom didn't know," I said quickly.

"Maybe, maybe not. But, she didn't believe *me*."

"Did he, um, was he...touchy?"

"Oh, yeah." She picked up her fork and resumed eating.

And, that's when I knew it had happened. I wasn't making it up.

I was the one you couldn't wake up, so I would "come to." I would notice that Daddy was in my room, or getting up from my bed. When he realized I was waking up, he'd leave. Something about him exiting my room in the morning made me think something was weird, but I was young, and I didn't know why. I think he fled before I was fully awake, because he knew I couldn't be trusted not to tell. He knew he couldn't control me because I was too independent. That's why I made him so angry. I couldn't be controlled...or trusted.

I remember one of my friends in Cary when I was growing up. Her name was Carolyn and she loved my daddy. She came over for one of his birthday parties, which I didn't think too much about at the time, because she and I ran off to listen to music after the cake. But, during the course of the party, he beckoned her to come sit on his lap. She walked over and he grabbed her around waist then pulled her up onto his lap. We were too old to be sitting on anyone's lap, but she would sit there on his lap for awhile, and I remember thinking at the time that it was odd.

All the things he was doing, the sexual abuse that had been right there just under the surface, well, I never put two-and-two together. I wasn't really available to him, and he couldn't control me, so that made him so angry. I wouldn't do what he wanted and he couldn't trust me to keep my mouth shut. He probably realized that I wasn't one to keep a secret. My sisters were more compliant. Sandy was the good girl, because she did whatever anyone told her to do. Aunt Nora called her the "robot girl." And he'd obviously done things to Judy, but when Judy tried to tell, she got shut down. When Judy said to Mom, I don't like the way Daddy kisses me, that's when my daddy lied, and my mom accepted his lie. I believe it was much easier for her to believe the lie, which sounded reasonable, than for her to consider the horror of the truth.

After that dinner at Judy's, she would call me on the phone, and we'd talk about it. It happened. It was real and awful. Judy blamed my mother, maybe even more so than my father, because Mom didn't rescue her from it. Mothers are supposed to protect their children.

Maybe that's why Judy always wanted to find her birth mom. But, I don't know for sure. I know there's blame for people who sit by and don't stop evil, but I don't think that was our mom.

Predators can be such chameleons. They can create honorable masks for others to see, while underneath there's darkness. I really don't think that my mom knew what Daddy was doing to us. None of us even knew what he was doing to the others, or at least I didn't know. It was a little unnerving for me to think about speaking out loud about such things, so, except to Judy, I never did. There are people who think of our father as such an honorable man, a godly man, who was a leader in the church and community. If people knew, then it would be a reflection on all of us as a family. We might be considered damaged goods if the truth ever came out. And, as his daughter, I didn't want to mess up his reputation and how people saw him. I didn't want to do that. Which is so weird, because it shouldn't have mattered at all. I know what he did. He knew what he did. But, until that dinner with Judy, I never talked about the abuse with anyone.

Judy had been looking for her birth mom for years. She started writing letters when she was in college to the Catholic adoption agency in New York City, where our parents had gotten her. But, the records were sealed and it was almost impossible to get anywhere in the pre-Internet age because everything had to be done by long-distance phone calls, which cost money, or by handwritten letters sent through the post office.

"Guys," Judy said, "I have some great news!" She was grinning like I've never seen before. We three sisters were having lunch in Garner.

"What is it?" Sandy asked.

"Guys, I've found my mom!"

We both looked at her, and I'm pretty sure our faces didn't match hers. She was practically bubbly.

Sandy spoke first. "What? What do you mean, 'your mom.' We have a mom."

I didn't say anything.

Judy countered, with a little less enthusiasm, "My birth mom, I found my birth mom. I've spoken with her on the phone."

"How do you think mom's going to feel about that?" Sandy asked.

"I told her already. Mom has always supported me trying to find her."

"I think that's a slap in the face," I said.

"It's not!" Judy shot back. "I found her, and I'm going to go visit her. She lives in Florida with my sisters."

"*We're* your sisters," Sandy said.

"I have two half sisters. My mom told them about giving me up for adoption, when they got old enough, even before I found her. Her husband knows, too, she told them before they were married. I'm not a secret. They *all* know about me."

"Whoa. Wait a minute, this is a lot to take in," Sandy said.

"I'm going to Florida to meet them. They want to meet me, and Hampton, too. We're going there over Spring Break."

"That seems a little fast. You don't even know these people," replied Sandy.

"If I don't, I will soon! They're my family."

"They're strangers, you don't know them. We're your family." Sandy was breathing in short bursts through her mouth.

Judy had gone from exuberant to miffed in the course of a minute. "You guys never get it. You don't understand me and never have. Mom is okay with this, I already spoke with her. And you should be okay with it, too."

"I'm never going to find another family, because I already *have* a family," I stated.

"And, that's good for you!" Judy spat. But, then she took a deep breath and exhaled slowly. "Look, that's what you choose to do. I'm choosing another way. I've found my birth mom and an entire extended family, and I'm going to visit them in Florida because I want to get to know them. And, you know what? They want to get to know *me*."

And, like that, we agreed to disagree.

A few weeks after Judy returned from Spring Break visiting her Florida family, Sandy called me. She said, "I have to tell you something, because Mom might call you. I made the mistake of saying something to her."

"What are you talking about?"

"I told her something about Daddy, and she said 'What?' And, I told her, 'oh, you know, when Daddy used to come into the bathroom when I was a teenager? He would come in when I was taking a bath, you know, to make sure that I was washing up right and getting really clean?'"

"And...?"

Sandy continued, "And, Mom was like, 'I don't know what you're talking about.'"

"And she didn't know?" I asked, though I knew the answer. I knew Mom didn't know.

"No, she didn't." Sandy confirmed. "She was completely in the dark."

Everyone always says that the other parent must have known, that they had to know what was going on. But, I think there are cases where the other parent doesn't have a clue because the abuser is such a chameleon.

I asked Sandy, "So, what did you tell her?"

"I told her some of the stuff he did to me and Judy, and she lost it. She had a royal freak-out. All the light bulbs came on. She said that she remembered that Judy had come to her about the way that Daddy kissed, and how Judy hated it."

"Yeah."

Then, Sandy asked me, "Do *you* have any memories?"

I replied, "Yes, I have memories of being touched, of him being in my bedroom."

Then Sandy got quiet. Tears came down her face as she swallowed to speak. "Christi, I'm so, so sorry! If I had known that he was touching you, I would have never gone to college! I would have stayed and protected you from him. I'm *so* sorry!"

"It's okay, Sandy, it's not your fault. It happened to all of us. He was sick."

"I wanted to take care of you. I've always wanted to take care of you!" Sandy always looked out for me.

"I know. You have. You did. You were there after he died and looked after me when Mom couldn't." It broke my heart that she felt she hadn't done right by me.

"I'm so sorry you had to go through it, too. You shouldn't have had to."

"None of us should have gone through it."

Daddy had a perversion that he masked with religious standing and a charming personality.

We ended the call, deciding that the three of us needed to go see Mom the next day. Sandy would call Judy, and we'd be able to discuss everything for the first time as a family. We needed to talk it through. It was in the open now, and even though I was still having glimpses of memories, probably due to the MS, at least I knew those glimpses were real and not some figment of my imagination.

It was an overcast day, with high, bright cloud cover, when I drove up to Mom's house. My sister's cars were already there. I parked behind Sandy's, and used my cane to hobble up the driveway. The smell of burning wood and the sound of my mom's voice led me to the backyard. My mother and sisters stood around a bonfire, but it wasn't a cheery fire, like one at a campground for roasting marshmallows. This fire had a purpose. Mom was in the process of burning every photo she had of Daddy. Mom pitched photo packets with their negatives and entire albums into the flames. Charred bits of old photos clung to the sides of the rock circle. Sandy looked horrified, but didn't move to stop Mom as we watched her throw a lifetime of memories into the flames. Judy stood by and didn't say anything or move, but I think I caught a slight upturn of her lips, as if she were satisfied that Daddy was getting his due, even if it was just paper images of him. And, I don't blame her a bit.

Mom was hysterical. "I would have shot him dead," she hissed through angry sobs, tossing another envelope of pictures onto her inferno. "If I had known, I would have shot him dead!"

Sandy comforted, "I know, Mom, I know."

"It's okay," I said flatly. I wasn't going to stop her from burning the family photos, but I wasn't going to help her burn them, either.

"When I die," Mom continued, with a sharp lilt to her voice, "I hope I go to hell, because I want to make sure, make *completely* sure, that HE IS THERE!"

Mom was always our protector, but she couldn't protect us from Daddy.

I think I knew how Mom felt, the anger and disappointment when someone you idolize falls from grace. My idol used to be Lance Armstrong, and I was so proud of him when he won the Tour de France, year after year. He beat cancer and struggled with his health issues, like me with my MS. He did so much for the sport of cycling. Cycling was so important to me, because it was about me overcoming my MS symptoms. I might walk with a limp and need a cane, but I could ride a bike, and that's when I felt whole. When the truth came out that Lance had cheated, and he had everything taken away from him, I took it personally. I was so angry with him and I felt betrayed. I had put him on a pedestal but he slid off of it, and mocked me in doing so. He had doped, and I was duped.

And, I think that's probably how my mom felt: angry and duped. She trusted this man who gave her such a wonderful life, yet he was taking advantage of her children. She thought we lived in a secure home, but the fox was in our henhouse and she was blind to it. It must have been like a gut punch. This larger-than-life man, this Mensa genius, the man who spoke four languages, who was the life of the party, who had a successful career with IBM, taught classes at NC State University, attended college at the Vatican, was a revered leader in our church and Knights of Columbus, adopted us children as his own and proclaimed his love for Mom, the man who was 'all that,' was really the wolf in sheep's clothing.

So, Mom had a cathartic fit, and created hell's own fire to burn his effigy, and we daughters stood by and watched our family illusion turn to ash.

CHAPTER 13

MIRACLES

Jesus told him,
"Stand up, pick up your mat, and walk!"
Instantly, the man was healed! He rolled up his
sleeping mat and began walking!
~*John 5:8-9 (NLT)*

Past

Apex, North Carolina, 2002

Christi, adult

It had been awhile, so I decided to go see my friend
Ann. After having lost her first salon due to her
ex-husband's mismanagement of taxes, she was now
renting a booth at another salon and some of my other
stylist friends owned booths and were working there.

On my days off I would usually pop into various
salons in the area to catch up and connect. Most of
the stylists in the area know each other because we've

either rented booths from each other, or we've leased booths to each other. It's a small circle.

I walked into the shop, and Sandra greeted me. We'd met when we both worked for the mother and daughter team of the laying-on-of-hands evangelicals, Gina and Flo Kidd. Sandra was the one who introduced me to Matrix color.

"Hey, giiiirlfriend!" Sandra said in her Southern drawl.

"Hey, you," I said, and gave her a big hug.

"I'm finishing up here—this is Lotus," she pointed at her client. "Ann's in the back." She crooked her thumb toward the breakroom.

"Hello, Lotus, you're in good hands," I said and walked to the back.

Ann took one look at me and exclaimed, "Oh, my gosh, you look amazing! You look *great*!"

"Thanks." I was complimented, but thought she was gushing a bit too much, even for ditzy Ann.

"Are you in remission?" Her expression was one of bewilderment.

"What?"

"Your MS!"

This took me by surprise. "Well, I haven't had a lot of flare ups, or exacerbations, I guess."

"You've had a miracle! You have had a miraculous healing. You're standing up straight, look at your posture. And, your face. You're, um, um, *vibrant*."

"Well, I've been biking and kayaking, you know, lots of exercising and stuff."

"You, Christi, have been healed by God, "Ann stated firmly. "God has healed you,"

"Things are going good right now, I'm active and fit," I explained trying to mitigate her theory of God's healing. I was doing all the stuff, why does He get the credit?

"This isn't possible without God, Christi! You're healed. Where's your cane?"

"Like I said, Ann, I've been really active, riding a lot." I had been doing the hard work, why give Him credit?

"Nooo, I'm not buying that."

Later in the parking lot, I sat in my car with Ann's words ringing in my head, and something changed in my attitude. I felt a warm presence in my car, but it wasn't the weather, as the day was cool. The warmth enveloped me but it wasn't a relaxing feeling, it strangely made me sit up and take notice. I felt like God's hands were on my shoulders and He was shaking me, saying, "Are you getting this, now? Do you see what I'm doing here?"

I realized that was how God had to reach me. He had to slap me across the face with the truth. I had been so selfish, I thought my physical fitness was all because of me. I thought I was the one who made it happen with my biking and kayaking. But, it was God. It *was* a miraculous healing.

The person to deliver that message to me was my scatterbrained friend, the last person who I would take seriously. God has used her as a vehicle for His message, and this proved to me that God was behind it. He always used the most unlikely messengers for His teaching. For me, He chose a flighty blonde.

I was surrounded by people showing me God's nature. Like, Gina and Flo Kidd and their praying over people for healing, and Phyllis Jewell who taught me that God wanted a relationship with me, but I never sought that out for myself. I never asked God to heal me, or make my symptoms disappear. I thought, like everything else in my life, if I were going to do it, I had to do it on my own. Trusting in other people, or even God, was not my forte.

How did these people have a relationship with God? There was a missing piece inside of me, that only God could fill, and I didn't even know it was there. God's hand had always been on my shoulder, but I was too independent and self-reliant to see it. He had been giving me miracles all along, but I didn't recognize it. He reached out to me, but I didn't know how to grab the lifeline He offered.

I think maybe I wrestled with God the way that Jacob did. Jacob had to confront all his weaknesses and acknowledge them, as I had to confront mine. My weakness was thinking that I had to do everything myself and that I couldn't rely on anyone else, especially God, to help me. When Jacob received the hip injury and he ceased struggling with God, only then did Jacob receive the blessing. I needed to stop wrestling with God and instead submit to God.

God had already done the work in healing me, and I was being selfish and human because I didn't give Him any credit. God took away my cane and made me walk straight. He gave me dexterity in my hands to do work. He was the one who healed me. Whether the gift of mobility would be temporary or permanent, I had to thank Him because He deserves the credit. How else is He going to bless me and bless my life, if I can't be grateful? I knew I needed to thank Him now more than anything else.

So, I did it. I thanked Him.

I had spent lots of time in PT, lots of time managing symptoms, lots of time managing medications, and then biking and kayaking. I was so proud of myself and my accomplishments. I was so focused on me and only me that I didn't see what God had been up to with my MS.

Thankfully, God put another human in my path who said the right words, someone surprising to deliver such a weighty realization, because Ann is a little bit of a ditzy blonde, though I loved her dearly. And it wasn't until I sat in my car after speaking with her that I let her words sink in. I had been given a gift: I had experienced a miraculous healing.

I'm sure biking and kayaking helped me get physically fit, but I had never before even been able to walk without a cane for any length of time. I had longed to have that personal relationship with God and hadn't realized that I was not really giving God the credit for what he had done for me. I think I had learned to not count on anyone but myself for so long and that included the Father I wanted a relationship with. Not even giving God a chance.

Also, I never wanted to say I was healed, because what if I got sick, again? Would that be a false testimony, if I claimed God healed me, but then I ended up in a wheelchair?

But, since God is good, He provided me with an answer. When you open your heart to God, you learn to understand how He works. God spoke into me, letting me know that nothing on earth is forever. He healed me, but it didn't have to last a lifetime. God healed me, and maybe it was for a day, a year, or decades, and that's up to Him. But, for the moment, I was healed. God healed me.

While, Sandy and I talked openly about Daddy's abuse and the fallout from Mom's bonfire (where she burned up every picture and artifact of Daddy) Judy and I spoke only once about it.

"I wish I could be like you," Judy had said to me, "forgiving and understanding about Daddy and moving on."

I thought a minute. She sounded angry, and it seemed that her anger continued to build, rather than dissipate after the big reveal. She was holding on to it, I reasoned.

"He's been dead for twenty years," I explained. "So who would I be hurting? I have to give it to God and let it go. You know, I have to believe in my heart because of his whole life, how he tried to live, that he was trying to get forgiveness. He was so active in the church and I think that was his way of making atonement."

Judy sighed. "I think you're wrong. He was sick, and I don't think he wanted forgiveness."

I nodded in agreement. "I could be absolutely wrong, yes, I could be. But, I might not be wrong. That's how it works for me, so that I can give him forgiveness. I have to see that he was a sick man and he had a disease."

"It was *more* than a disease," she said briskly.

"It was a disease *and* it was a sin. And, it was his fault. But, I'm only hurting myself if I hold onto that anger."

"The anger is justified."

"Yes, it is!" I agreed. "But, I can't stay there in that anger. I have to move on from that place. Because how else am I supposed to move on and grow?"

"I wish I could forgive him," Judy told me, "but I can't."

I felt like she wanted to forgive him, but it was just too big of a step. I could understand that. "Maybe you're not ready," I said. "It's okay. But, just remember that forgiveness isn't about the other person, it's always about us."

I thought about it later; that it may be different for Judy and Sandy than for me. Since I could not be trusted to keep secrets, Daddy might've been drawn to do more to the both of them, who wouldn't speak out and could be trusted. In fact, Judy had spoken out and was shut down. Maybe Daddy knew that prevented her from saying more. With my sleeping issues, I'm sure there are things I can't remember that perhaps my sisters remember vividly. Their paths might be harder to walk because of that and might take more time to deal with the aftermath. Still, I knew that forgiveness should always be the ultimate goal, regardless of our circumstances. Forgiveness is not for the abuser, but to bring peace to the abused.

God led me to forgive Daddy. It was important for my own sake. It's never good to live in the past and be a victim, because that would only keep me down. I would rather be a survivor than a victim, otherwise, how else could I continue on with my life and live each day to the fullest? I couldn't do that as a victim. But as a victor, I'm strong, I'm capable, and I can accomplish so many things in my life. I can own a business, bike around Cuba, and kayak in the rapids. There's nothing that can stop me except my own limitations.

God healed my MS symptoms, and I gave Him the full credit for that. The medications helped. The physical activity helped. But those things wouldn't reverse the atrophy in my right side or allow me to stop using a cane to walk. It had to be healing by God. And, in the same way, God healed me from my father's abuse. I was able to forgive my daddy because of God's grace in the situation. He made it crystal clear that I would hurt myself if I held onto that pain. I wasn't giving Daddy a pass, I was giving myself one.

I was sitting on my stool at work, talking with one of my clients, Frieda. I had just come off of a 'recovery week', which was a week I'd taken off from cycling after a 250-mile ride. I told her that I needed to start back bike riding because I was gaining weight, and feeling tired, but I was having trouble with motivation.

"When I get on my bike, I'm starving, and I feel like I can't get any traction. But, I really need to ride to lose this weight."

Frieda said, "Are you pregnant?"

"No way!" I said, knowing how impossible that would be. I had been told the chances of that happening were zero to two percent.

That evening, as I got in my car, where I do my best thinking, I asked myself aloud, "Am I pregnant?"

I didn't get an answer to the question, but I knew I had to find out. Driving home, I stopped by the pharmacy and picked up an at-home pregnancy test. That night I took it, but I couldn't tell if I could see a blue line or not. I didn't want to say anything to Mitch about it then. Since the directions said to use morning urine, I decided to wait until morning and do it again with the second test in the box. First thing in the morning, I took the test. But, it looked the same. It was a thin blue line, hardly discernable. I showed it to Mitch, and he said that he could barely see a line. He wasn't sure, either.

Was I seeing a line, because I wanted to see one?

After the ectopic pregnancy and the hemorrhaging, I was told that I had less than a two percent chance of getting pregnant. I thought there was no way that I could be pregnant. It might be hormones. I deemed the test result as "inconclusive."

A few days later I was at the doctor, and I told her about my symptoms and the test. She said, let's do a *real* test. So, they stuck me with a needle, for like the millionth time in my life, and processed my blood while I waited.

After a few boring minutes in the exam room alone, Dr. Sue walked back into the exam room. She said with a big smile, "Christi, you are most certainly pregnant."

I wasn't sure what to think about that, because having a baby was not in my plans any more. I'd given up that dream, and filled my life with so much else. I was a business owner, and that took a lot of time. I planned to cycle in Cuba. I was going to take another kayaking trip. I'm a woman who cycled 5000 miles a year. Mitch and I were recovering alcoholics. I didn't even know if I knew how to change a diaper, or when to burp a baby. Was that even a thing, or was that only in movies?

Dr. Sue handed me a few brochures and told me to call Dr. Friedman to discuss MS treatment, and my OBGYN immediately to set up my first appointment. She wanted the OBGYN on top of everything from the get-go because of my ectopic pregnancy. She said, there was a great chance everything would be fine with this pregnancy, because it usually is, but they would need to monitor me more closely.

I looked down at a smiling baby face on one of the brochures. Sweet blue eyes peeked out from a yellow blanket, and I realized that nothing else in my life mattered. I was going to have a baby.

I was glad to be pregnant, but it was nerve-wracking, too. Coming from a home with sexual abuse, I was worried I might do something to hurt my own child. So, I spoke with my friend Sharon. We had met working at Northridge Charter Hospital.

"I'm afraid I'll be the same with my kid."

"Christi, no, you won't. You won't, because you're not that person."

I believed her, and I think God spoke through her at that moment. I needed to hear that I wasn't going to hurt my kid like Daddy had hurt and confused us.

Chapter 14

Throwing the Baby Out With the Bathwater

I knew you before I formed you in your mother's womb.
~*Jeremiah 1:5 (NLT)*

Present Day

Cary, North Carolina, Summer

I was angry at my bio brother Glenn for not taking a DNA test when he told me that he would. I waited for a while for him to do it, only to find out he didn't want to do it, and probably never was going to go through with it.

I understood that Glenn and his wife, Roberta, might've felt threatened by my sudden appearance on the scene. I'm not sure he believed me when I said that it wasn't really my intention to find a family. Yet, here we were. I think he might have thought that I was after money or property. And, I got that. If I had been raised differently, and had different life experiences, then maybe I would have been suspicious, too. It's that I was raised to stand on my two feet, and make my way in the world. I wasn't looking for financial help or my share of someone else's pie. I had my own business and was doing fine. I didn't need anything. I'm not sure he ever had the opportunity to experience that type of security. I think he might have always needed or wanted help. I don't blame him or even pity him, but I understand that he can't see the world the way I see it, so he would question my motivations.

Still, I was angry at him for not telling our father about me. As if he had that right. I was hurt that he put a wall between our dad and me, but then I realized it wasn't anyone's place to put up a wall. I'm free to make my own decisions and I could contact him myself. It was time my dad knew about me. *Besides, I was the oldest!*

It was early summer in North Carolina, when the first of the humidity starts pressing down and the sun seems like it's hovering right over your head. The plants and grass were still dark green, and hadn't experienced the toll of the season. It was my day off, and I sat at the kitchen table, in the cool of the air conditioning. A plate of chicken salad sat next to my laptop opened in front of me. I logged onto Facebook, and went straight to Glenn's profile. My mind was made up. I looked for a Michael Mercado on Glenn's friends' list, and clicked on the profile.

I sent Michael a message in Messenger. *Hi. I took a DNA test and it turns out my mom is Wilma Faye Tidwell, and that you're my dad. I've already contacted your son, Glenn, and my aunt Karen. I'd like to talk to you, too.*

All day, I waited for a reply, but he never responded. He didn't the next day, or the following day, after that, or even the next week. It was heartbreaking. He didn't want to connect with me. Maybe he really was a 'rough guy,' like Glenn had said. Though I wasn't exactly sure what that meant. Was he a powder keg and did he explode easily? Or, was he anti-social and failed to get along with people very well? I knew both types well. Whatever his disposition, I knew it didn't matter. We were only going to be talking through Messenger, so I could easily delete him out of my life with a click of the mouse.

I was grumbling to my friend Bruce, who was also my client. He was sitting in my salon chair and I was filling him in on the latest of my DNA adventure.

"I've messaged him, but he won't answer. Why do you think he's not answering?"

"Well, are you guys 'friends' on Facebook?" Bruce asked.

"No," I replied, "why would he be my 'friend?'"

"If you're not 'friends,' then your message goes into a different folder. He might have missed your message altogether."

"Really?" Technology and I aren't compatible.

So I sent Michael a friend request. And, waited.

A few days later, I noticed something unusual. "John, look here!" It was early morning, and we hadn't gotten up out of bed yet. I was still lazing under the covers and scrolling through my Facebook feed. I noticed that Michael had accepted my friend request. He had been reacting to my earlier posts with "likes."

I turned the screen to show John. "What's he *doing*?"

"He's checking you out to see if you're legit," John replied.

Ping. I got a message. It was from Michael. *Is your salon permanently closed?*

I typed back. *No, we moved to another location and changed the name slightly*. And, then I thought, really, Christi? Your first message to your biological dad is about business?

He wrote back. *Let's talk*.

I sat straight up in bed, catching my breath. My dad wanted to talk to me. My fingers moved clumsily on the phone. *Okay*. He responded with 10 digits.

"John, he sent me his phone number. I have my father's phone number!" I was freaking out a bit. From being despondent over not hearing from Michael, to having him send me his contact information was a little overwhelming.

John asked, "Are you okay?"

My face must've given me away. I threw the covers aside to get out of bed. "Um,m I don't know."

"Are you going to call him? What are your thoughts?"

"I need a cup of coffee." So, I texted Michael's cell. *I need a cup of coffee.* I had no idea why I texted him that.

Then, I went to get a cup of coffee, because, apparently coffee was the most important thing at the moment. Thankfully, the coffee maker was set to automatically brew and I had a fresh pot waiting for me in the kitchen, which I had just discovered that I desperately needed.

I called to John while I was pouring coffee. "Should I brush my hair?"

"Is it a video call?" He said with a touch of sarcasm.

"No."

He laughed at me. "Then, I don't think it matters."

"Right." I walked back into the bedroom with my cup.

John had moved into the chair by the window. "Would you rather sit in the chair?" He started to stand up.

"Nah," I waved him down. "I'm going to sit on the side of the bed like I always do." I felt more comfortable there with my phone and a cup of coffee on the bedside table. I took a deep breath. "Here goes." I dialed the number he'd given me and he answered on the second ring. "Is this Michael?"

"Yes, but call me 'Mike.' Is this Christi?" he said. He had an accent from somewhere up north.

"Yeah, it's me, Christi."

And, just like that, we started talking. It should have been the most important phone call of my life, but after all the build-up of excitement and fear, it was a conversation between two people. I don't know why I thought it was supposed to be like fireworks or something special, but it wasn't. It was a normal phone call where two strangers met for the first time.

Over the following weeks, through texts and phone calls, we got to know each other. He told me about the past, about Wilma Faye (who he called 'Wilma') and about how I was given up for adoption. Giving me up for adoption was certainly better than the alternative: they could have ended the pregnancy. I'm grateful they didn't because it gave me the opportunity to live my life.

Wilma Faye Tidwell was one of the eldest children in a large, poor family that lived in Jacksonport, a rural town in Arkansas. Her dad, Carl, was a guitar player and traveled with popular Memphis recording artists, and her mama, Billy Jo, kept house, had babies, and tended a small but fruitful garden on their property.

The year was 1967. Young men were plucked from their homes and drafted into military service to fight the war in Vietnam. Television brought the social and political strife of the era directly into people's living rooms. Every night, Americans watched news reel footage of the peace protests and civil rights protests happening in large cities across the country. Rioting and looting in places like Detroit, where the National Guard was called in to restore order, were common images viewed by families gathered around their small screens.

Wilma Faye's family was too poor to own a television, but a diner in nearby Newport boasted an old black and white TV above the counter. Ten cents would buy a Coke and Wilma Faye would sip the soft drink through a paper straw and stare at that small screen, seeing a world quite different from the one in which she lived. She wanted nothing more than to see that world for herself.

At the age of 16, Wilma Faye decided to leave home. Well, she ran away. She grew up in rural Arkansas, with few opportunities and a lot of barely filled plates on dinner tables. For her family, she knew it would be better for her to leave because there would be one less mouth to feed. There wasn't much in the way of a future for her in Jacksonport, except to move to Memphis, but that didn't sit right with Wilma Faye. She wanted to see the world, and travel far away from the soybean and cotton farms of Jackson County. She set her sights on Camp LeJeune in North Carolina, where service men had access to the world. Wilma Faye hitchhiked from her hometown in Arkansas to Jacksonville, North Carolina. In the late sixties, hitchhiking was common, allowing people to travel across the country with very little cash.

She found a job working near Camp LeJeune. Mike wouldn't say what she did when I pressed, so I let it go. Maybe he didn't remember. It was there that she met Navy Corpsman Mike Mercado. It was love at first sight, and they were inseparable. She thought she had found her ticket to see the world, but Mike wasn't happy in the military and wanted out. He hated LeJeune and North Carolina, which he called 'North Cackalacky.' Mike told her that he and his buddy Louie were set to be discharged soon, and they were heading back up to New York. He invited Wilma Faye to join him. She said yes.

It was in the town of Olean in New York that Wilma Faye got pregnant with me. She and Mike weren't married, yet. Being unmarried, poor and pregnant in the sixties didn't give a woman a lot of options. You could have the baby and either get married or put it up for adoption, or you could get an illegal abortion. According to Mike, Wilma Faye didn't want to get an illegal abortion, so they decided together that they would put up the baby for adoption. I don't know if that's true or not. I know they were poor. They were living off Wilma Faye's meager salary, and Mike was in college studying to get into medical school, working two jobs himself.

Mike said, "When your mom and I were first together, we didn't have a pot to piss in or a window to throw it out of."

I wasn't sure about Mike's version of events. He made it sound like putting me up for adoption was both

Wilma Faye's and his decision, but everyone on the other side of the family, in Arkansas, said that Wilma Faye would never give up a daughter, because she always wanted a daughter.

In *my* family, my adopted family, I grew up in a world with a lot of lies and misconceptions for many years. I know what it takes to keep people's mouths shut up about an issue. I know what goes into it. But he didn't say anything other than he and Wilma Faye decided together, so I didn't press him on it. We'd just met, after all.

Only Wilma Faye and Mike know the truth: whether they chose to give me up for adoption together; or, whether it was Mike's ruse (like some in Arkansas believed) that he used his medical connections to trick Wilma Faye into believing the baby had died. Hospitals used gas back then for mothers in labor, to help ease the pain, and it made them loopy. She could have been too doped up to realize what was going on. Or, she could've simply told her relatives in Arkansas the baby had died because none of them would have understood. I'm sure that giving a baby up for adoption was a foreign concept to her large, rural family.

Was Mike's version of events how it actually happened, or is that how he wanted to remember things? I believe that we can settle ourselves on something we can live with. Did he manage things in a certain direction because he had a little bit of clout because he was the native son of Olean? Or was that not a part of it at all? Maybe I'd never really know.

The only one who could tell me another part of the story would be Wilma Faye, and even if she were alive to tell us, then it would only be her perspective of what happened. Because that's the funny thing with memory; you can never truly remember the truth. You only remember how it made sense to you.

I've decided that 'the truth', whatever that is, doesn't matter. It doesn't change anything today. The fact remains that they're my biological parents, and I'm their kid. I guess I'm really glad they didn't choose abortion. I'm here today because they chose to have me and place me for adoption. They created my life, and they let me live.

It's odd to me that the very people who create a person, can choose whether that person lives or dies. Two people have sex, create a baby, and then they get to pronounce sentence on the baby: life or death. As a person who was adopted, I'm more profoundly grateful for the people who choose to let their babies live than most people, I guess. When people don't think too deeply about it and they say, "oh, it's just a clump of cells," it's probably easier to make the 'inconvenience' go away. But, I wasn't a clump, I was a person. Given all the childless couples who really want babies who can't have them, why not give babies a chance at life, and the couples who want them a chance to be parents? That's what makes sense to me.

But then again, the world doesn't make sense because it's imperfect. It's not our home, our home is with God in Heaven. So why would the world make sense on something like this?

Mike and Wilma Faye weren't married when they gave me up for adoption. It wasn't until a few years after I was born and given away that they finally tied the knot. Mike graduated from college and went on to medical school. He chose the dental track of medical school and became an oral surgeon. He told me the reason for a dental degree over a medical one: "I didn't want patients dying on me and I got weekends and nights off."

It's ironic that my biological father turned out to be a dentist. The braces I got in France wrecked my teeth because no one took them off, at least not until I got back to the States, and by then, my teeth were ruined. As an adult, I've had to undergo major cosmetic and reconstructive dentistry. My husband John calls it his 'Mercedes smile', because of the amount of money we've spent on my mouth.

Mike and Wilma Faye had my brother Glenn in the mid-seventies and divorced four years after his birth. Wilma Faye met Frank, and together they had William. And, that sums up my list of my siblings: Glenn my full-blooded brother, William my half-brother, and Sandy and Judy my adoptive sisters.

The only kink would be if Daddy—Alan, the one who adopted me—actually did have a second family in France. But, I guess that's something I'll never know. Even if someone in France—like a child or grandchild of that woman with the bright, red lipstick and a black hat with a netted veil who attended Alan's funeral in 1985—took a DNA test, it would never link back to me or any of my siblings. We weren't Alan's biological children, so there's no DNA to match. The mysterious woman from France at Daddy's funeral will forever remain a mystery.

Mike was faithful in writing and calling, and he *immediately* got a DNA test! That test proved conclusively that he was my father. We talked and texted a lot. On one call, I told him that we'd just celebrated a big milestone. Back when I found out I was pregnant for a second time, after losing my first baby, I had a rainbow baby. A rainbow baby is a baby that you have after the loss of a child and they are a symbol of renewal and hope from God. I had a healthy baby boy. And, that baby boy, my son Ian, had just celebrated his fifteenth birthday. Mike asked to speak to him and I didn't see a problem with that, but I kept it on speaker, because this relationship was so new. I didn't think he would say anything inappropriate to Ian, but I wanted to listen in all the same.

"Looks like I just missed your birthday. Happy birthday, buddy."

"Well, you've missed that and fourteen others," I said, then felt a little bad about it, and quickly added, "I'm kidding," But, then I made it worse by saying, "Well, not really."

I thought to myself, Christi, that was so rude. I knew it was rude and I couldn't believe I said it, but I said it. Telling myself to 'shut up' would have been better.

Ian and Mike chatted for awhile. After the phone call, Ian said to me, "You and Mike are alike. You talk the same."

I told my friend Donna about Ian talking to Mike.

"And, they hit it off?" She asked.

"Yeah, they did." I asked her about my comment to Mike, and if she thought I had been too rude.

"He can't expect you *not* to have some snarkiness about your position," she responded.

I think she was right. I had a right to be a little bit snarky, given that I was having such trouble convincing other relatives what I knew to be true, that I was the dead baby. But, now we had Mike's DNA test. There was no further question of my status.

The odd thing about these DNA tests is that they link people by blood, but not by heart. Your heart is linked to others because you know them, not because you share their blood. It's the shared experiences, the love and laughter, and hard times, too, that link us to others. It's not the DNA in our cells. People get so hopped up on 'blood relations' and 'biological family' that they forget that we're all related, all of us humans. Does it matter whose sperm connected with whose ovary to create a person? Maybe, maybe not. The only real family is the one that supports you, that takes care of you, that loves you, and goes through hardships with you. It's the experiences that connect us, not DNA strands.

Mike told me that he is currently married to a wonderful woman, Debi. He never had any more kids, other than Glenn and me, and both he and Debi are now retired. He told me that they were in the process of moving from Maryland to Delaware.

When he ended each call, he said, "Love you, Sweet Lady." It kind of bothered me because he said he 'loved' me. I couldn't trust that. I wish I felt like I could return his sentiments, but it didn't feel right. I've had to be too protective of my emotions to let myself get caught up in something so new.

I wanted to ask him some things. Like, how are you going to tell me that you love me and now your life is complete, when I was born and you threw me away? I'm the baby you threw out with the bathwater. How am I supposed to feel about that? He doesn't know me, or know who I am.

He's so lucky that I'm not the kind of person that would hold that against him, because I know a lot of people who would hold a huge grudge. And, that grudge becomes the scars that they carry with them wherever they go, the ones they want to show everybody. Sort of like, look at my pain, I'm so hurt, now give me sympathy. But, I'm not like that. It's not who I am as a person, because I believe it only holds people back from living a good life. One thing I have learned through my years and experiences is that you can't live a good life by constantly needing sympathy. You can't move forward if you're stuck in the past.

We've all done stuff in our lives that we're not proud of. That's how I can feel more generous toward Mike. We've all made mistakes that we regret. I believe his pursuing a relationship with me had to be a good thing. If I held his actions as a young man against him, how did that help me? How did it help him? By holding onto that anger or resentment or whatever-you-call it, who was it hurting? It might hurt him, maybe, but it definitely hurt me. So it made no sense to be angry or bitter. Instead, it made sense to me to look into the relationship and see if it developed.

One of my dear longtime clients who I've done hair for forever recently moved to Colorado. I was telling her all about the journey and I shared Mike's texts with her. She said when she first read them, it ticked her off. She said it felt like he was being too close, too fast. But then she started rereading them, and she got a different impression.

"It seems like he's really trying to reach out to you. One thing I notice is that when you and he text back and forth to each other he constantly says 'I love you,' and

'I care about you' and such, but I've never once seen you reciprocate. Why is that?"

And I told her, "I can't, because he doesn't know me and I don't know him."

Summer turned to fall, when the pumpkin patches and corn mazes opened up, and everyone had their trick-or-treating fun. I was planning the final details of the Thanksgiving Day meal we were going to have at our house instead of going to Martha and Pa's. Bishop and Mrs. Collander were going to join us, and I had Ian this year. I sat on my screened-in porch, sipping coffee and listening to the neighbor kids play pirates in the woods. Mike and I talked on the phone about this and that.

"The best thing for us to do," he said, "is for Debi and me to come to North Cackalacky and visit you."

"North Cackalacky?"

"I hate that state. But, I love you and I want to see you. How about if we come down for Thanksgiving?"

Thanksgiving? Thanksgiving was three days away.

"Um, sure," I answered, but not totally sure why I agreed.

"Then it's settled. I'm finally going to see you face to face."

I thought that was a funny thing to say. Didn't he see me in the hospital when I was born?

CHAPTER 15

GOD'S LEFT TURN

Honor the Lord with your wealth and with
the best part of everything you produce.
Then he will fill your barns with grain, and your
vats will overflow with good wine.
~Proverbs 3:9-10

Past

Cary, North Carolina. 2005

Christi, adult

In AA you are told to work on a relationship with
a 'higher power', and that doing life on your own
doesn't work, and it hasn't worked for me. I knew that
the 'higher power' was God, but I had never really let
Him take the reins. I knew there was more to cultivating
a relationship with Him, but I didn't know how to get
there on my own. I had always seen various people
who were faith driven and had an understanding of God

and this 'higher power'. People like Gina and Flo Kidd and Phyllis Jewell, who gave me a new understanding outside my Catholic faith. Also, a client of the Kidd's, Judy Jesse, was a big part of those conversations we had at the salon. What these women had seemed almost unattainable for me. I could stop wrestling with God. I could thank Him for my miracle healing, and I could even forgive my daddy, but I didn't know what to do next with my relationship with God. My own Catholic upbringing was thin on having a relationship with God, and heavy on rituals. I felt the path to having God control my life had to be through church.

I'd been attending various churches and denominations since I started my Bucket List, but none had felt right or like 'home' to me. I had been riding my bike past a church in the outskirts of Cary called Crosspointe Church, but I hadn't noticed it was there until one day I had a flat tire right in front of it. I pulled into the parking lot to fix it and as I looked around, I felt something special there. My son, Ian, had just turned three years old, and I thought he should start attending Sunday School. Since Mitch wasn't religious, it was my job to introduce Ian to God, and what God could mean for him.

That Sunday, I decided to take Ian and check it out. Crosspointe was housed in a newly built industrial building, and walking through the doors felt like walking into a business operation, not a house of worship. There weren't crosses or other Christian emblems on the walls, only oversized portraits of smiling people working in the community. To my left was what looked like a hot tub framed by a backdrop of river rock and fake greenery. I stared at it for a minute, because it seemed so out of place surrounded by steel beams and commercial-grade carpet. Then, I realized it was a baptismal fount for full immersion, which was quite a bit different than the fount in my home church, where the priests would dip a golden cup into the holy water and pour it over the babies' heads.

In the back of the two-story atrium, were a line of tables with coffee and doughnuts. I filled my cup with Starbuck's coffee, and fished inside an open Dunkin's box to pull out a powdery doughnut. I gave Ian half and I took a bite of the other half. He looked up at me with bright blue eyes, and I patted his mop of curly brown hair as he proceeded to stuff the entire half doughnut into his mouth. *Boys.*

After wiping the powdered sugar from his face, I followed the signs to the preschool room, which was through a secured door on the other side of the building. A man was standing at the entrance to the hallway, allowing entrance to only adults with kids. The preschool room was filled with rambunctious kids and lots of toys. And it was really loud. A little blond-haired boy ran up to us. The boy took one look at Ian and said, "Ian!" And, I was taken aback. It was his buddy Howie from preschool.

"I guess they know each other," said a smiling woman with dark eyes and long dark hair.

"Yeah, they go to preschool together," I offered.

"Great, then he already has a friend. I'm Kayti, I'm the teacher." A girl with golden brown pigtails and greenish blue eyes ran up to see who was coming into the class. "And, this is my daughter Kaytlin. Kaytlin," she said bending down to open the baby gate to let my son inside, "this is Ian." She slapped a nametag on his back as he walked through, which they do to prevent the kids from messing with them. Both Kaytlin and Howie grabbed Ian, and they all ran off to the toy cubbies.

"Looks like he'll be fine," she said, handing me a sticker.

"Thanks," I said, feeling weird that I would collect my son with a ticket like he were a piece of luggage at the bellhop station.

I walked into the sanctuary, which was a shock, because it was actually a basketball court that was converted for worship. The nets had been hoisted up by pullies, and black folding chairs were laid out in neat rows in front of a stage backed by a large projection screen. The theme was definitely 'modern Christian', with a rock band worship team and a preacher who got teary preaching the Gospel. It was lightyears removed my parents' church. It was energetic and exciting. Plus, Ian had a great time with his friends. So, we kept going back.

Things were getting very stressful at home. I had started grabbing the audio cassettes from previous sermons at Crosspointe and would listen to them in my new Subaru during my commutes. They gave me peace and kept me grounded when dealing with Mitch. For some reason the more I had been searching for a relationship with God, the more annoyed and difficult Mitch had become.

During the week, I was watching different ministers on TV, including Joyce Meyer and a pastor named Creflo Dollar who had fallen ill numerous times, but the Lord kept pulling him through. I loved to hear his sermons because he got to the point with clear ideas. He knew Scripture, taught on the Word, and his messages spoke to me. I needed somebody like that in my life; someone to tell me exactly what to do and what was missing. I still was looking for something to ground me.

One of the things he talked about was tithing. As a Catholic, I didn't read the Bible much, so I didn't truly understand what tithing meant. I watched Creflo Dollar's show and in one message he explained the concept of tithing. I never thought about it before, and then suddenly, it seemed like the biggest deal in the world; something I had to do. The Lord put it on my heart that there was an amount to the tithe, or more accurately, to the gift, and that was fifty dollars. I felt I was being told to make a donation to Crosspointe for that exact amount.

Which upset me because I was saving money to help me escape, for when I planned to leave Mitch. I wasn't planning on leaving Mitch any time soon, but I knew if I had to get out, I would need the money I saved to survive as a single mom. I had maybe 650 dollars saved, but I needed much more, enough for rent, deposit, utilities and other necessities. I was making decent money at the salon, but it wasn't enough to strike out on my own, yet. I needed a larger nest egg so I could feel comfortable walking out with a child in tow.

Once a week I would drive to see my mom, who had moved to Smithfield to be closer to my sister Sandy, and I would pass through the intersection with Highway 55, the road that led up to Crosspointe. And, every time I drove past it, God tugged on my heart that I needed to give my money to the church. It made no sense to me because didn't God know that I needed to save money so I could get out of the abusive relationship? But, still, God kept tugging at my heart to give that fifty dollars.

One day, when the sun was bright and seemed more cheery than I felt, I was driving to see my mom. Ian was asleep in the back in his car seat, and I had the radio on softly and the traffic was light. I should have been in a good mood, but I was dreading that upcoming intersection, because I knew that God was speaking to me. He wanted me to be obedient, but I hadn't been. I wouldn't give the fifty dollars to my new church because I couldn't afford to let it go.

When I reached the intersection, I was fully prepared to grit my teeth, bear the twinge in my stomach,
and drive straight through to Mom's. I knew that the
stab of guilt I always got would go away as soon I
passed through the intersection. I had played out this
drive-by dozens of times, and, like all the others, I
expected it to be another *Groundhog Day*.

But something odd happened: I turned left. I
made a left turn up Highway 55 leading to the church.
Instead of going to my mom's house, I drove directly
to Crosspointe.

What are you doing, Christi? I couldn't believe I'd
turned the wheel.

I drove up to the church and parked, then reached
into my purse for my wallet. I had exactly fifty dollars,
which is amazing because ATMs only dispense twenty
dollar bills. So, how had I ended up with fifty? It was a
mystery I never solved.

Then, I remembered that it was a weekday. Would
anyone be at the church? How could I possibly give my
fifty dollars to the church if they were closed? I looked
around at the parking lot. There were a few other cars,
and I wondered if there weren't other people inside
the building.

I prayed, "Lord I don't know why you're having me
deal with this. What do I do?" Tears filled my eyes and
blurred my vision. I couldn't figure out what God was
doing. Something about this church, at this moment in

time, was important to God, and it was so frustrating to me. I was supposed to be going to Mom's, and I'd be late.

Most people go to church because they want to connect with fellow Christians, but not me. I never wanted to connect with anybody in the church. It's where I could drop my kid off in preschool church, and then go sit in the back row and drink my coffee. I didn't want anybody to talk to me; I only wanted to learn about God. I was at a place where I desperately needed to be invisible and this was my Sunday routine.

Also, I didn't want questions. Some moms asked me pointed questions about my son, because of the way he acted. That's a mom's life: our conversations revolve around asking and answering questions about our kids and raising kids. But, I had no answers for Ian. He exhibited unusual behavior in front of other people, and I didn't want to talk about it. I wanted church to be somewhere where I could sit and not be forced to interact. A place where I could learn what the Bible says, and follow God.

I couldn't wrap my head around doing something other than attending church on Sunday mornings and learning Scripture. In other words, I couldn't imagine 'giving', when all I wanted to do was 'take'. I wanted church to be a place to feed me, not the other way around. I stared down at the fifty dollars that sat in my lap and I started to cry. I didn't know it at the time, but God was molding me.

As I sat there crying, I thought up a plan. I was going to walk over to the entrance, and if the doors opened, then I was going to throw the money inside and run away. I wanted my part in this deal to be over. Then, I would be right with God, and He'd know that I'd done what He asked and I could move on.

While I was sitting there with tears streaming down my face, I saw one of the pastors of the church, Jon McClarnon. He had been walking toward the church from his car. He looked over at me, and in a few quick strides, he was knocking on the window of my car. He wore athletic shorts with a Duke basketball team t-shirt, and leaned a worn basketball on his hip.

I rolled down my window.

"Can I help you with something?" he asked. "You look troubled." He obviously didn't know me from anyone, but there he stood, ready to assist.

I couldn't believe that Pastor Jon, the one talking to me was the same one that I attended church to hear preach each Sunday and listened to the tapes of his sermons in my car. He preached with such emotion, he was captivating. And, now he stood at the door of my car. It had to be a 'God thing.' It had to be one hundred percent orchestrated by God. Which made me cry more. In front of him. This was totally out of character for me.

I grabbed a takeout napkin and wiped my eyes. I took some breaths, steadied myself and handed him the money. "I was told to bring this to this church, and give it to you, or give it to the church. So, if you can take this money, um, that would be great."

"Uh, okay. Do you want it to go to a special ministry or a general donation?" I know I'd shocked him, but he was composed.

And, then I started sobbing again. "Don't ask me, ask God! He's the one that made me come here!"

He nodded sympathetically. "That happens... Are you alright, do you need to talk to anyone?"

"No, I'm fine," I sobbed, "I had to do this."

"And, you'll be okay?"

"Yeah," I said, wiping my face with the damp napkin which was falling apart. "I'm fine, I'm fine."

And, I think I was.

On the way to Mom's, after I'd collected myself, I prayed, "God you are so in control. You needed obedience and I gave it. And you wanted to make sure that I understood that it was about you, and not about me. Thank you. Amen."

The next day, I wrote Pastor Jon a letter and I told him that I was the woman in the parking lot, and relayed the story of how God made me take a left turn. I resisted making a donation, but I did it, even though I needed the money.

One Sunday after service, I went up and introduced myself to him.

He shook my hand. "We're baptizing a bunch of people today, would you like to join them?"

"Oh, no! No!" I cried out. But, I realized I had startled him, so I said less sharply, "I'm not ready."

It scared me to think of doing it. I was used to water poured over babies' heads, but full immersion baptism as an adult was another thing.

"You let us know when you are, okay, Christi?"

God was getting involved with me, and I was perplexed. Why would He bother with me, and the mess that I am? I'm a rebel. I constantly wagged my finger at God, like I did Daddy. But God didn't back off.

When I was pregnant with Ian, and we knew the pregnancy was viable, I told Mitch I couldn't continue to live in this single wide trailer. With Mitch's stuff stacked everywhere, and the small space, there was no room for a kid. The only way for us to get a house, I knew, would be for me to take the lead. So, I did. I contacted several local modular home builders, but none of them would adjust their plans to make the house handicap accessible. *How could it be so difficult? Don't handicapped people have rights?* With that wheelchair looming in front of me, I needed to ensure my house had special accommodations, because I had to be able to function on my own. I found a builder in Virginia who would work with me to modify their plans. I hired them to build a three bedroom house, with a full attic and a three-car garage.

I thought that Mitch could use part of the garage for his stuff, and I could park my car in one of the bays. But, that never happened. The garage was soon filled with all of his things, and the trailer, which sat only a few feet from our new house, was still brimming with Mitch's who-knows-what. I think they call that hoarding.

Things with Mitch were up and down, and having a kid in the house made things more complicated. But, at least we were in a house that had room for the three of us.

Because of his moods, I asked Mitch to go to marriage counseling...for the *third* time. I thought it was important that I at least try to make our relationship work for the sake of Ian. A friend of mine recommended an excellent couple's therapist and we went to see her.

We met at the therapist's office because we both had left our places of work for the meeting. Her office was in a small complex north of Cary. I met Mitch in the parking lot because he was waiting for me. He didn't want to go in until I got there. We entered the front doors and walked down a long hallway until we found the door with her nameplate. It read "Susan Tibbetts" with a bunch of letters after her name. I guessed that was because she had a lot of degrees, like my sister Sandy, so she must be good.

"Hi, we're Mitch and Christi, here for Dr. Tibbetts," I informed the receptionist. She took my credit card and gave us a bunch of paperwork to fill out. I took pen to paper, but some of the questions stumped me. How could I put into words what was going on? I left them blank.

"Christi? Mitch?" A short, stocky woman with gray hair and kind eyes introduced herself as "Susan." She called us back into the office with a sound machine in the hallway by the door.

Everything about her office yelled, 'calm.' The walls were a calm cream color. The furniture was soft, with a calm floral pattern. The lighting was dim and calm. I felt like I was in a spa.

"How can I help you, today?" She asked, as if she were going to take my order in a restaurant.

"Um, we're here for marriage counseling…?" was all I could think of to say.

She laughed a little. "I figured that. What's hurting the most in your marriage right now?"

Man, she got to the point. "He's angry and I'm trying to raise our son," I shot out.

"I'm *not* angry," Mitch said in tone that showed otherwise.

"I see. Tell me about your end goal, then. What do you wish to accomplish through therapy?"

307

And we spent the next half hour debating the outcome of therapy. Mitch didn't see anything wrong, and I couldn't see anything right. I talked about how his angry outbursts hurt Ian and me, and how he didn't do anything to help raise our son. He talked about how I was always working and never had time for anything else. Susan mentioned some compromises we both might want to make. She and Mitch talked a lot about those, and he was very resistant to everything she had to say. I think he might have been taking her suggestions for change as attacks on him as a person. The more she offered ideas, the more agitated he became. I could feel him starting to flare up.

"I think it's worth looking at some of these things that we can do, Mitch," I offered.

He stood up in a huff. "I get it now, you're both against me!" he yelled, and stormed out of the room, slamming the door behind him.

The therapist and I stared at the doorway for a minute, but since I'd seen this before, and she was, well, a therapist, we both quickly recovered.

"What's going on with Ian?"

I was taken aback. My husband had stormed out of our marriage counseling appointment and she wanted to know what was going on with my son? She must have misstated his name. "You mean, Mitch?"

"No, I want to know about your son Ian."

I explained that Ian was in therapy twice a week, but we had yet to determine a definite diagnosis. He was highly intelligent, and they would give him puzzles, and each one he completed he went on to a harder one, and they finally had to cut him off when he reached into the high school level ones. They said he was operating at a genius level. I knew that, because he was completing multiplication problems when he was four years old.

However, he was having a difficult time with social skills. If you asked him a complex question, he could answer it. If you gave him multi-step instructions, he could follow them. But, if you asked him if someone was happy or sad, he would have a hard time figuring it out. If you asked him to figure out non-verbal clues, he didn't have a clue. He understood how the world worked, he just didn't understand people.

"I'm hearing that he has a problem with social cues. Tell me, does he keep to a routine? On his own, not with your prompting. Does he have to do things at a certain time, or say, in a certain order?" Susan asked.

"Yeah, he's very methodical about things. He gets upset if things are changed up."

"Has anyone given you a preliminary diagnosis?"

"Some say it might be Asperger's, others say he's 'on the spectrum.' When you have a different kind of child, you learn new terms."

"Christi, if your son has a high probability of diagnosis of Asperger's, then, I want you to know," she pointed to the door, "that the apple doesn't fall from the tree." She explained what that meant for the both of them and their relationship with me. She told me that I had control of Ian's treatment and therapy, but not Mitch's.

"You know I'm not shocked to hear that Mitch might be the same as Ian. When you were talking, I had a vision come to me, and it's this: I feel as if my marriage has been like we're in a dinghy, and we're swirling around in the water. Water is pouring into the dinghy, it's going to flood us, and my job is to keep bailing the water out of the boat. My job is to keep us afloat."

She looked at me for a while and sighed with some sort of resignation. "Then you have some decisions to make. How long will you try to keep bailing water out of that dinghy? And, more importantly, are you willing to let Ian watch you do it?"

God put that image in my head, where I saw myself bailing water out of this little boat and that I couldn't paddle forward because I was too busy bailing. But, what I failed to do was look around at who else was in the boat. Ian was in that boat with us. It wasn't just between me and Mitch anymore, because we had a child now. What I did mattered to Ian.

Mitch didn't understand that he needed a counselor. But I knew we needed one. We worked our way through five different ones, until the last counselor said that he didn't even want to discuss anything with the two of us. He wanted Mitch to come back alone for individual therapy. The counselor said that there was no point in the two of us talking to him because Mitch needed therapy. Mitch was angry about being singled out and never went back.

I was in church and they announced that they were going to be performing baptisms in a couple of weeks. And, in an instant, I went from wanting nothing to do with full immersion baptism, to wanting it more than anything.

The church had me sit down with the worship pastor, Stephen Claybrook, to talk about my baptism. So, I sat in his small, dark office upstairs in the church offices. The walls sported music-themed artwork, and the room was packed with large, flat monitors, assorted computer equipment, and an electronic keyboard connected to it all. Behind his desk, lined up on the wall were about six guitars and a couple of amplifiers. It was a musician's paradise.

We talked about what it means to be baptized. Turns out, baptism isn't some supernatural experience. It doesn't save you, or make you a better Christian, and the water isn't even 'holy!' When you get baptized, it's a public statement that you will live your life obedient to Christ, and trust and follow Him.

Pastor Stephen and I read Matthew 28:19-20 together: "Therefore go and make disciples of all nations, baptizing them in the name of the Father and of the Son and of the Holy Spirit, and teaching them to obey everything I have commanded you. And surely I am with you always, to the very end of the age."

We talked about the logistics of the church's baptism and what to expect. I had to bring a towel and wear clothes that could get wet, but no white or light colored t-shirts. And, I thought, duh, we don't need a wet t-shirt contest at church.

As I was about to thank him and leave, Pastor Stephen asked if my husband would come to the baptism.

"Oh, *Mitch*?" I was a little agitated. I didn't want Mitch involved. Church was my safe place and I didn't want him here, not since he rejected it. "You know, he won't come to church. I've asked, but he won't come."

"Do you mind if we pray about that?"

Despite not feeling it in the least, I said okay, and we prayed about it.

Later, I was talking to my friend Denise, who I dragged to Crosspointe on occasion, and I told her, "Can you believe that he wanted me to pray?"

She said, "Maybe that's a good idea, Christi."

Denise had grown up in a strict Christian family. She had her head wrapped right around God, and she had modeled tithing to me. She was in financial straits, but she still put money into the tithing box whenever we went to church together. Since Denise was on board with Pastor Stephen's directive, I figured she probably had the right idea. So, I prayed about it.

The next day, I called out quickly to Mitch, on my way out the door, "Oh, by the way, I'm going to be baptized this weekend, and you can come if you want to, or if you don't, that's okay. Bye!" And, I left for work.

The following day, Mitch confronted me. "What is this baptism? What do you have to do at this church, do you play with snakes?" He was curious, not angry. He wanted to know more about it.

So, we had a conversation where I basically repeated back to him everything Pastor Stephen had told me about baptism, and Mitch was genuinely interested.

Later, I asked God, "Lord, what are you doing?"

Mitch showed up for my baptism, and I would have liked to say that I wasn't surprised, because I knew that God was in control, but I couldn't say that. I was shocked. Mitch never went to any other church thing with me, and I'd tried. Actually, at my baptism, I almost had an audible conversation with God. God said to me, you made it your job to bring Mitch to Christ, and it's time that you realized it's *my* job, not yours. We were to show the way, to make the introduction, but it's God's job to bring people to Christ. And, God told me that day.

I didn't feel any different after being dunked (in a dark t-shirt, of course). But, by showing my faithfulness, and letting God do His job, His work and getting out of His way. I knew that God would make things happen. I'd always felt like I didn't know anything about God because I learned about the rites and the expressions of the Catholic faith, but not about God himself. I learned that I had to get out of God's way and let Him do the work He needed to do. I can't do His job; I could only do mine.

It reminded me of Saul/Paul on the road to Damascus, where God blinded Saul to get his attention. God said, "that's the guy I want, I want Saul to do my work, and he'll be known as Paul." So, God radically changed Paul on that road by blinding him. That was how God worked in me when I had gone blind myself, and how He shaped me through the people he put in my path. That was what God did when He made me take that left turn to donate fifty dollars at Crosspointe Church. Highway 55 was my road to Damascus because that's when I first responded.

When Mitch came to my baptism, things didn't change. Every time I came home, I would feel the tension, and God put it on my heart to start humming. I would be in the kitchen, and I would be humming gospel songs. I hummed all the time. It made me feel better and removed the friction in the air, at least for me.

Not too long after I got baptized, Mitch wanted me to sell the salon because he said it took too much of my time, so I sold my unimaginatively named Salon 329, but I stayed on as a stylist and rented out a booth from the new owner. That worked out for a while, but then I decided to try something different. I took a corporate job at the Umstead Hotel and Spa.

The Umstead was a new hotel, designed to be the Triangle's first 'five star' resort. It was built adjacent to SAS Institute, one of the area's largest employers. The location and opulent appointments catered to international business executives, scientists and other VIPs coming to the SAS campus. James and Ann Goodnight, who were majority owners in SAS, approached the Ritz-Carlton and Four Seasons to build a hotel near the corporate campus, but both luxury hotel chains declined. The Goodnights were sure that Cary could support a luxury hotel, so they hired their own architects and designers and built a 12-acre resort themselves.

I got hired by a friend of a friend to be on the team to get the Umstead Spa up and running. It was an amazing place. I really enjoyed the process of setting up the spa and working with the great team there. The only drawback was that they didn't have a hair salon, and since hair was kind of 'my thing', and the start-up phase was over, I decided to see if I could find another corporate opportunity that involved hair.

A woman came in to get a pedicure at the Umstead, and while I was talking to her, I told her that I had owned a salon before. This piqued her interest. Her name was Hannah, and she was the department head at the salon at a new gym and fitness center called Spirals Fitness that was being built in the Triangle. She asked me if I would help set up their salon. I said, sure. So, I left the Umstead, and went to work for Spirals as lead stylist, where I helped hire the first team of stylists.

Before the salon opened, Hannah was escorted off the property by security. The buzz around the salon was that she had tried to blackmail one of the bigwigs of the organization, and he called her bluff. I wasn't sure whether to believe that or not but it was bizarre.

Since the company hadn't given me any information on my insurance or other benefits, I called Hannah's cell to find out what was going on. I needed to know how to sign up for insurance, and what paperwork they needed, but everyone I spoke with at corporate in Arizona couldn't or wouldn't tell me what to do.

"Hannah, I can't put all my eggs into one basket, I need to know what my insurance situation is. I'll be happy to work part-time there until they can tell me more, but I'm not going to work without benefits."

Instead of helping me get information, she fired me. And, I thought, they escorted you off the property, but you're firing *me*? The situation stunk up a storm. I was glad to be done with them.

The next day, when I took Ian to preschool, Fred, one of the Spirals big wigs was there dropping off his son. He ran up to me. "Why are you not on our team anymore? Why did you leave?"

"Fred, Hannah fired me."

"What? She's gone, how did she fire you?"

I shrugged. "She did."

"We need someone to run the salon--say, I've got to rush to a meeting, but I'll call you!" he yelled back at me as he left.

A couple of hours later, Fred called me and told me that he wanted me to run the salon.

"Fred, I don't even know how to run a computer."

"Look, right now your job is to make your staff happy, because of all this turmoil." Hannah wasn't the only one to go, the corporation was having trouble finding the right people. "So, make your staff happy. You can do that, right?"

"Sure." I wasn't that convinced, but I knew how to run a team. And, I needed a job. They let Ian attend pre-school there for free, so that was a huge bonus.

As I knew would happen, I couldn't figure out the computer system Some nights I'd be there until 2 a.m. finishing up the paperwork and computer entries. I realized pretty quickly that I was in over my head. The work was impossible for me to do with my lack of technology skills, at least without training.

I decided that I hated corporate America, so after a year of struggling with the computer and the paperwork, I made the decision that I would give my notice and open another salon. Sometimes you have to stick to your strengths, and running my own salon was something I knew how to do. I did some research into some spaces in Cary, and put some feelers out with friends to see what was open and what others were planning on doing. I vowed to leave Spirals as soon as I found a space.

In the morning, my phone buzzed. "Hello, Christi? This is Mavis from Spirals. I have a question for you: are you planning to open up a salon?"

I froze. How could they possibly know? Then, I got mad. I told her, "I don't think it's any of your business."

She gave me some canned speech about ethics and the law, and I told her again, that my plans are none of her business. I had already written a letter of resignation, so I needed to hand it in.

After I hung up, I told Mitch that my days at Spirals were over. I headed over to Spirals to get my things, and took some black trash bags with me to cart stuff home. When I arrived at the gym, they had posted security personnel at the door. It was Tiny, someone I'd gotten close to over the past year and someone who was anything but Tiny. He singled me out as I tried to enter, and prevented me from getting inside the building.

"I'm not allowed to let you in. I'm sorry, Christi."

"But my things are inside, and I'm going to get them, then I'll get out and stay out. I promise."

"I'm sorry, but you're not allowed inside. I've been given orders to keep you from the building."

"Listen, you can watch me, if you want. I only want my things."

One of the big wigs that I didn't know interrupted us. He was posturing like men do who think they're more important than everyone else. "You must leave the premises now, or I'm going to call the police."

Angry and frustrated, I stormed back to my car. I texted Cleo, one of my stylists in the Spirals salon. *They won't let me in to get my things.*

Cleo texted me back. *Penny has your stuff – she emptied your station.* Penny was the new manager they'd hired to take my place.

I called the gym manager, Jim, but it went to voice-mail. I left him a message for him to call me right away and that it was a legal issue.

Then, I called my friend Denise, because she was working as a paralegal. I asked her advice. I knew she'd know what to do. She said, "Don't leave. Stay in the parking lot until you hear from Jim. If he doesn't let you in, stay there, and *we'll* call the police."

It made me feel better to know I had at least someone on my side. I had a lot of money wrapped up in the equipment at my station that was mine. They had no right to keep it from me.

After awhile of biding my time sitting in my car, Jim returned my call. He greeted me with a fake upbeat tone in his voice. "Hello, Christi! What can I do for you?"

"You can let me come inside and get my things," I told him, "because you obviously know that I'm out here in the parking lot. I'm kind of surprised things have gone like this, but I'm not leaving until you let me get my stuff."

"I can't let you come into the building." His mood had changed.

"Well, I'll tell you what, Penny has my things and they're my property. So, either you can get them for me, or I can get a policeman, and we'll come in there to get my property!"

I realized what had happened. They were scared that I was going to take all the hairstylists with me when I left, because I never made anyone sign the non-compete contract. The non-compete was a contract that corporate insisted everyone sign, but I told the stylists *not* to sign it. I knew that people ended up staying in bad situations because they had a bad contract that prevented them from working in their industry for a certain amount of time. That's what non-competes do: they prevent employees from being competition to their company which means they can't work. But, stylists are different. We have our client base and we take it with us when we leave. It sparks the question: "Are these my clients or your clients?" In my mind, a stylists' clients belong to the stylist, not the salon.

Jim sent Tiny out to escort me into the building. They had put my things in a big box, and I went through everything, to make sure it was all there. I made the manager and Tiny both stay there with me while I looked, then Tiny walked me outside.

"Thanks, Tiny." I gave him a half-hug juggling my box.

"Sure thing. We'll miss you."

"I'll miss you, too."

Sandy stopped by the house on her way to work to drop off Ian's jacket. I had left it at Mom's in Smithfield and I needed it because the temperature was supposed to drop again. She rapped on the screen door.

"C'mon in!" I yelled from the kitchen.

"Where's the kiddo?"

"At preschool. I'm heading there in a hour to get him."

"Here." She threw Ian's jacket on the couch, and walked over to give me a hug.

"Have a seat. Want some coffee?" I asked.

"Sure, I got a few minutes."

I poured her cup and handed it to her, when Mitch walked out from the bedroom. He took one look of us at the table and muttered something under his breath.

"What?" I asked with a bit of attitude. I didn't really want to know what he said, but I was so mad that he was mad, so I poked him with the question because I knew it would annoy him.

"Never mind," he said tersely, and grabbed the pistol from on top of the bookshelf and walked out, the screen door slapping shut behind him.

My sister Sandy looked me in the eyes and said, "You know, the way I see it, he's going to kill you. And then he will kill Ian, and then he will kill himself. That's all I see as the outcome of your situation."

Her words hit me like a gut punch. I didn't know what to say. I slowly shook my head.

"Christi, I'm not the only one who thinks that way."

And, I thought, is this how people see me and my situation?

CHAPTER 16

I'LL APOLOGIZE NOW

Love is patient and kind. Love is not jealous
or boastful or proud.
~1 Corinthians 13:4 (NIV)

Past

Cary, North Carolina, 2010

Christi, adult

I left Mitch, because it was time.

Mitch cared about me, but he didn't know how to show it. I don't think he ever knew how to love others, but he didn't want to be alone so that's why he always had a partner. The longer I was with him, though, I could see that he was jealous of me, but that didn't mean that he didn't care about me, because he did. Maybe he needed someone to care about, and I was available.

Sometimes we find ourselves in circumstances and it takes a while to figure out how to handle them. I was sixteen years old when we met. For me, as far as Mitch was concerned, I learned how to handle it, and how to cope with it. I didn't have a life with him. We did things at the same time, but never together. We biked and raced and kayaked, but those were things we did side-by-side, not together. Mostly I did my own thing, and he was another person in the house. Which worked, until there was a third person in the house, Ian. Then, I had a reason to get myself out of there. I didn't want Ian to grow up thinking that this was a healthy marriage. We both had our issues, and I believe that we teach people how to treat us.

I believe that God gives us a timeline to act on certain events in our lives. It was the same with Sandy when she told Mom what Daddy did to her. It was time to deal with the family secret. Sometimes God gives us reasons to not handle things at the time other people say it should happen. People will ask, "why didn't you do that earlier?" because it seems so obvious to them. But, maybe it wasn't our time to do it. There is a time for everything, like it says in the Bible.

For everything there is a season,
   a time for every activity under heaven.
A time to be born and a time to die.
   A time to plant and a time to harvest.

A time to kill and a time to heal.

A time to tear down and a time to build up.

A time to cry and a time to laugh.

A time to grieve and a time to dance.

A time to scatter stones and a time to gather stones.

A time to embrace and a time to turn away.

A time to search and a time to quit searching.

A time to keep and a time to throw away.

A time to tear and a time to mend.

A time to be quiet and a time to speak.

A time to love and a time to hate.

A time for war and a time for peace.

~ Ecclesiastes 3:1-8

Maybe earlier, emotionally, I wouldn't have been ready to walk out on Mitch. Maybe, emotionally, my mom wouldn't have been able to handle the revelation of abuse. We need to insert God in our circumstance of what's going on with us, even the world-at-large today. When we start thinking that we're in charge, we forget about what it means to be a Christian and live in faith. We're not on other people's timeline for what actions we take, we are on *God's*.

God told me to leave Mitch to save Ian, so I did.

I had to start out on my own, both professionally and personally.

As for work, I needed to get my salon up and running. I had rented a retail space in Cary, but it was a brand new building that needed to be upfitted. Despite it being an empty shell, the space had a light airy feel and the location was perfect. I found a contractor, who took on the project. I designed the layout and decor, because I knew how to best utilize the space and style it. I ordered stations and counters, ceramic sinks, swivel salon chairs, faucets and other hardware. I popped into a local lighting store in downtown Cary to purchase upscale fixtures, which he and his crew also installed. When the space was finally finished out, I put in the final details such as flowing sheer curtains, modern wall art, and large floor vases filled with bamboo. After months of work, one again I had my own salon and it was gorgeous. It took a lot of my savings to make it happen, but it was all mine.

As for housing, I had enough remaining money to get an apartment for Ian and me in Cary, but it took much more of my savings than I thought. There were so many expenses, including a car repair, that weren't in my initial budget, and on top of that, Ian needed school clothes and supplies for Second Grade. It was tight and the money kept flowing out of my account at a heart-stopping speed.

I was scared. So I prayed, "Lord, I don't know how I'm going to make this happen, and I know this is my path, but you have to help me. I don't know what I'm going to do!"

I sat in my car in the parking lot in front of my new salon. I had signed a lease to for this space and had to trust that the Lord would provide. I had enough clients to pay the rent on the business, but not the apartment rent. I needed more stylists to join me, and pay booth fees so I could afford to live. Not having Mitch's income as a backup made me really nervous.

I knew that Victoria and Kathy were going to join me in my new venture. I'd decided to call it Papillion, which means butterfly in French. I didn't come up with the name, though, because I probably would have named it the street numerals again. It was Linda, a fellow patient advocate, who came up with the name Papillon for me at a round table discussion at one conference. I loved the idea of the butterfly. That was me, I was the butterfly. I'd been in a cocoon for so long, it was time re-emerge and spread my wings.

I went into the salon, and Victoria was in there setting up her station, across from mine, of course. Kathy had chosen one down the row. I looked at the empty stations, housing a few products to make it look like they were owned by other stylists. But, I knew there weren't any stylists renting those stations. Placing product at empty stations was a customer service trick to make clients feel comfortable so they don't wonder if you're about to close your doors. But there was no worry about that, because I couldn't afford to close my doors. This was it. This was my savings and my livelihood. I had three rooms to use for a nail artist, massage therapist and esthetician, plus the six hair stations. It had to work. Ian was my priority and I needed to be financially stable.

Two hours after my prayer in the parking lot, I got a phone call from a woman named Sharon. She was friends with Mindy, who I had hired as my receptionist at Spiral Fitness.

"Christi, Mindy told me you were looking to rent a booth."

"Yes, I have a booth available."

"Well, here's the thing. I need to make a decision to where I'm going because my lease is up. And, I need to make it quickly."

"That's fine

"When can I come talk to you?"

I told myself to be calm and cool, but that didn't work. "Well, you could come now!"

And, she signed that day.

Moments after Sharon left, a friend who'd I met through Victoria called me. Her name was Sherry and she was full of energy. "Christi, I thought about it, and I'd love to sign a contract!"

I could feel my shoulders relax. All I could do was give the glory to God, because He made it happen. With four stylists and me, I could keep Papillion running, and support Ian as a single parent.

I took Ian on a vacation that summer before school started. We went to the beach. I thought he needed some normalcy in his life since we'd moved from the house in Apex to an apartment in Cary and he was about to start at a new elementary school. It was a lot of upheaval for him. A vacation sounded like something that normal people do, so I drove him to the beach and we stayed at a small hotel a few blocks from the ocean. The whole adventure wasn't much more than watching TV in a rundown hotel, grabbing some cheap meals, and playing in the sand and the pool, and collecting shells, but it was a vacation.

We were eating hamburgers at a shack off the beach highway. The place was decorated in surf boards, old photographs of local surfers, and faded tiki grass.

Ian said, "Mom, I don't even know if I believe in God, and I only go to church because you make me."

My kid was like a mini-adult in some of the things he said. It was then that I realized that I couldn't be responsible for Ian's faith, any more than I could be responsible for bringing Mitch to God. It's a person's own journey, and there comes a time for kids when they have to give up their parents' religion and form their own relationship with God.

"Ian, look, my mom and daddy made me go to church. You know, my father studied at the Vatican to be a priest, so we didn't have a choice. I hated it because it didn't have any meaning for me, and when I was 13 years old, I said 'when I get old enough, I'm not going to go.' It was because I saw the hypocrisy of the people in the church and I said, 'this is baloney.'"

Some people may think it odd to be so blunt with a seven year old, but Ian was not a normal seven-year-old kid. He had taught himself to read when he was three. He was already testing at the college level in problem solving puzzles and his IQ was off the charts. So, our conversations weren't the normal 'mom and little boy' chats.

"Was it, ba-baloney?" he asked, trying out the word.

"No, and something I'll never make you eat, however, the fact that I didn't want to go to church didn't discount all that I had learned there. When I got older, I was so extremely grateful for the background in Jesus and God that my parents gave me. There were times when I was at the end of my rope, you know, when bad things happened to me, and I knew where to turn. I knew how to get back 'home' to God."

"But, can I quit?" he asked.

"No. As long as I go to church, you will go to church. Because you always need to be able to find your way home and I need to help plant that seed in you."

"I don't understand it," Ian told me.

"It doesn't matter if you understand it right now. In fact, if you don't understand it, I think you need to listen more."

"I listen." He gave me that petulant look.

330

"Ian, you go to school, you go to the doctor, and you go to church, because these are the places that help you as a person. In church, that's where you gain an understanding of who God is, and who He can be in your life. Part of your well-being is to have a strong faith in the Lord because that will back you up every time."

Ian took a big bite of his burger and chewed thoughtfully. "So, I hafta go to church to get better?"

"Yes, I'm a big stickler in that, Ian. I don't let you take a day off from school, and I don't let you choose not to go to the doctor. It's the same with church. I don't let you choose to not go to church. I make the rules because I'm the parent. I don't have to justify the rules. You have to accept that I'm doing it for your benefit, like God does for us. Sometimes we don't like His rules, but the rules exist for our benefit. God's not a dictator Ian. Everything He guides us is for our advantage. One day, it will be important to you."

It was one of those parenting moments that I loved. I was able to speak truth into my boy. I can't believe I said it that bluntly, either. It was like God one-hundred-percent put those words in my mouth that He knew Ian needed to hear.

My mom was having knee replacement surgery, so my sister Sandy kept me updated on her condition. I got a call from Sandy in the mid-afternoon saying that Mom was out of surgery, but she hadn't woken up yet. I told her I'd be over after I finished my last client. I visited her that night, but she was really tired and not responding, which was expected and typical. That is, until it had gone on for two days.

Sandy, who had followed Mom's career path and become a nurse herself, confronted the doctor. We were both in the room when he came in for rounds, and Sandy practically yelled at him, "You need to figure out what the hell is going on, because my mother isn't waking up!"

I looked at Mom. Her eyes would open, but she wasn't seeing anything. She laid there like she was in a coma or something, but I knew that couldn't be it because they would have told us if she was in a coma. Something was wrong.

The doctors put her through various tests to figure out what was going on with her, while Sandy, Judy and I took turns sitting vigil at our mother's bedside.

She finally began to speak, but she spoke in numbers not words. "4, 3, 2, 1..." she would recite, as if she were playing solitaire. It was driving us crazy. Sandy and I vowed if she came out of it, she would never play cards again.

One morning days later, I was sitting at her bedside before heading into work and I asked her, "Can I read you the Bible, Mom?" I didn't expect her to answer, but I asked anyway.

I was going to Hope Chapel Church in Apex, because Pastor Jon had moved on to another church. They set out Bibles at the front entrance for anyone to take if they needed one, and I had grabbed one because I didn't have one at home. I read it like a book. I would dive into the stories of people's lives, like Moses, David or Paul, because they were a mess and God used them. And, if God could use them, maybe God could use me, too. I loved reading about these people from the Bible who gave me hope.

So I went down to the parking lot to get a Bible from my car, and realized I had about four of them in there. I found that interesting—it was like I had planned for that moment. I grabbed three of them and went back to my mom's room. I had one for me, one for my sister Judy and one for her daughter Hampton. That way, we could all read the Bible to Mom.

When I read those stories of people's lives in the Bible to Mom, her eyes flickered and I knew I was reaching her.

After all the tests, the doctors determined that she'd had a stroke on the operating room table. They were finally able to give her the proper treatment and she started to come around. She spoke in words instead of numbers for the first time, and then I knew she was going to be okay.

However, due to the stroke Mom couldn't walk, and since she couldn't walk, she couldn't do physical therapy after her knee replacement. Which meant that she would never walk again. So, instead of me being in the wheelchair, it was my mom. She moved in with Sandy, so Sandy could help take care of her. It was hard on Sandy, and just as hard on Mom, because Mom always took care of us.

Until Mom couldn't.

"You know, you've got to get 'out there,'" my friend Tiffany told me as she worked on her client.

"Out there, where?" I picked up a comb and shears.

"Dating. A friend of mine is getting married and she met her husband on Christian Mingle."

"I don't know about that. Online dating? Seems kind of weird."

"Lots of people are doing it. Give it a try. Go on! Your life can't consist only of work and being Ian's mom."

"I'll think about it," I promised.

I more than thought about it. I went home that night and set up an account on the online dating site. Maybe it was a bad idea, or maybe it would lead to something. I had nothing to lose.

After entering in all my information, I heard back from a few men. I dated some of them, and I discovered that I was really bad at dating. I didn't know what to talk about, or how to act. They seemed to be disinterested and maybe it was because I wasn't sure what I was supposed to do. The last time I dated was in 1986 and I was sixteen years old. What did I know about dating? I was clueless.

The next time Tiffany came in, I had a question for her. "This guy was texting me all the time, and now he's not. Is he blowing me off?

"Yeah, he probably is," said Tiffany.

"See that's why I don't do this. I don't do good with rejection. So, I'm not doing this any more."

I went home to cancel the service. I didn't need the constant rejection from guys, I'd already gone down that road. And, I still didn't understand the rules of the game so how could I play?

While I was online to cancel Christian Mingle, I noticed that a man had looked at my profile. I studied his picture. He wore a suit and tie, and had silver hair with vibrant blue eyes and a nice smile. His online name was "Flying Squirrel."

Then I thought: he's looking at my profile while he's at work, why is he doing that? Even, though I was doing it, myself.

I messaged him. *I saw you looked at my profile. I'm Christi.*

He wrote back. *I'm John. I did look at your profile, and it sounds like you're really busy and congrats on your business ventures.*

We proceeded to text back and forth for about thirty minutes.

He asked, *Can we talk?* So, I gave him my number

And we talked on the phone for nearly an hour. It was so easy to talk to him. I felt like we were old friends catching up.

"I see the State Fair is open," he said, "and, you have a son. Have you taken him to the fair?"

I replied, "No, I'm not taking him to the fair."

"Why not?"

"There's no way I'll ever take him, because this is what will happen: we'll get to the carnival games, and we'll get stuck there, because he just knows he's going to win. And, I'll keep giving him money, and he'll keep trying to win. We'll get stuck there for two hours before he finally gives up and I buy him a twenty dollar toy."

He laughed. "I see. Say, if you're free tonight, I'd love to meet you."

"I have my son," I explained.

"Well, if you can get a sitter…?"

"I guess I could drop him off at Miss Cindy's day-care place." I thought that maybe some of his friends who also frequented Miss Cindy's would be there, like Kaytlin, or Howie and his sister Anna. Miss Cindy ran a drop-in daycare place in Apex, and it was a blessing for those of us without regular sitters on call. She had renovated a strip mall space to be a kids' dream, filled with toys, climbing structures, dress ups, computer games, and other fun games and toys. She always had a schedule for the kids, which included movie nights on the weekends. For a small charge, she would order dinner to be delivered for your kid.

John and I met in the Olive Garden parking lot, and the first thing I noticed was his smile.

He said, "According to your profile, I know you like surprises, so let me surprise you with where we're going tonight. C'mon, I'll drive."

I immediately texted Tiffany. *I'm getting into the car with John.* I gave her a description of the car and told her where we were. That was just in case he tried to kidnap me or something. I was a little nervous, but he seemed okay.

John turned to me in the car and asked, "Do you mind if we pray?"

And, I immediately relaxed. *This is going to be okay.*

So, we prayed and we started driving. He took me to the State Fair.

"When I asked you to pray, I knew you were going to stay in the car or you were going to leave," he confessed as we walked around the fair eating fried everything.

We had so much in common, that we were constantly saying, "I do that, too!" He put his arm around me and was touching my side, and I thought that it felt really nice.

"I want to tell you about your profile. It's not that welcoming. You pretty much say, 'I have my business and my son, and I'm really busy. I have so many plates in the air, and I might have time to fit you in my schedule.' That's not very inviting."

"I did write that, didn't I?"

"Yes, because you sounded like you don't want to date," said John.

"Thanks for letting me know so I can change my profile."

"I really wish you wouldn't."

"Oh?"

"I'm having a really great time tonight. And, I'd like to see you again."

"I'd like that, too."

"Thank the Lord. I didn't know what your reaction was going to be." He was a forty year old man, but all men are teenage boys wondering what the girl is going to say.

As he was driving me back to my car, he said, "I would love to invite you to a barbecue."

"Okay..."

"It's tomorrow night. I work for the state and my pal at work is having people over at his house."

"Okay, sure." *I just met this guy and now I'm going to meet his coworkers?*

The next day, I went to buy myself some new jeans for the event, and I realized I had a problem. On Christian Mingle, you have to be divorced. I had been separated for almost three years, but I wasn't divorced. I was so afraid about how Mitch was going react to receiving divorce papers, that I never did it. I was just like Mitch's ex, Linda, who stayed married to him, even as she lived separately, because she didn't want to rock the boat. In my mind, Mitch was a time bomb waiting to go off, so I also stayed married but lived independently of him.

I realized I had to be honest with John, and come clean about my situation. It was scary, because I really liked him. He was such a genuine man, a good person, but this could drive him away. Everything hung in the balance, and the results of my telling John could go one way or the other.

"I have something I need to tell you," I said, before we left for his friend's house. "I'm still married."

"What!?" I could tell there was shock in his reaction, and hurt there, too.

"But wait, let me tell you why. He's a scary guy. You never know how he's going to react. He's not in my life, except for my son, and not even much for that. I had to tell you before you drove me somewhere, in case you want to call it off."

He sat and thought for a minute. Then, he said, "You guys are really done?"

"We're more than done," I replied.

"Okay." And, he drove me to his friend's house.

Within 48 hours of meeting, we both knew that we would end up getting married. There was something else I needed to tell him.

"I have something else I have to tell you. I have MS. I don't have symptoms anymore, and I believe I'm miraculously healed by God, but the lesions are still present on my MRIs."

"Well, I have something, too. I have an involuntary tremor that they haven't diagnosed yet. How are you going to feel if I get sicker?"

"Probably the same that you'll feel if I get sicker."

And we both laughed. That was the moment we knew we would handle whatever happened in the future together.

John was totally different than anyone I'd ever met. He was such a good man who had so much happen to him in his life. He experienced bad past relationships with women who cheated on him and stole from him. His strong faith in the Lord wove through every area of his life and sustained him in those bad times.

He told me that when he met me he thought, "Lord, either she has a bad drug problem or she's very tired." I was very tired, of course, working all the time and raising my son on my own. It was never my desire to be in a relationship with anyone because I knew my major life focus was Ian. My life consisted of trying to run a business and figuring out Ian's issues. But, God put John in my life as a gift to me.

I said to John, "I feel like I should apologize to you now, because for so many years, I learned how to guard myself. So, I feel like I'm going to say something that will offend you, and I should apologize now. Part of protecting yourself from others is learning not to be affected by things and to put a protective shield up, and sometimes that comes out wrong. The shield can be an affront to other people."

"It's going to be okay, Christina," is all he said. Like Victoria and my mom, John called me by my given name.

Bible study became important to me and I could share that with John. Before I got to know God on a personal level, I couldn't have a legitimate, intellectual conversation about the Bible with anyone. With my Catholic upbringing, I simply didn't know enough about it because we didn't read it at home. I could never have a legitimate conversation about what was in the Bible because I didn't know what was in it. But, now I read and studied the Bible. It's a tool God gave us to learn about Him and how to live.

It was through Bible study that I had an epiphany. When I started having more intimate moments with God, I realized that He had been directing my life *all along*. He was there, even as I ran out of the church, and even as I shunned Him. He was still there, helping me through the horrible things, and beckoning me back to Him.

He protected me from Daddy's abuse by making me unpredictable, unpliable, and half asleep. He saved me from addiction by putting it on my heart that I would drink and drug myself to death if I didn't stop at an early age. He kept me safe in my abusive relationship with my ex. He gave me Ian to raise and help determine which therapies were best for the kid with the Mensa IQ who was lightyears ahead of his classmates in school work, but behind in social skills. He helped me endure my MS treatments, and performed a miracle by healing me of MS symptoms. He helped me forgive Daddy who abused me. He helped me run a business to support myself and Ian. He brought me John. God did it all.

God gave me the tools to work to go forward each phase along the way, but I took the steps. We always have to step out in faith.

One day I called John, and I said, "Pray for me, because I have to go pick up Ian from his dad's and I don't know if I have enough gas to make it."

"You know, Christina," John said, "You would walk over there before you would let me help you. I could come bring you some gas right now if you wanted me to. But, you wouldn't even call me to ask for gas. For prayer, you called, but not for gas."

"I know, I know, but I never want anyone to do anything for me, because in the past there's always been a price tag attached to asking for help."

"There's no price tag with me. I want to take care of you, Christina."

I wanted to be with John for the rest of my life, and praise the Lord, John felt the same way. We both knew we were going to get married and we knew it was God who brought us together. We were too 'messed up' as people and we never would have found each other without God. In fact, our meeting was *because* of God.

I was still married to Mitch, and that was a problem. John told me that he didn't want to have the relationship with the three of us. I had to make a choice. I had to put on my big girl pants and be willing to take a chance that God would protect me, Ian and John. Mitch didn't want anyone else to be teaching or taking care of me. He was twelve years older than me, and didn't like the fact that I might rely on someone else to help make choices, like God or John. So, I knew there would not only be push-back, but maybe violence.

I had gone without child support or anything, because I didn't want to make waves. It was easier to keep the sleeping lion quiet and not wake him up.

John gave me the courage to serve Mitch with divorce papers. I asked for child support. It took time, and lawyers and hacking out a final deal, but we finally reached it. Mitch was angry, but I was elated. Legally, I was a single woman.

Victoria and Kathy took John out for coffee to see what his intentions toward me were. They raked the poor guy over the coals.

Victoria explained it to him directly, "John, if you ever do anything to hurt Christi or break her heart, I will hold you down and Kathy will eff you up, you got it?"

Of course John agreed, and he was grateful that I had such loyal friends who cared about my well-being.

John and I got married outside on a sunny afternoon, and Ian was part of the ceremony. It was a wonderful day of union. We hired an electric violinist and someone to play the saxophone, because we loved jazz music. John's two sons and my sister Sandy also stood up for us.

John also helped Ian with his social skills. He gave Ian the book *How to Win Friends & Influence People* by Dale Carnegie. Ian devoured the book, taking the lessons to heart and thereby increasing his social IQ.

John loves to tell people about something I told him early on. He says, "When I met my wife, something she said to me was that God took seven days to form the earth, but He didn't need seven days. He did it for us, so we could understand that things need to happen in a certain order."

Now, I felt like my life was finally 'in order'.

It wasn't all smooth sailing, though. We had some trying times because Mitch more than once physically attacked John.

One time, Mitch lost his job because of it. He was working for the Town of Cary and he punched John in the face while we were at the doctor's office. We had been doing Mitch a favor because we were taking Ian to the doctor, when it was Mitch who should have done that. Ian needed vaccinations before heading to Word of Life youth summer camp.

Ian was in the waiting room when Mitch hit John, and that was a disaster because Social Services got involved. They were called because a minor had witnessed the domestic attack. People who work in healthcare are mandated reporters. That means if they see something, they have to report it to the correct agency. It doesn't matter what the circumstances are surrounding the incident, they have to report it. It's the law.

John agreed to drop the charges against Mitch if he took anger management classes. John always wanted to solve things peaceably. As far as we knew, Mitch took them because they were court-ordered.

But, when the town where Mitch worked found out about the attack, they fired him. And, there went my child support.

Ian gave a stick of gum to the boy who lived next to us in the apartment complex. His name was Ty, and Ian and he became close. I was really happy because Ian had a friend.

Ty's mom had moved so often that Ty lost count after naming for us twenty different elementary schools he'd attended. His mom was such a good person, but had trouble figuring out how to raise her son, navigate social services, and buy food and pay rent. She was overwhelmed and thankful that we loved and took care of Ty.

He eventually moved in with us when we left the apartment for Smithfield, because his mom wanted John to provide a father figure role in his life. John and Ty had a father and son relationship.

John, Ian, Ty, and I moved into a new house in Smithfield to be closer to my mom, and to help Sandy take care of her. John's folks lived nearby, so much of the family was in one place. I put Ian in a charter school in Johnston County and Ty went to public school. As the boys got settled into school, John was eventually diagnosed with Parkinson's Disease, which meant a lot of doctor visits. Ian needed his own appointments, so I was busy with schedules at home as well as the salon.

A lot was happening all at once, so I decided to go to a counselor to help me get through all the upheaval and changes. I always thought of myself as independent and strong, but I decided counseling might be a good place for me. The counselor and I talked for a while, then she said, "You suffer from PTSD." It seemed odd to me, until one day I felt that intense pressure.

I had gotten back from the hospital, the second time John had been admitted due to his Parkinson's. Ian was with his dad and his aunt, because they were going to watch him in a talent show, and then meet me at the drop off place.

Since Mitch had assaulted John, we only met in public places, and our usual place was the McDonald's on Highway 64. It was about a forty-minute drive to Smithfield, but a fifteen-minute drive to Mitch's. I figured if I set the location close to Mitch's house, he'd be more willing to meet for pick up, making the transitions easier for everyone. Picking up Ian at Mitch's was always challenging. When it was dark outside, Mitch wouldn't turn the light on. I would have to stumble my way up to the house in the dark. And, he never packed up Ian. He was never ready to go, so I had to go inside and pack up Ian's things. The McDonald's drop off place fixed that.

I was glad that Ian was with his dad, so I could focus on getting John home from the hospital. After I got John home, I called Mitch.

"I'll meet you at the drop off in about an hour," I told him.

"I'm not leaving the house."

"You have to bring him to the drop off."

"I'm not going to."

"Mitch, stop making this difficult, it's right down the street."

Mitch said, "Call Social Services then."

And, I thought, well, the only thing that Department of Social Services has on us, is Mitch punching out John. So, how's that going to work out for Mitch? They'd come after him not me. I hung up the phone, not wanting to get into it. It was late, and I was tired. I went to bed.

In the morning, I drove up to Raleigh and went into the offices of Social Services. I stood at the reception desk, looking at the woman who was trying to be helpful, but I could tell she was as stressed as I felt.

"I wish we could help you, but we can't."

"What do I do?" And, uncharacteristically, I started crying in front of her because it brought back everything I had already dealt with. I felt like an elephant was sitting on my chest, and I felt paralyzed. It was overwhelming, the stress of what was going on with John and his Parkinson's, and Ian stuck at his dad's, a dad who wouldn't meet me at the designated drop off. It came to a head in the form of sobs.

"I'm so sorry, I really am. But, we simply can't advise you."

I went out the parking lot, and I called the school. "I want you to know where Ian is; he's at his fathers. We've had a *situation*,"—I didn't know what else to call it—"and he'll be at school as soon as I can get him there." As the primary custodian, I was responsible for getting him to school. They didn't care that I couldn't pick him up yesterday from his dad's, they only cared that he didn't show up for school. I envisioned the Truancy Officer paying me a visit.

After driving back to my house, I called the Apex Police Department, because I thought, maybe they could help me.

A woman with a clipped voice answered the phone. I explained the situation and her voice relaxed. "Okay, here's what we can do. You call us about 15 minutes before you get into Apex, and as long as we have an officer available, we will have the officer drive over and meet you at the address." Thank God for small town police departments.

I called the station when I got to Apex, and then waited down the street until I saw them drive up in one of their large, black SUVs. I pulled into the driveway, so I could get Ian, and the police SUV followed me, but didn't pull into the driveway. The driver cocked the vehicle at an angle at the end of the drive.

Since I had left Mitch, he'd let the place deteriorate. Weeds stood three-feet tall in the front, bushes overtook the windows, that had closed blinds, and the trailer next to the house was mostly obscured with overgrowth. In the front was a large, barbed wire enclosure, which I knew was for a garden, but since there was no garden, it looked creepy. The property looked abandoned and Stephen King worthy.

I walked over to the SUV. Inside was a feisty, young black woman who looked around and shook her head. "I can understand why you didn't want to drive up here *alone*."

"Yeah." And, I had to almost laugh because I thought, well, my son was in there, so what did that say about me as a mom?

She asked, "Do you have dealings with your ex-husband?"

"Well, not for a while, because he actually hit my current husband."

She nodded and jumped down from her seat, then walked up to the front with me, but stayed back a few feet when I knocked on the door. Ian answered, but as I started to walk inside, the officer said, "Ma'am, please leave the door open behind you."

I nodded and went inside. Mitch wasn't even there. He'd left Ian alone.

CHAPTER 17

THE FIRES OF HELL

O Lord, if you heal me, I will be truly healed;
if you save me, I will be truly saved.
My praises are for you alone!
~ *Jeremiah 17:14 (NLT)*

Past

Smithfield, North Carolina, 2016

Christi, adult

My mom passed away and it was the hardest thing. I lost my protector, my rescuer, my champion; my mom who loved me to the moon and back.

It's odd how when you lose someone you love, and you see something you want to share with them, and you reach for the phone, only to realize that phones don't dial Heaven. That's how it felt all the time. I would want to call her, or text her, or go visit her, but I couldn't. I loved her so much that I could still feel her, even when she wasn't still on the earth.

Three weeks after Mom's funeral, my stepson, John-Mark said to me, "Will you make some of your famous chicken parmesan?"

"Sure!" I told him. We were going to have a get-to-gether with John's parents and the entire family. I was excited to have something to do and to be needed. It felt wonderful to be included and wanted.

I planned to make a ton of my specialty dish so everyone could have plenty to eat. I decided to put it together beforehand so it would be ready to go, and when we got down there, then all we'd need to do was to put it in the oven.

I had about ten pounds of chicken breasts that I had dredged in flour and seasoned on both sides, and then left them on a platter on the counter while I got out the pan.

Ian came home from school alone because Ty was visiting his mom. Ian walked into the kitchen and I stiffened. Every time he got back from his dad's house, he had some attitude, because Mitch put ideas in his head. So, Ian had been a jerk for a few days. That morning, I'd told him to have a good day at school, and he'd replied, his voice dripping with sarcasm, "I'm sure I'll have a good day *at school*." And, I stated brightly, "Well, I'm going to have a good day, and I hope you have one, too."

He was being a teenager, and I wanted to pop him one.

"Wow, Mom, whatcha doing?" Ian was back to his jovial self.

I relaxed. "Making chicken parm for Saturday at Martha's and Pa's."

"Yum," he said, not looking at me, but grabbing an apple and a bag of chips. He sat down on a barstool by the breakfast counter separating the kitchen and living room, and he switched on the laptop, quickly getting lost in whatever grabbed his attention.

I turned on the stove and added a mixture of grape-seed oil and olive oil to my twelve-inch skillet. I filled up the pan about half-way to the top, and left it to heat up. Meanwhile, I picked up the platter of chicken to start frying it. I would fry the chicken, then drain it, and build my casseroles of chicken parm using the freshly fried breasts.

"Mom!" Ian yelled.

My skillet was on fire. Tall flames licked the micro-wave above the stove.

"Get water!" He came barreling into the kitchen.

"No, no not water!" I corrected, knowing what water would do to an oil fire. "Look, move away! I'm going to get it outside!"

What I should have done was put the pan in the oven and shut the door to starve the flames of oxygen. But, I didn't. You think about these things later.

Instead, I grabbed the pan, and ran to the front door. The flames, fueled by excessive air, leapt higher, and fiery oil splashed on my arms as I headed for the door. I was almost all the way down the corridor to the front door, when I dropped the pan. Now I'd left a trail of burning oil behind me, and it was all over my arms, but all I could think of was that I had to pick up the pan. So, I bent down and picked up the pan.

"Open the front door!" I screamed at Ian.

There wasn't much left in the pan, because most of the oil had splattered all over the house and me, but I still grabbed the pan and threw it out the front door. Then, I ran back into the kitchen and turned on the cold water, and stuck my burning hands and arms into the cooling fresh water. The skin on my arms was bubbling up.

Normally, I'd have sent Ian next door to get an adult to help with the situation, but we had recently moved into the neighborhood, so we barely knew our neighbors.

"Ian, call John. *Call John.*"

I looked at my arms, and I thought that if I could keep my hands and arms in the water, I'd be okay. I'd be fine because it didn't hurt in the water.

Ian called John and put it on speaker, "John, Mom was in an accident, we had a fire."

"Is your mom okay?"

"No, she's burned."

"Call 911 and take care of your mom, I'll be right there."

The fire department was the first to arrive. They came barreling in the front door in full gear, with axes and breathing tanks. They assessed the situation and two of them flanked me by the sink.

"Ma'am," one of them said, "do you mind if we take off your wedding ring?"

"What? Why?"

"If your hands swell up, they'll have to cut it off. It'll be easier if we take it off now."

"Okay, but don't lose it!"

The ring was so special to me. John's father, Pa, designed the ring for John's mother, Martha. He bought all the stones for it, and went to a jeweler to design the ring. Since she'd gotten sick with Parkinson's, she didn't wear it anymore, and when John and I were ready to get engaged, Pa told John to buy the ring from him and give it to me. John had asked me if that was okay, and I said that it was more than okay. It was so special to me because Pa had wanted me to have it. So, John bought it from his dad, and gave it to me as my wedding ring. We had to have the stone lowered from it's high setting, because I kept getting it caught on everything. It doesn't look as grand as it had when I first received it, but it was still the most beautiful ring I could imagine.

EMS arrived a short time later, and agreed that removing the ring was a good idea. The lead EMT asked me my name, and put her hand on my back in a comforting way. "Christi, we're going to be taking you to the UNC Burn Center, so you're going to have to take your hands out of this water."

I was so scared to take my hands out of the water, and I knew it would hurt beyond belief. But, I also knew that I wasn't a child, and I had been through so much in my life up until this point, that I could do it. I took my hands out, and Ian says that I screamed and screamed, but I had no memory of it.

My limbs were on fire. I could only see red. If I could have left my body at that point, I would have, because there was no relief from the torture. If this was hell, it was the worst part of it. This was the place where my mom wanted my daddy to live, and I thought, no, I wouldn't wish this on anyone, not my worst enemy and no matter what they did.

The EMTs put me on a gurney and wheeled me outside, where a crowd of my neighbors had gathered. "We have to wait until my husband comes!" I yelled out.

"Christi, we have to take you now. We have to get you to the burn unit *right now*."

As soon as they secured me in the ambulance, they gave me medicine, and little by little, relief washed over the searing pain.

Ian said to me, "Mom, you go. I'll tell John what happened. It's okay, you have to go."

I was so proud of him and how he acted, handing a horrible situation with such maturity and calm.

Before they closed the doors, John drove up. I could see his white car careen around the corner. He had made the thirty-minute drive in less than fifteen minutes. John got out of the car, and ran over to the open back door of the ambulance where Ian stood.

"I caught the kitchen on fire!" I told him. The medicine had kicked in, and I was feeling really loopy. "I ruined the carpet! I'm sorry, I ruined it. Oh, oh, and the fireman's got my ring! Get my ring!"

"It's okay, honey," John said.

"And I didn't get to cook the chicken!" I told him. "I battered it all. Don't waste the chicken! Don't waste it!"

"Don't worry about that. You go. I'll get Sandy to stay with Ian. I'll meet you there!" John turned to the EMT to get instructions on where to meet us. The UNC Burn Unit was about an hour and a half away.

They closed the doors and took off. The EMT gave me more medicine, but I kept going on and on about the chicken. I could hear the EMTs talking amongst themselves. "If I'd given this much to a 300-pound man," one said to the other, "it would have put him under the table." Still, I kept babbling on about the chicken, my ring, canceling clients at work, and on and on about everything that didn't matter.

They wheeled me into the main emergency room, and it was so busy that they had people lined up in the hallways. I was singing by then, because I was so high on the medicine. I sang some gospel songs because

I thought they'd make everyone feel better. John had arrived and stroked my head as I sang.

After a few hours, John-Mark and Anna, my stepson and his wife, came up to see how I was doing. They told us that they would stay at the house overnight and take care of Ian. All I said to them was, "Be sure you cook the chicken, because I have all this chicken and it's sitting on the counter and I don't want it to end up in the trashcan."

Because the burn unit was full and they didn't have a bed for me, they left me in the hallway. John told me later they didn't move me for over five hours. Finally, they realized I needed to be put somewhere, so they put me in the burn ICU. I was undressed and gowned, and placed back onto a gurney. A nurse wheeled me into a room called 'the tank', that was sort of like an operating room. I had a bad feeling about the place, because I had an inkling of what they might do. The room consisted of a flat stainless steel table, where they laid me out with nothing but a sheet over me.

A woman in full protective gear, head to toe, entered the room. I told her, "If you're going to do what I think you're going to do, then you better give me a lot of freaking drugs, or you're not touching me!"

They debrided and excised the burned, dead tissue of my arms, layer by layer until unearthing healthy bleeding tissue and I experienced a new kind of hellish pain. Because I had third-degree burns, I had to have it done every day. I didn't have to go to the tank every day, but they had to debride my burns every day.

After I learned about what my fellow patients were going through, I realized I didn't have it as bad as others. Being in the burn ICU, you could hear the cries and screams of the patients, and it was unnerving. Their wails echoed through hallways. I wanted to fix them, but I couldn't.

John told me about meeting a man in the waiting area, whose son had gotten burned by gasoline, and they weren't sure if he was going to make it or not. His lungs were severely damaged. It was tough to realize that other patients around me might not leave that place, that the burn ICU was their last place to live.

The people that worked there were amazing. They were incredibly kind people with enormous reserves of compassion. They worked with people who didn't even look like people because they'd been burned so badly. I think you have to be born with that sort of gift to work in a place that dreadful.

I kept going over and over what happened and what I could've done differently. I wanted to give it another shot, another try with a different outcome. Put the pan in the oven. Use a fire extinguisher or flour. Anything but run out of the door with flaming oil.

On day two of my hospital stay, John showed me a picture. It was of Ian, John-Mark and Anna sitting at my kitchen table and smiling for the camera with their forks raised in the air. They were eating my chicken. I had to laugh, because what else could I do?

I thought I was healing so well because of the debridement treatments. My burns were pink flesh with red dots. I looked at the doctor assessing my wounds, and I expected a great appraisal. Maybe I wouldn't need plastic surgery.

"Christi, we're going to have to do grafts," said the doctor.

"Whaat?"

"We're going to do split-thickness pigskin grafts on your burns."

That didn't sound good. It turns out it was actually the weirdest, most bizarre thing I could imagine. They adhered pigskin to my burns. It was actual pigskin, and it was so stereotypically North Carolina, with our love of all things pork.

Ian scrunched up his face when he saw me. "Mom, you look like a zombie."

I did. It was grotesque. Thankfully, after a few weeks, the skin eventually peeled and fell off, leaving much better, well, at least better than before, skin underneath.

I stayed in the hospital over a week. When they sent me home, they gave me and John detailed instructions for care. John would have to come into the shower with me, and help me clean my wounds. If I were a single person, I don't know how I would be able to treat myself. He would join me in the shower, and take a wash cloth and wring it over my arms, and I would cry as he did it, because it hurt so badly. I don't know how he had the strength to do that, he was amazing.

With the pigskin sloughed off, they gave me a bio-material to apply between my burns and bandages. The material was really expensive and promoted healing. After that, I moved on to special acute burn gloves on top of the bandages. I went to the burn center at UNC in Chapel Hill every week for months, then once every two weeks for another six months.

It was a year of my life in recovery and it was a hard time, but it was a sweet time too. I learned to trust John more, because I had to have faith that he would take care of me. And, watching Ian handle the accident and aftermath on his own, I really saw him grow up during that time. I was so proud of him, how he stepped up and helped me when I was hurt.

John would have to change my dressings, three times a day. Each time he did it, it took 45 minutes, and it was so painful.

At first, I didn't know if I would be able to work again. My thumb and index finger were starting to fuse. I had to do exercises to keep them from melding together. But, eventually I healed, and with therapy and adhering to strict bandaging protocols, I regained most of my prior mobility. That allowed me to work again.

The scars became less prevalent as time went on. In fact, few people comment on them today. Usually only children and people who work in the medical field notice my scars. They're the ones that will say something to me about them, but not negatively, always in a curious manner. How did I get them? What happened? Kids ask, do they hurt? I tell them the truth, that once they hurt so very much, but then the scars came and made my hands and arms feel better.

I use the burn story to teach safety. I like to tell people about my accident to remind them to keep a fire extinguisher in their kitchens, and keep it accessible. I don't want anyone to go through what I went through. There's enough pain in the world without bringing it on yourself.

CHAPTER 18

DAD AND THE GO-GO DANCER

Children are a gift from the Lord;
they are a reward from him.
~Psalm 127:3(NLT)

Present Day

Smithfield, North Carolina, Thanksgiving

John was at church, working on the sound system. His IT experience lended itself to volunteer technical work for the church and other charities. I called him and said, "You're not going to believe this. Mike and Debi asked to come for Thanksgiving."

"Thanksgiving's in three days."

"I know. Um, and I said 'yes.'"

"Okay." I loved that about John. His heart was always big enough to handle whatever came our way. He asked, "Where are they going to stay?"

That put me behind the eight ball. I no longer had a real bed in the guest room, because I didn't want anyone else living with us. John's son, John-Mark moved in with us to finish his college classes while we were living in the apartment in Cary. When we moved to our house in Smithfield, Ty moved in with us. When he graduated high school, he, too, moved out. That's when I got rid of the bedroom set. I didn't want anyone else to feel comfortable and move back in with us. I needed my house back.

The problem with accommodations was that Mike and Debi had an 11-year old golden retriever who was like their kid. Since they couldn't stay with us, I had to find them a hotel that was dog friendly. The only hotel in the area that allowed pets was the Super 8 in Smithfield. Which is, well, a Super 8. In Smithfield, North Carolina. I couldn't imagine that this dentist, his wife and their dog would stay at a Super 8. I should tell them about the Umstead, where I helped set up the spa and which also takes pets. I thought it would be better suited for someone used to the nicer things in life, but it was over an hour's drive away. I didn't want them to have to drive that far. So, I told Mike to make reservations at the Super 8.

They came to NC the day before Thanksgiving. It took them six hours to make a four-hour drive because it poured rain the entire time they drove down the I-95 corridor. It was still raining when they arrived, so they came into our house with a seventy-five-pound soaking wet dog. I grabbed a bunch of old towels and met them at the door.

"Hi, Mike!" I yelled, "Here's some towels!" I shoved the towels at them, and couldn't believe that my first interaction with my biological father who I'd never seen before was to throw towels in his face.

They came in and John helped me take their coats and hang them on the backs of the barstools to dry, and we set their wet umbrellas on the back porch. Ian took the towels and dried off their dog, Augie, who licked Ian's face.

Mike, now free of his wet coat, gave me a big hug "Hi, Sweet Lady!" He held me for a moment. Then, released his embrace. "This is Debi." He pushed me toward her.

"Hello, Debi," I said, giving her an awkward hug.

"Great to finally meet you, Christi. This is Augie, don't worry, he won't get into anything, all he ever wants to do is to lay around and be near us."

Augie was a sweet, old dog who was very quiet and padded around the room until settling himself into a corner.

I started the coffeemaker to serve everyone, and Mike pulled out a liter of Seven-Up and a bottle of Canadian Club from a bag he'd brought. He turned to me, "You don't mind if I..." he left it hanging.

"No, help yourself. I'll get you a glass and some ice." It didn't bother me. I went to many dinners and parties with friends who drank alcohol. I knew why I needed to stay sober, and I was comfortable with that fact locked tightly in my head. I wanted to live, and if I started drinking, I would drink myself to death. God was good in reminding me of that every day.

We decided the best thing to do for dinner was to go to the local Chinese restaurant. So, Ian and his girlfriend joined us, and John said the blessing at the table.

Mike reminded me of my daddy, Alan, in the way he commanded a room, and told stories that everyone wanted to hear. He told us about their volunteer work with the Naval Academy, and how they would take in cadets who couldn't go home for the holidays. They had to sadly leave all that behind when they moved to Delaware. He told us about how he worked for the Navy as an oral surgeon, but couldn't stand it, and got out to start his own private practice. He told us stories about patients, and weird cases that he'd had. We were like kids at his feet listening to his stories.

The next day was Thanksgiving and we had invited our friends, Bishop John and Mrs. Hortense Colander, to join us. Now, Miss Hortense is about eighty pounds soaking wet, and she's also fearful of dogs. When they made their way up the walkway to our house, Augie started barking. Despite his calm demeanor, his bark is loud and deep and a little scary, especially to those who are unnerved by dogs. I thought when she heard him bark, she was going to turn around and go home, but she proceeded to the door, even if she was taking careful steps. Once Augie realized she was friend and not foe, he stopped barking, and padded over to sit at her feet. When she saw he loved a scratch, and was gentle and friendly, Miss Hortense relaxed.

Throughout the day, the sweet dog would get lost in the room. This was funny because he was so big. But, we'd ask, "Where's Augie?" and everyone would scan the room for him, until we'd spot him in a corner or under a table. I thought he was like that because he was so old, but Debi told me, "No, he's always been that way; a gentle giant."

John's son, John-Mark and his wife Anna joined us for dinner, along with our friends Teresa and Allen. Mike gave a toast for our dinner, and thanked us for our hospitality, even if he had to come to 'North Cackalacky' to see us. He spoke of the importance of family, which included close friends, as he nodded to Miss Hortense and Bishop John and Teresa and Allen, and talked about how reunions can happen under the strangest circumstances.

We filled our plates with the bounty of the table, green bean casserole and mashed potatoes, roast turkey, cranberry jelly, rolls with jam, and sweet potatoes with brown sugar and pecans.

Mike leaned over and said to me, "Seeing you right now, Christi, now I can die. I know you're okay and I know where you are. I can touch you, speak to you and hug you. I feel so complete now."

I smiled as he squeezed my hand. I wished I could reciprocate. But, I didn't have those same sentiments. I had to guard my heart and my emotions. If this thing was going to blow up, I didn't want to be a part of the hurt.

After pie, we collapsed in the living room. Mike and Debi were amazed at Ian, their first and only grandchild.

Ian was sitting next to me, and I pointed at him while addressing Mike, "Ian told me a few weeks ago that he wanted to be an emancipated minor."

Leave it to a teen, I thought.

Mike's eyebrows shot up, and he rubbed his chin. "Oh, reeeally?"

Ian, said, "Yup."

Mike looked at him thoughtfully, then said, "Ian, I've had enough time to be around you, and I see that you're a very bright kid. You're probably more intelligent than all your peers. But, let me tell you what's going to happen. You're going to get a couple of buddies, and you're going get your own place, and you are all going to think you're cool and independent and you don't have to follow your parents' rules. And, you'll be okay for about two weeks. But, then, you know what?"

"What?"

"You are going to be acting as your friend's 'parent'. You're going to be the one who's making sure that they're going to work to pay their part of the bills. You're going to be the one that calls the landlord to fix the toilet or the AC or whatever's broken. And, you're the one who's going to get screwed over by your buds who won't hold up their end of the bargain."

"Oh," said Ian. I could tell he was processing what Mike told him.

"Yeah, 'oh.' That's how it's going to go down, and you'll be the one scrambling to pay the bills and not go broke, and your buddies will take off leaving you holding the lease on an apartment that you can't afford."

In my Christmas card later, I enclosed a thank you letter to Mike for his conversation with Ian. John and I couldn't say things like that to Ian without getting brushed off. But Mike could, and it made a difference. Ian got it and understood it. Mike and Ian had spoken with each other a number of times on the phone leading up to Thanksgiving. Through those calls, Mike had built up enough credibility with Ian so that Mike's words held value.

Ian went into his room to play his guitar, and left us adults to talk.

John said, "You guys are so easy going, it's a shame you're not staying with us."

I chimed in, "Yes, it would be great if you could stay, but we don't have a real bed in the guest room anymore."

Mike said, "It's okay. We travel so much that we bring an inflatable mattress with us."

They drove up to our house the next morning, and said, "We're moving in!" They canceled the hotel and stayed with us for the rest of the time. We didn't know how it was going to work out, but it was so comfortable being around them that I was glad they decided to stay.

It wasn't until that third day, that I finally felt comfortable asking Mike about the past.

"Hey, Mike, did Glenn tell you about me?"

"Yeah, he called me and said that this girl had contacted him, telling him that she's his sister. And, right then, my heart lurched, because I knew it was true. I think Wilma had hinted to the boys, or at least to Glenn that they might have a sister. So, I told Glenn that, yes, he did have a sister."

"So, he spoke with you about me, and you confirmed it for him?" I asked.

"Yes, he told me you'd contacted him, that's why I wasn't surprised when you contacted me."

"Why did Glenn try to keep me from the family?"

"Well, Glenn was executor of his mom's estate and he was concerned about the implications to the estate of another heir. Some wills have a clause that included all heirs, even unknown ones."

That was interesting. I hadn't thought about that.

Mike continued. "Wilma owned over a dozen properties in Arkansas, that she'd purchased from money she got from her guy Frank. The taxes hadn't been kept up since her death, though, and those properties were going to be sold by the state for the tax money. Frank had decided that he wanted those properties, so he's made a move to pay the taxes on the homes."

I pondered that. It sounded like a good investment. "Maybe I could go down to Arkansas, and put my name in the ring, and try to get those properties."

"Christi, do not get involved with those properties, or anything to do with Frank. Frank is an evil person. Stay away from him."

Despite Mike's warning, I still thought about acquiring those properties. But later, I thought, well, I found out about this family, and some of them live in those homes she purchased. Do I really need to make enemies of my newfound family? I probably could make a move and get a lawyer. But, why? Especially if it causes ill will. I wouldn't want that.

"In the end, Glenn won't get the properties, but your half-brother William may get a piece of them someday. Frank bought a house for Wilma, and William currently lives there as Frank's son. I don't know if Glenn has a part in that or not." Mike held out a picture. "This is your brother Glenn as a kid." Debi and Mike had brought a bunch of pictures, and we were looking over them on the coffee table.

"Oh, cute. You know, he was supposed to get DNA test, but he didn't."

"He didn't need to. I knew you were my daughter. Plus, I got the DNA test, so we know for sure. And frankly, I could take one look at you, and know you were Wilma's. Here, you can see it in this photo."

He handed me a picture of Wilma Faye pregnant with me. It was odd, to see me in the belly of a woman I didn't know.

"Her name isn't Wilma Faye," Mike said. "She went by Faye. I always called her Wilma, though." He looked at the picture in my hand and touched my shoulder. "I put you up for adoption, because I was young and selfish. I made a mistake and I was wrong. I'm sorry, Christi, will you forgive me?"

I nodded. It wasn't until John told me later that Mike had apologized that it registered for me. I don't know why I couldn't hear it at the time.

"You always wonder where your child is," Mike continued, "I wondered and wondered, and I wanted to find you. And, here you are. I have you back now. And, here you are in North Cackalacky and this is where we started. This is where it all began, and you're here. I now have family in North Cackalacky," Mike said, and sort of chuckled. He hated North Carolina, but here he was back in the state because of me, because he had a daughter living here.

"Karen said that she was close to Wilma Faye," I offered, trying to tease more information from him.

"I don't know Karen very well. She was a baby, then not much more than a girl when she lived with us. I was busy with school and work, so I don't remember much."

"She lived with you two?"

"For a time, but that was later on. Your mom and I hooked up in North Carolina all those years ago in Jacksonville area. I was in Camp LeJeune, which I hated. I hated everything about the place except for Onslow Beach. There was an Acey-Deucey Club, where they served quarter beers. We would go there and dance and meet women and drink lots of beer."

"What's an Acey-Deucey Club?" I asked.

"It's a tiki bar for Second- and First-Class Petty Officers. The place is all decorated like it's the 1940s. They play swing music and serve fancy cocktails with umbrellas for the ladies. We men drank quarter drafts."

"Did you meet Wilma Faye there?"

"No, that was before. Wilma and I met later."

"Miranda contacted me, and she's your brother's daughter, right?"

"Don't talk to her. She's crazy. My whole family is nutballs."

"Tell me about your family," I said, thinking they can't all be 'nutballs.'

"My father, Ray, grew up an orphan in the Bronx, and his mom died in childbirth, and his dad had a Merchandising Distribution center in Ponce, Puerto Rico. So, Ray was raised by his godparents. He used to get into trouble with the police for fighting. The local cops would say, 'Hey, Ray, you like to fight?' And, he would reply, 'Yeah, I like to fight.' And, so instead of carting him off to jail, they put him in a boxing ring. And, that's how he became featherweight Golden Gloves champion. But, World War Two came along, and he got sucked into service."

"My mother grew up on a farm in Pennsylvania, where she was one of nine kids. Her father emigrated from Italy when Mussolini took over, and they sailed to America on the ships with the girls they were supposed to marry. But, when he arrived, he and the woman he was pledged to marry didn't want to get married, so they went their separate ways. He met my grandmother in Pennsylvania. He worked forty-five years on the Erie Railroad. He used to take care of and manage the Kinzua Bridge, the highest railroad viaduct at the time. When my grandmother and grandfather married, they had a large family. They eventually settled and worked on the farm. You know what? When we were young, we didn't go on vacation, we went to work on that farm. My vacation was hard labor!"

I said, "That sounds awful!"

"It was! I've got two older and two younger brothers. I was the monkey in the middle. We were all in the military. We were rough and tough boys, so my dad, the boxer, would put a rope ring in the backyard, and we'd get into the ring and punch each other out. And, my mother would always scream at him that the police were going to come and take us away. We grew up in Olean, New York."

"When did you leave for North Carolina?"

"When I was sixteen. It's funny, Wilma left home when she was sixteen, too. She was bull headed and stubborn, and I am, too, so we butted heads a lot. That's probably why it didn't last. She was a great lady, a really special person, but our personalities were too strong for each other. She left home—a runaway's what you'd call it today—and she just took off. She hitchhiked all that way. It was kind of normal back then, but today you'd get murdered if you did it."

Mike continued his story. "So, I left home when I was a junior in high school, and my friend Louie and I went down to Florida. We planned to hitchhike Route 66. We were going follow the TV series and go to California, but one day we were walking around and a guy comes out and asks us, 'Hey, you want some free coffee?' And, we said, if it's free, we'll take it. Because with money so tight, you didn't turn down free coffee. He ended up being a Navy recruiter, and told us he could get us to California faster than bumming rides on Route 66. He told us that we'd be stationed in San Diego. So, we signed up on the spot. And, we were shipped out to a most gorgeous area of the country."

I poured us more coffee. Mike was on a roll and we were a rapt audience.

"I spent two years in Navy and two years in Marines. I became a Navy hospital corpsman, and if you go into Marines, it counts as your 'at sea.' So, I didn't have to do duty on a ship. I was in the medical technical field, and I wore a marine uniform with Navy insignia. They shipped me overseas to the Mediterranean, which I really enjoyed, but then I came back to Camp LeJeune. And, I *hated* it. I couldn't get the hell out of there fast enough."

"Is that when you met Wilma Faye?"

"Yeah, Wilma had gone up to Camp LeJeune with a friend, who was shacked up with a guy there. Wilma decided to stay because of the wide availability of men in the area. She got a job at a place called Birdland, which—now, Christi, I don't want to offend you..."

"You won't offend me," I promised. I was sitting on the edge of my seat.

"Well, Birdland was a go-go club. And, Wilma now, she was a topless go-go dancer. Guys went into Birdland, you know, like guys do. My best pal, Louie, had a gal who also worked at Birdland, so when Louie went to the club, I went, too. In Birdland, they put the girls into these oversized birdcages suspended from the ceiling, about six feet off the floor. The bar bouncers would put ladders out, and the girls would climb up into the birdcages. The girls would then dance around in white go-go boots inside the cages. I saw Wilma up there, and I wanted to meet her. And I did meet her. So, that's how your dad hooked up with a go-go dancer."

We all laughed at that. I could picture the young Marine with a go-go dancer on his arm.

"My pal Louie was from Kingston, New York, and since I didn't want to go back to Olean, I went up to Kingston with him. I took Wilma, and Louie took his gal. When we got up there, Louie went to register for classes at Ulster County Community College. The admissions guy asked me why I wasn't registering, too, and I told him that I didn't have a high school diploma. He said, 'you've served your country, I know you have to have some smarts to do that. Tell you what, you take some classes and if you do well, we'll let you stay, and you can get a degree.' And that's how I ended up in college without a high school diploma."

"You never finished high school, and yet you're an oral surgeon?" asked John.

"That's right. I ran away when I was still in high school. When we got up to New York, that's when Wilma got pregnant with you," he said, looking at me. "You were born at Benedictine Hospital. I've told you this before, but we were so poor we didn't have a pot to piss in, or a window to throw it out of."

"I understand, things were really tight. I've been in tight positions before," I explained.

"Christi, we didn't want to, but we had to let you go because we were so unstable. We weren't married and we lived in a little, bitty trailer in a trailer park that we were sharing with Louie and his girl. I had two jobs, a night job at Drug City, and a day job at Kingston City Labs, plus I was going to college. The only way that Louie and I could study was to pull all nighters. We napped, but we never slept. He had two jobs, too. Years later, Louie became a board certified cardiologist. He was in charge of the Catheter Lab in Philly. He had gone to Temple. Your mom should have been his partner, they were both more suited for each other and they both smoked like two or three packs a day. Louie and I were closer than brothers. He ended up dying of cancer."

Mike drained the last of his coffee and continued. "I learned how to study and I did good. I went for two years, but I took too many science courses, so I couldn't get an Associate's Degree, then I went to University of Kentucky, but I hated it there, so I transferred to Harper College in Binghamton. After that, I got a free ride going to SUNY Buffalo. I had to choose which path to take in medical school, so chose to be a dentist. You see, the upside of being a dentist is that no one dies on you, you get weekends and holidays off, you get to work on mouths instead of butts, and they still call you 'doctor'. This reminds me, I have to tell you about the best honor I've ever received."

I stopped him. "Hold on. I have to get us all more coffee and some *pie*!"

Debi and I went into the kitchen and served up the last of the Thanksgiving pies and I brewed some more coffee.

"This is fun," she told me, and squeezed my arm. "You know, I've always known about you. Mike told me about you, and he hoped that someday he'd get to meet you."

"Really?"

Debi nodded. "Yes, yes! He never stopped wishing that you would turn up in his life."

I thought about that and wondered if Mike had ever looked for me. Instead of asking, I plated pie slices. "Mike sure has some stories."

"He's on a roll. He loves to talk."

I chuckled. "Oh, I can tell."

When we had fresh cups of hot coffee and plates loaded with pie and whipped cream, Mike continued his tale.

"So, the best honor I ever got was thanks to my lovely wife here, Debi. She was driving up the road, listening to Billy Joel and the DJ on the radio said that Billy Joel was being given an honorary degree from Rutgers University, and he never finished high school, but he was going to be given an honorary college degree due to his contributions to music. Debi was listening to this, and got the bright idea of calling up the Superintendent of Schools over in Cattaraugus County where I went to high school."

"Yes," piped in Debi, "I called the Superintendent, and told him that my husband never graduated high school, but he's a doctor now. I asked him if there was any chance that he could give him an honorary high school diploma at his 50th High School Reunion."

Mike took over. "Even though I never graduated from Olean High School, I still attended reunions over the years, because I had so many good friends."

Debi chimed in, "Mike gets along with people and has a lot of friends!"

Mike said, "That's true. Well, at the reunion, they sat me up front at the head table, and I couldn't figure out what was going on. The Superintendent of the Schools walked up to the lectern, and presented me with a high school diploma."

Debi said, "Mike was so overwhelmed that he was crying."

"I couldn't even speak. And, for a long-winded guy like myself, *that* was a feat," added Mike, and we all laughed. The guy could talk.

"I looked out at the audience," Mike said, almost getting choked up, "and they were cheering and clapping, and as I wiped away my tears, all I could manage to say was, 'Well, it only took me fifty years. Thank you.' I have some weighty degrees, but my most honored one is that high school diploma."

The story touched me. "Mike, that's awesome. Debi, that's really amazing what you did."

"If anyone deserved it, he did," said Debi smiling at Mike.

I was relaxed and feeling closer to Mike and Debi, so I thought I should ask the question that had dogged me since I found out about my biological family. I took a deep breath. "Mike, there's still this one thing I don't know. Wilma Faye told everyone in Arkansas that I had died. What's the truth? Did Wilma Faye know about me or not?"

"Of course she knew about you, she gave birth to you!"

"I mean, did she know about giving me up for adoption? Was she awake afterwards?"

"Yes, yes, she was awake. She held you in her arms when we named you."

"You *named* me?"

"We were in the hospital, and we got to hold you for all of two minutes, and they said, 'you have to give her a name.' So, I thought about it, and said, name her after her mother, call her Wilma. Then, I thought, well, she can't be Michael, but she could be Michelle, so I said, name her Wilma Michelle. That was the name we gave you before they took you away."

"You're as creative as me," I told him in a deadpan.

"I thought it was pretty good," he said, sticking his chin out in defiance.

"This is funny, because the first business I owned, I was trying to think of a name for it, so I named it Salon

329. Then someone asked me, 'what does 329 mean,' and I said, well, um, it's our address."

Mike laughed. "Okay, okay, so creativity isn't a family strong suit."

I was curious, however. "But, why did you name me if you were giving me up for adoption?"

"They needed a name for the birth certificate, I suppose."

"The birth certificate that I have has my adopted name on it. But it doesn't have any other information."

"They probably gave you a new one, when you were adopted. You said you were adopted by a Higgins. That's odd, because they told us that you were supposed to be adopted by Dr. Diacovo, a physician, and his wife. They were a nice Italian couple, Catholic, who had already adopted a few other babies. You were supposed to go with them."

"That's weird, I wonder why I didn't?" I took a sip of coffee.

"Yeah, I don't know what happened, or why you ended up with the Higgins family. But, we thought you'd be with the doctor and his family."

I wondered what happened in those nine months that I was in foster care. I wondered if the family who took me in, decided not to keep me, and, for whatever reason, released me back into the system. Or, maybe the Diacovo's were the foster family, that's why they gave their names to Mike and Wilma Faye.

"Over the years, Wilma wanted to find you, so I helped. I helped her look for you several times after she and I split. She always had you in her heart, and she always looked for you. I hired professional investigators two or three times to find you, but the records were locked up. It was impossible to find out any information. Your adoption records were sealed and we didn't have much to go on. Everything in the sixties was secretive. She had a good heart, Christi, she wanted to find you."

"Oh, my gosh, that's amazing." I couldn't think of anything else to say. I was overwhelmed. And, I believed him. Wilma Faye knew I was alive, and she looked for me.

Mike leaned over to me and said, "We always knew that you were out there, and we hoped that one day you'd pop up. And, guess, what? You did!"

Epilogue

Two Years Later

*I*n 2019, John, Ian and I went to Delaware to visit Mike and Debi. We would have seen them more over time, except that 2020 happened, when travel and gatherings were restricted due to the COVID-19 pandemic. Cell phones kept us connected.

Mike calls Ian once a week. He calls me once a week, too. He is part of our lives.

It was a sour rainy day in a winter of constant rain in North Carolina. Mike and I were chatting for a bit between my client appointments.

"I refuse to take the position as the oldest," I told him. "I've always been the baby and it works better for me."

"Okay, you can be the baby, Sweet Lady. I'll let you do that."

"Good, because I've already decided that."

"Say, Debi and I are thinking of heading to Florida in a couple of months. We thought we'd stop by for a visit on our way."

"That sounds great. C'mon down!"

"Excellent, we'll make a plan of it. I'll call when I know the dates. Now, I know you've got to get back to work, so I'll let you go. Love you!"

"Love you, too!" I blurted out.

And, as I hung up I realized it was the first time I said that I loved him. I sat in the silence of the break-room for a moment and thought about that. I was able to tell Mike I loved him, not because he kept telling me that he loved me, but because I finally meant it.

I was no longer the family's 'dead baby'. I was Mike and Wilma Faye's daughter.

AFTERWORD

For I know the plans I have for you," says the Lord.
"They are plans for good and not for disaster,
to give you a future and a hope.
~Jeremiah 29:11 (NLT)

*H*i, it's me, Christi. Well, it's been me all along, but my friend Cat took all my scattered thoughts and put them in order, you know? Just so they'd make sense to people outside my own brain. Everything in this book is true as I remember it. It all happened to me.

My story is bittersweet because with all the bitter, there was always sweetness.

I worried about how my sisters, Sandy and Judy, would feel about me talking about our daddy's sexual abuse. Cat and I were getting to the part of the book where we needed to write it or nix it, so I thought I should consult them. I talked to my husband John about it, and he agreed with me that I needed to have a sit down with my sisters. I didn't want to do anything that would hurt my family, so I took a leap of faith: if either Judy or Sandy had a problem with the revelation, then we'd leave it out of my story.

Sandy already knew that I was working on a book, but she didn't know what it was about. I hadn't had a chance to talk to Judy at all, so it was new information to her. When we finally got together to have lunch, and I shared with them that I was writing my memoirs, they asked what that meant. I told them that it would be a story about me growing up, the different trials and successes in my life, and other things that have happened to me. The book would be about my journey and my renewed faith. I told them, of course, part of the story was going to be about Daddy. I wanted to make sure that they knew that, and that they were okay with it, because my sisters are my sisters. Family is not about blood, it's about the people who have been in your life, and who have your back.

I was amazed that Judy immediately said that she had no problem putting out that kind of information about that time in our lives. Sandy said she didn't have a problem with it, either, but she was concerned about how it would affect people who knew us and our family. She wanted to protect the integrity of our family. She didn't want to hurt those friends, or alter how they felt about us. Sandy also wondered if people would think we misled them about our family by keeping secrets and not 'coming clean.' Sometimes, it's not about *what* happened, it's about *how* it was managed. We talked that out for a bit, and I'm happy to say that my sisters backed me 100 percent in being able to share my own experience with what happened during that difficult time, and what happened to us all.

I dedicated this book to my mom—my adoptive mom, Nurse Amy—because she was my real mom. Many people think that birth moms are 'real moms,' but only if they raise and lead you. My mom told me what it meant to be adopted: she said I was lucky because I was chosen. Then she told me that they really wanted a boy, but it was okay that they got a girl. And, they were so happy that they got me. She never made me feel anything less than being her daughter. She was always my mom, and no adoption papers or DNA tests that show my birth mom was Wilma Faye affect Amy's status as my *real* mom.

My sister Judy looked for her birth family, but I never did. And, when I accidentally found them, I was glad my own mother, Amy, had already passed away. She died a year before I connected with my birth family, and that was God protecting me, I believe, because I don't know what it would be like for me to have to explain this to my mom. I don't think I could do it. I wouldn't want to hurt her or dishonor her. She was always there for me, all my life. Not sharing her DNA doesn't make her less than my mom, and you know what? It probably made her more 'my mom' because she had to choose to love me.

My mom was the one who came and rescued me when I ran my sled into the woodpile. She was the one who bought me trendy clothes when I didn't fit in. She planned a birthday party and made fellow classmates show up when I was lonely and without friends. She got me into the treatment center, and busted me out when she felt I was ready. She gave me my career as a stylist. She helped diagnose me with MS, get me access to great doctors, and help with my treatment. She rushed to meet me at the hospital when I lost my baby. She was there for Ian's birth. She saw me come back to God, and marry John. She was my everything.

Did we fight? Yes. I was a pretty awful teenager at one point, so, yeah, we fought. Was I brat? Maybe, at times. Weren't we all? I gave her some attitude. She wasn't a saint, though, and I know that. She was a woman—a human—and she had bad days, and bad months and bad years. But she was my mom.

If you're looking for your birth family, your mom or dad, or siblings or whoever shares your DNA, remember that they are strangers. You'll have to cultivate a relationship with them over time. Your adopted family might not be perfect, and mine certainly wasn't, I mean, my daddy molested us girls, but you can't use the excuse that they didn't live up to your expectations to shut them out of your life or replace them with strangers, unless, of course, the abuse is still ongoing. Then, you have to protect yourself and get away from abusers or people who are hurting you.

With my adopted daddy Alan, gone, and having reached peace with his being the chameleon while hiding the molestation of us from everyone, I think it was easier for me to accept creating a relationship with my biological dad, Mike. He certainly has love for me, and never forgot me through the years. Long after the divorce, he even helped Wilma Faye try to find me. Now, even a few years after that first phone call, we've become much closer. We've visited each other's homes, and we call and text each other regularly. He even calls Ian. Ian has an amazing grandpa now, one who listens and gives advice. Ian says Mike sounds like me, and I think he's right, because we're both stubborn and direct.

It was God who put all this in motion and saw it through to the end. I've been through a lot in my fifty-plus years, but God was always there for me, even when I didn't see Him, or when I ran away from Him. I fled the Catholic religion, but God still pursued me. That's what God does: He pursues us. Everything in the Bible points to Jesus, who reconciles us back to our Father. God goes after us, is passionate about us, and wants to know us and spend time with us. Jesus is 'Emanuel,' meaning "God with us." God wants us, all of His children. He's after you, too, and all you have to do is answer His call.

God showed me that I was going to kill myself with alcohol and drugs if I kept going. I had to get sober or die. I believe God cured me from MS, for as long as

He sees fit. He helped me have a baby, Ian, when I was told I couldn't get pregnant. He helped me deal with the sexual abuse from my daddy, and the rape when I was in high school. God helped me to get out of my abusive relationship with my ex-husband, and protected Ian and me when I left. He helped me make my peace with those things. God went through it all with me, even as I was faltering in my faith, even as I had given up on Him. He was there for me. And, He can be there for you, too.

This book is more than my story. It's my testimony. It is my testimony to what God did in my life, and an example of what God can do in yours. He's there, wanting you to reach out. If He can do all that He's done for me: the healing, guiding, and making things happen. He can do anything for you, as well, according to His will. All you have to do is believe, to accept Jesus as your Savior. It's not that complicated.

Know that God loves you and has a plan for you. He desires to have a relationship with you and to walk with you. He wants you in the fold. We have a God-sized hole in our hearts that only He can fill. We need to understand that man is sinful and it's our sin that separates us from God, who is perfect and holy. Sin hurts God because it keeps us from Him. We need to realize that God sent His Son to die for our sins. Christ bore our sins on the cross, so that we can be restored into a relationship with the Father.

Saul (later named Paul), on the road of Damascus, shows us faith. You see, he was faithful, but not to Jesus. He needed to flip that around. Saul was an extremely faithful person, but had a wrong kind of faith. That's how he justified killing Christians. He was putting his faith in the wrong place, in the Roman government. He just needed to put it in the right place: in God. He had all the skills that God needed him to have. God made him lose his eyesight to turn him around, to show Saul that he was blind to God. By making him blind, then he could truly see.

I went blind because of my MS, so I know that panicked feeling of being blind, and how it makes you vulnerable. You have to rely on others to take care of you. You have a lot of time to think, and use your other senses. My sense of hearing and touch really came alive. I remember sitting in the trailer, listening to the cars stream by on the highway and wondering why I never heard them before. I remember feeling a soft blanket that, over time, had pilled with use, and thinking to myself, "how did I not know this blanket had all these little bumps?" Being blind means you can rediscover the world around you. And, that's why God's gift to Saul was blindness.

The loss of eyesight gave Saul some private time with God. God was able to use it to show Saul that God had complete power and that Saul should submit to Him. God showed Saul that He had a plan for his life. After the three days of blindness, Saul came out again into the light to look around, and the world was completely different: Saul was immediately baptized. God got Saul, later called by his Roman name, Paul, to do the Lord's work through faith and he ended up writing a lot of the New Testament. My story is like Paul's story, as are all of our stories. God gets our attention in various ways, and we can either ignore Him, or accept Him. God gives us free will because he wants us to choose Him.

If someone doesn't have the capacity for faith, they can't believe. You can't have faith out of an emergency. You can't pray when things are bad for God to fix everything, then when things calm down, you ignore God again. I know that when I'm willing to put my faith in God, in the good times and the bad times, that He'll come through. He may not work it out the way I want, but God will finish the task.

We don't make good decisions ourselves, so that's why we need God. We teach people how to treat us, like when I was with my ex-husband. I taught him that he could treat me poorly.

We think we know the best answer, but God always knows the best answer. Sometimes we think we need to pull somebody out of the gutter, but sometimes they need to sit in that gutter for a while, and feel uncomfortable in order for them to come to know God, and realize that they need to change. If they don't have enough pain or muck under their boots, they may never see their need for God. That's why God blinded Saul on that road to Damascus, so that he would be vulnerable enough to listen.

And that's important, because not everyone will listen. Sometimes, in that gutter, people make a personal choice to ignore God. There's nothing we can do about that. You can lead a horse to water but you can't make him drink. I know that sounds trite, but it's true. You can't make someone believe or follow God. They have to choose it themselves. The gutter has to be mucky enough, the pain great enough, and the desire to fill that God-sized hole strong enough.

God leads us and steers us where He wants us to go, but we need to listen. For instance, John and I belonged to a certain church and we'd been trying to get a ministry going for youth, but we kept hitting roadblocks along the way. I thought it had to do with us not being in the 'inner circle' at the church, and that's why we couldn't get the program up and running. You have to have the right influence in any organization to get things done. But then, one day, I was talking with someone who said to me, "You know, when I left this other church, it was because my time there was done, and God took me somewhere else." That's when it dawned on me that the failure to launch had nothing to do with us not being in the 'inner circle.' Maybe it was because it wasn't the right place for our ministry.

So I called John, and I said, "You know, I've been thinking that this church is not where we're supposed to be right now." And, he replied, "Yes, that sounds right." God had been moving on both our hearts, but we didn't listen because we were too busy trying to get the ministry up and running and concentrated on what we wanted, not what God wanted for us.

God will put us where He needs us, but then we have to come through. We have to step out in faith and do the work. I learned that I had to do my part, too, not rely on God to get it all done. In John Chapter 5 there's a story that brings that thought home to me.

John 5:1-15 says:

Some time later, Jesus went up to Jerusalem for one of the Jewish festivals. Now there is in Jerusalem near the Sheep Gate a pool, which in Aramaic is called Bethesda which is surrounded by five covered colonnades. Here a great number of disabled people used to lie—the blind, the lame, the paralyzed. One who was there had been an invalid for thirty-eight years. When Jesus saw him lying there and learned that he had been in this condition for a long time, he asked him, "Do you want to get well?"

"Sir," the invalid replied, "I have no one to help me into the pool when the water is stirred. While I am trying to get in, someone else goes down ahead of me."

Then Jesus said to him, "Get up! Pick up your mat and walk." At once the man was cured; he picked up his mat and walked.

The day on which this took place was a Sabbath, and so the Jewish leaders said to the man who had been healed, "It is the Sabbath; the law forbids you to carry your mat."

But he replied, "The man who made me well said to me, 'Pick up your mat and walk.'"

So they asked him, "Who is this fellow who told you to pick it up and walk?"

The man who was healed had no idea who it was, for Jesus had slipped away into the crowd that was there.

Later Jesus found him at the temple and said to him, "See, you are well again. Stop sinning or something worse may happen to you." The man went away and told the Jewish leaders that it was Jesus who had made him well.

This story makes me think how easy it is to forget God's miracles. The paraplegic man could have made many different choices after being granted the ability to walk, yet he chose to go straight to the Temple. And even though he had made that reverent choice at first, Jesus still spoke to him, and reminded him that he still has a personal choice to make going forward. He tells him to go and sin no more.

This is a reminder to me of how easy it is for me not to take personal responsibility for the choices I make.

Even when we are given wonderful, life-changing gifts, it's easy for us to fail to do our part. In the last sentence, Jesus reminds him that worse things may happen even than before. It is not that Jesus will bring bad things to us, but that we would be bringing it on ourselves. This would not be a 'God thing,' because it would become a 'me thing'. I'm the one that suffers for my sinful choices.

Earlier in this scripture the man stated that every time he tries to get to the water, someone beats him to it. I almost feel that he was missing his chance because of the sin he was carrying, which ties to the warning Jesus gave him at the end of the passage. Even crippled people can sin. We can all sin, but we can't use our circumstances to *excuse* sin. I could have easily excused sin or turned against God because of any one of my circumstances: Recovering alcoholic and drug addict; rape victim; sexual and physical abuse victim; patient with MS; mother who suffered a miscarriage; divorced single mom; woman who faced financial ruin a few times, and was horribly burned. I could certainly justify turning away from God.

But, that's not what happened.

This book is about my transformation through God. I have been sober for over three decades. I have found peace from past abuse. I was miraculously healed from MS—in fact, I should be in a wheelchair right now, yet my husband with Parkinson's leans on me these days. I have a wonderful son, Ian, a musician, who graduates high school this year. My arms have healed from the burns, and my salon, so far, is surviving the Covid-19 pandemic. God transformed me and led me as a blind woman, not physically blind but spiritually blind on my road to Damascus.

God gives us each an opportunity for our own personal transformation. God doesn't complicate things. We humans have an ability to complicate everything, but He makes things simple: *trust Him and follow Him*. I proved to myself a long time ago that when I am in charge of things in my life, I don't always make the best choices. I'm better off trusting God and not having to be responsible for everything, everyone, and fixing the problems of the world. Through God, anyone can live life joyfully.

The Lord had placed it on my heart that He wanted me to give my testimony in some larger way than the small groups I was reaching. But in the last five years or so, He told me, it's not time. Sit back and wait. We all have to realize when it's not the time, it's not the time.

But, then suddenly it *was* the time.

My client and good friend Janice and I had talked for years about how I should do it through a book. One day she came in to the salon for her appointment, and she told me it was time to call my writer friend. I stalled because I didn't want to make the call. I didn't want to open the lion's cage, because I knew that once out, the lion could never go back inside. Janice said she didn't want to hear it, and so she gave me a deadline. Before her next hair appointment in a few weeks, I had to contact my writer friend.

My writer friend is Cat, and we met fifteen years ago when her son Howie was in preschool with Ian. God planted a seed with us, all those years ago. While our boys would mess around on the playground, we'd sit on a park bench and complain about lack of sleep, potty training, and playgroup drama. Cat told me, "we should write a book together." I thought she was crazy, but I went with it.

"What would we write about?" I asked.

"I don't know, *anything*!" she replied, because she's always looking for possibilities.

We went over the various topics we could write about: kids, business ownership, the salon, different industries, and other stuff. In the end, we left it up in the air. And, it stayed there. For about fifteen years. We went our separate ways, as our boys grew up. They went to different schools, and we lived in different towns. We stayed in touch over the years, sometimes meeting for lunch, but mostly checking in now and then.

Because I'd promised Janice, and I could feel from God that the time was right, I contacted Cat. Her cell number had changed, so I messaged her on Facebook, where we'd kept in touch over family pictures and posts. She agreed to meet me at Bosphorus, my favorite Turkish restaurant in Cary, for lunch.

It was God's perfect timing because I was ready to tell my story, and Cat was ready for her next gig.

I believe that God knew that Cat's parents were going to die, and she was going to use her inheritance to buy a business, run it for a few years, and then sell it in March of 2018. I mention that date for a reason, because it was the exact date that I learned I was the "dead baby." When she sold her business, Cat decided to go back to writing full time. And, in the summer of 2018, when she and I reconnected over house-made pida bread and Baba Ghanoush, she mentioned that she was looking for a new project.

I told her, "Well, I guess I'm your new project!"

Christi Hales
Smithfield, NC

NEXT STEP

*G*od gives us free will so that when we come to Him, it's our choice, not His demand. Which means, you need to make a decision. Would you like to receive God's forgiveness and be restored into a relationship with God who loves you beyond measure?

If you have chosen to accept God into your life, and Jesus into your heart, then pray this prayer written by the late Rev. Billy Graham:

"Dear God,

I know I'm a sinner, and I ask for your forgiveness. I believe Jesus Christ is Your Son. I believe that He died for my sin and that you raised Him to life. I want to trust Him as my Savior and follow Him as Lord, from this day forward. Guide my life and help me to do your will.

I pray this in the name of Jesus. Amen."

(Courtesy of the Billy Graham Evangelistic Association through 'Peace With God.' Visit www.peacewithgod.net for more information.)

"Dear friends, let us love one another, for love comes from God. Everyone who loves has been born of God and knows God. Whoever does not love does not know

God, because God is love. This is how God showed his love among us: He sent his one and only Son into the world that we might live through him. This is love: not that we loved God, but that he loved us and sent his Son as an atoning sacrifice for our sins." ~1 John 4:7-10

CPSIA information can be obtained
at www.ICGtesting.com
Printed in the USA
LVHW010846190522
719178LV00006B/51